AQA German
Higher

GCSE

Roy Dexter
Helen Kent
David Riddell
Sue Smart
Kathryn Stanley
Marcus Waltl

D1368856

Nelson Thornes

First edition published in 2009 by Nelson Thornes Ltd

This edition published in 2013 by:
Nelson Thornes Ltd
Delta Place
27 Bath Road
CHELTENHAM
GL53 7TH
United Kingdom

13 14 15 16 17 / 10 9 8 7 6 5 4 3 2 1

A catalogue record for this book is available from the British Library

ISBN 978 1 4085 2176 2

Cover photograph Fredrik Arnell / iStockphoto

Illustrations by Kathy Baxendale, Mark Drasey, Tony Forbes, Abel Ippolito and Dave Russell

Page make-up by Hart McLeod, Cambridge

Printed and bound in Spain by GraphyCems

Contents

Context – Lifestyle, Topic 1 – Health
1.1 You are what you eat 1.2 How healthy are you? 1.3 Tobacco, alcohol and drugs

Context – Lifestyle, Topic 2 – Relationships and choices
2.1 Relationships with family and friends 2.2 Future plans regarding marriage / partnership 2.3 Social issues and equality

Context – Leisure, Topic 3 – Free time and the media

3.1 Free time activities   3.2 Shopping, money, fashion and trends
3.3 Advantages and disadvantages of new technology

Context – Leisure, Topic 4 – Holidays

4.1 Holiday possibilities and preferences   4.2 What to see and getting around
4.3 Past experiences, future plans

Context – Home and environment, Topic 5 – Home and local area
5.1 Types of homes and what is in them   5.2 Where you live and what the area is like
5.3 Life at home day to day and on special occasions

Context – Home and environment, Topic 6 – Environment
6.1 Current problems facing the planet   6.2 Local issues and action

6 Contents

Reading

Learning vocabulary

Writing

Getting ready for the exam

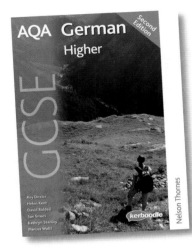

Building grammar knowledge

Listening

Developing exam strategies

Speaking

Understanding how the exam works

The AQA GCSE German exam is divided into four main subject areas, called **Contexts**. This book is divided up in the same way, with colour-coding to help you know where you are. Each Context is divided into two **Topics**, making a total of eight Topics to study during the course.

| Lifestyle | Leisure | Home and environment | Work and education |

The exam is divided up according to the four **Language Skills**: Listening, Speaking, Reading and Writing. Each one of these has its own separate exam, either in the form of an end-of-course paper or as a Controlled Assessment.

Writing (30%) (Controlled Assessment)

Listening (20%) (Exam)

Speaking (30%) (Controlled Assessment)

Reading (20%) (Exam)

AQA GCSE German

📖 Reading

The Student Book contains plenty of German reading material on the kind of subjects that come up in the GCSE exam. A headphones icon means the texts are also recorded so that you can compare the spoken and written word. The activities that follow the reading passages are similar to the types of questions you'll encounter in the exam.

🎧 Listening

Some activities only have a headphones icon. This means they're for developing listening skills and you won't see the words written down. The recordings are available from the Kerboodle book – just click on the icon next to the activity. A few of these recordings also exist as video, to help to bring the German language alive.

🗨 Speaking

Your ability to speak in German accounts for 30% of your final mark. In every Topic there are activities that are designed to build up the skills you need for your Speaking Controlled Assessment while using the language you have just learnt.

✏ Writing

Many students think that Writing is the hardest part of the exam, but it doesn't have to be if you are properly prepared. Each Topic contains carefully structured tasks that will help you to develop the skills you need to maximise your grade.

V Learning vocabulary

You can't get away from the fact that vocabulary has to be learnt in order to do well in the exam, so we are giving you help with this in various different ways.

- Vocabulary lists – For each section where new language is introduced there is a list of up to 20 useful words that come up in the tasks. There are also recordings to help you learn to pronounce each word correctly. Why not start by learning these?

- Vocabulary tasks – Every Foundation spread starts with a vocabulary activity. You might work on these together as a class, or you can use them for practice and revision at home.

- Context lists – AQA have made lists of words that come up in their exams, one for each of the four subject areas or Contexts. We have put these lists in Kerboodle and added English translations.

- Interactive activities – If you learn well by getting instant feedback, why not try out the vocabulary builder in Kerboodle?

G Building grammar knowledge

Understanding grammar is the key to building your own phrases. AQA GCSE German helps you to consolidate your grammar knowledge in a logical way.

- Grammar boxes outline the grammar points you need to know for the exam.

- Activities next to the boxes provide instant practice, before you have had time to forget what you have just read.

- Interactive grammar activities in Kerboodle give you more practice.

- There is a Grammar section with verb tables at the back of the Student Book, to refer to whenever you need to.

> ### Using *man*
> *Man* means 'you', 'one', 'people', 'we or 'they', used when you aren't referring to anybody in particular. It is followed by the same form of the verb as *er / sie / es*:
> *Man darf im Restaurant nicht*
>
> **Grammatik** Sei

Language structure boxes

These tables provide the scaffolding you need to construct different sentences for Speaking and Writing. On Kerboodle you will find editable versions matched to most of the Student Book Topics, allowing you to get creative by adding your own ideas and vocabulary items.

Ich treibe	immer	Sport.
Ich spiele	oft	Tennis / Fußball / Go
Ich gehe	ab und zu	schwimmen / joggen.
	selten	
	nie	

 **Hinweis** **Accessing Groundwork Student Book pages**

Where you see this link icon in your book, this means you can access Groundwork pages, offering more basic activities and grammar practice for revision or catch-up work, directly from your Higher Kerboodle Book.

Developing exam strategies

Getting a good grade at GCSE German is not just about how much you know; it is also about how you apply this knowledge in the exam. Throughout the book you will find strategy boxes that are linked to exam-type activities. Read them carefully and use the suggestions to help you improve your grade.

Use pictures to help you focus

The pictures in questions 1 and 2 tell you whereabouts in the advert to focus. The fact that for both questions there is a (3) means that each time there is only one item that is not mentioned. Make sure you write down three letters each time.

Strategie 1a

Getting ready for the exam

At the end of each Context, you will find an Exam Practice section. There are four of these in the book. They give you:

- further practice in the sort of Reading and Listening questions you will meet in the exam
- recaps on Reading and Listening strategies, plus a few new ones
- some sample tasks for Speaking and Writing Controlled Assessments, with example answers
- exam technique advice to explain everything you need to know about AQA Controlled Assessments
- some grade boosters to tell you what you need to do to push up your grade.

Grade booster

To reach grade A, you need to ...

- Write 40 to 50 words per bullet point, conveying a lot of relevant information clearly, e.g. bullet point 5. You could give a lot of information and details here. However, try to limit yourself to 40–50 words and focus instead on quality of communication so that you don't neglect the other bullet points of the task.

 **kerboodle**

Kerboodle offers an innovative, blended range of products to help engage teachers and students alike. It can be purchased as a whole learning solution or in parts, depending on the needs of each school, college, department and learner.

Kerboodle for AQA GCSE German includes differentiated resources focused on developing key grammar, vocab, listening, reading and writing skills. These engaging and varied resources include videos of native speakers, self-marking tests, listening activities with downloadable transcripts, interactive vocabulary builders, practice questions with study tips and comprehensive teacher support.

Our AQA GCSE German Kerboodle resources are accompanied by online interactive versions of the Student Books. All your Kerboodle resources are embedded to open directly from the book page.

Where appropriate there are links to support Groundwork and Higher activities.

Find out more www.kerboodle.com

Log into Kerboodle at live.kerboodle.com

Numbers 1–20, ages and days of the week

Ich habe zwei Schwestern und keine Brüder. Ich bin fünfzehn Jahre alt, aber Marlies ist achtzehn und Claudia ist neun.

Jan

Ich habe zwei Brüder und eine Schwester. Karl ist elf Jahre alt und Michael ist sechzehn. Gabi ist erst sechs Monate alt.

Monika

Meine Geschwister sind älter als ich. Ich bin vierzehn Jahre alt und Hans ist siebzehn. Brigitte ist zwei Jahre älter als Hans.

Susanne

1a 📖🎧 Read the texts above and answer the following questions in English:

1. How old is Jan's younger sister?
2. Who has two brothers?
3. How old is Susanne's brother?
4. Who is the youngest person mentioned?
5. How old is Monika's older brother?
6. Who doesn't have any brothers?
7. How old is Brigitte?

Wie alt bist du?	*How old are you?*
Ich bin ... Jahre alt.	*I am ... years old.*

0	*null*	11	*elf*
1	*eins*	12	*zwölf*
2	*zwei*	13	*dreizehn*
3	*drei*	14	*vierzehn*
4	*vier*	15	*fünfzehn*
5	*fünf*	16	*sechzehn*
6	*sechs*	17	*siebzehn*
7	*sieben*	18	*achtzehn*
8	*acht*	19	*neunzehn*
9	*neun*	20	*zwanzig*
10	*zehn*		

1b 💬 Work in pairs. One person makes a statement based on the texts above and the other identifies who it is. Then swap roles.

Beispiel:

> Ich bin achtzehn Jahre alt.

> Du bist Marlies.

2a 📖🎧 Read Lena's plans for what she will do when she is on holiday. Then put the sentences into the order she will do them (her holiday starts on a Monday).

a Am Mittwoch kaufe ich Souvenirs.
b Am Sonntag spiele ich Tennis.
c Am Dienstag spiele ich Fußball.
d Am Samstag mache ich eine Bootsfahrt.
e Am Montag gehe ich schwimmen.
f Am Freitag gehe ich kegeln.
g Am Donnerstag mache ich eine Stadtrundfahrt.

Montag	Monday
Dienstag	Tuesday
Mittwoch	Wednesday
Donnerstag	Thursday
Freitag	Friday
Samstag / Sonnabend	Saturday
Sonntag	Sunday

2b 📖🎧 Now write down in English what Lena is going to do each day. If you are unsure of some of the activities, look them up in the glossary.

2c ✏️💬 Using Lena's sentences as a model, write down what you do each day. Then work with a partner. One person asks the other what he or she does on a particular day. Then swap roles.

Beispiel:

> Was machst du am Mittwoch?

> Am Mittwoch gehe ich schwimmen.

Days of the week

If you want to say on which day you do something, use *am* followed by the day:

Am Montag gehe ich schwimmen. – On Monday I am going swimming.

If you do something regularly on a particular day, miss out *am* and add *–s* to the day, but don't give it a capital letter (unless starting a sentence):

Wir gehen samstags zum Fußballspiel. – We go to the football match on Saturdays.

Grammatik

Numbers and dates

1a 📖 🎧 Read the description of a city in Germany. For each of the following statements write **T** (True) or **F** (False).

1 There are 32 underground stations.
2 The city has 270,000 inhabitants.
3 There are 41 youth clubs.
4 There are 22 parks available.
5 The city has 300 buses.
6 On the roads are 59,000 cars.
7 There are 3 major stations.
8 There are 56 schools.

> In meiner Stadt gibt es zweihundertachtzigtausend Einwohner. Wir haben fünfundneunzigtausend Autos und dreihundert Busse auf den Straßen. Es gibt auch vier große Bahnhöfe und zweiunddreißig U-Bahnstationen. Für die Kinder gibt es sechsundfünfzig Schulen, aber wir haben auch einunddreißig Jugendclubs und zweiundzwanzig Parks.

1b ✏️ Work out the answer to these sums in German and write the answer in words.

Beispiel: **1** siebenundzwanzig

1 acht + neunzehn =
2 fünfzig – zwanzig =
3 fünfundneunzig – dreiundvierzig =
4 einundzwanzig x vier =

2a 📖 🎧 Three famous people are saying when they were born. Match up the year of birth with the name of the person.

a Ich heiße Michael Ballack und bin Fußballspieler. Ich bin am sechsundzwanzigsten September neunzehnhundertsechsundsiebzig in Görlitz geboren.

b Mein Name ist Barack Obama und ich bin Präsident der USA. Ich bin am vierten August neunzehnhunderteinundsechzig in Hawaii geboren.

c Ich heiße Heidi Klum und bin Fotomodell. Am ersten Juni neunzehnhundertdreiundsiebzig bin ich in Bergisch Gladbach geboren.

| 1961 | 1976 | 1973 |

21	einundzwanzig	60	sechzig
22	zweiundzwanzig	70	siebzig
23	dreiundzwanzig	80	achtzig
29	neunundzwanzig	90	neunzig
30	dreißig	100	(ein)hundert
31	einunddreißig	200	zweihundert
40	vierzig	201	zweihunderteins
50	fünfzig	311	dreihundertelf

836	achthundertsechsunddreißig
1,000	(ein)tausend
2,000	zweitausend
2,009	zweitausendneun
3,684	dreitausendsechshundertvierundachtzig

Dates

When talking about a particular year, include 'hundred' and 'thousand':

1995 = *neunzehnhundertfünfundneunzig* (nineteen hundred and ninety-five)

2001 = *zweitausendeins* (two thousand and one)

Note that there are two ways of saying when you were born:

*Ich bin **1995** geboren.*

or *Ich bin **im Jahre 1995** geboren.*

Grammatik

2b 🗨 Work in pairs. One person names a famous person to the right and the other person gives his or her date of birth.

Beispiel:

> Du bist Angela Merkel. Wann bist du geboren?

> Ich bin am siebzehnten Juli neunzehnhundertvierundfünfzig geboren.

Wayne Rooney, 24/10/1985	Angela Merkel, 17/07/1954
Daniel Brühl, 16/06/1978	Britney Spears, 02/12/1981

Telling the time, months and birthdays

Wie spät ist es? / Wie viel Uhr ist es?	What time is it?
Es ist ...	It is ...
Uhr	o'clock
Viertel nach	quarter past
Viertel vor	quarter to
halb	half **to**
halb neun	half past eight
Mittag	midday
Mitternacht	midnight
um	at
zwischen ... und ...	between ... and ...

1a Put the sentences below into the correct order, then note down each time in figures.

Beispiel: **a** 7:30, ...

a Ich frühstücke um halb acht.

b Zwischen sechs Uhr und sieben Uhr am Abend mache ich meine Hausaufgaben.

c Um Viertel nach zwei esse ich zu Hause zu Mittag.

d Um ein Uhr verlasse ich die Schule und gehe nach Hause.

e Zwischen halb elf und zehn vor elf quatsche ich mit Freunden in der Pause.

1b 🖉 Write down the correct times in words for each of these clocks using the German 12-hour clock.

Beispiel: **1** *Es ist zehn nach zwei.*

@Grammatik

24-hour clock

The 24-hour clock is often used in German. When you use the 24-hour clock you need to add the minutes as a number, for example 15:10 is *fünfzehn Uhr zehn*.

Januar	January
Februar	February
März	March
April	April
Mai	May
Juni	June
Juli	July
August	August
September	September
Oktober	October
November	November
Dezember	December

2a Match up the dates on the calendars with the birthdays.

Beispiel: **a** 3

a Ich habe am einundzwanzigsten Mai Geburtstag.

b Ich habe am siebzehnten November Geburtstag.

c Sie hat am dritten Januar Geburtstag.

d Sie hat am ersten Dezember Geburtstag.

e Er hat am achten Oktober Geburtstag.

@Grammatik

Birthdays

To give your birthday, you say *Ich habe am [number] [month] Geburtstag*. The numbers you use (*ersten, zweiten* etc.) are called ordinal numbers.

Seite 189

2b 🗩 Interview at least eight people in your class, asking them when their birthdays are. Each person has to answer using a full sentence.

Beispiel:

Wann hast du Geburtstag?

Ich habe am siebten Juli Geburtstag.

Classroom equipment and colours

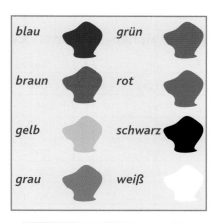

blau		grün	
braun		rot	
gelb		schwarz	
grau		weiß	

1a 📖 🎧 Read the description of Elke's bag, pictured above. Rewrite the text correcting the five errors.

> Elke geht zusammen mit Paul in die Schule. Sie hat eine blaue Schultasche. In ihrer Tasche hat sie ein schwarzes Etui und zwei Hefte. Ein Heft ist rot und das zweite Heft ist weiß. Ihre Sportschuhe sind grün. Sie hat auch ein Lineal, einen blauen Kuli und einen gelben Bleistift.

1b 🖉 💬 Use a dictionary to find the German for ten items you associate with a particular colour. Write the words down and swap lists. Write down an appropriate colour next to each word on your partner's list, then check that you both agree.

Beispiel:

> Die Banane ist gelb, nicht wahr?

> Ja, die Banane ist gelb. Ist der Apfel grün?

> Nein, der Apfel ist rot …

Adjectives

Grammatik   Seite 178

Adjectives which follow the noun they describe do not change.

*Die Tasche ist **grün**.*

If the adjective is placed before the noun then its spelling will change.

*Die **grüne** Tasche kostet €2.*

2a 📖 🎧 Read Paul's text, then copy and complete the sentences.

Paul

> Hallo. Ich bin der Paul. Wenn ich in die Schule gehe, habe ich viele Sachen in meiner Schultasche. Für jede Stunde habe ich ein Heft und ein Buch. Zum Schreiben habe ich einen Kuli und einen Bleistift. Natürlich kommt mein Lineal auch in die Tasche. Montags haben wir eine Stunde Sport und dann darf ich meine Sportsachen nicht vergessen.

das Buch	book
das Etui	pencil case
das Heft	exercise book
das Lineal	ruler
der Bleistift	pencil
der Kugelschreiber / der Kuli	ballpoint pen
die Tasche (Schultasche)	bag (schoolbag)
Sportsachen (pl)	things for sport (PE kit)
Sportschuhe (pl)	trainers

1   Paul hat viele Sachen in seiner _____ .

2   In jeder Stunde schreibt er Aufgaben in sein _____ .

3   Wenn er schreiben will, kann er einen _____ oder einen _____ in der Tasche finden.

4   Am _____ ist seine Tasche immer voll, weil er seine _____ braucht.

2b 🖉 💬 Use a dictionary to find the German words for 10 other things in your classroom or schoolbag. Compare your lists in pairs.

Beispiel:

> Hast du eine elektronische Tafel?

> Nein, aber ich habe ein en Overheadprojektor …

Gender

Grammatik   Seite 174

All nouns in German are either masculine, feminine or neuter. In a dictionary this will normally be indicated by m., f. or n.. Gender determines which articles (words like 'the' and 'a') are used before nouns.

German pronunciation

🎧 The alphabet sounds

A	ah	B	bay
C	tsay	D	day
E	ay	F	ef
G	gay	H	hah
I	ee	J	yot
K	kah	L	el
M	em	N	en
O	oh	P	pay
Q	koo	R	air
S	ess	T	tay
U	oo	V	fow
W	vay	X	iks
Y	oopsilon	Z	tset

🎧 German pronunciation

Many consonants are pronounced the same as in English. The ones you need to take extra care over are:

j	ja, jung
qu	quälen, Quantität
v	viel, Vater
w	wie, Wasser
z	zu, Zeitung

Some consonants are the same as in English except when they appear at the end of a word. Then you need to pronounce them differently:

b	ab, Dieb
d	Kind, Hund
g	Tag, sag

Pay attention to the following consonant combinations:

ch	machen, Tochter
sp	Spanien, spannend
st	ständig, Strand

The ess-tset (ß) is used in place of *ss* after a long vowel or diphthong, and has the same sound; *ss* is used after a short vowel.

> *Er heißt Felix. Er **isst** gern Pommes.*

Umlauts on *a*, *o* and *u* change the sound of these vowels.

A	lachen	Ä	lächeln
O	mochte	Ö	möchte
U	unter	Ü	über

With vowel combinations, make sure you don't confuse the following:

ie	viel	ei	weil

Typing German accents

Use the following PC shortcuts:

Ctrl + :, then a	ä	Ctrl + :, then Shift + a	Ä
Ctrl + :, then o	ö	Ctrl + :, then Shift + o	Ö
Ctrl + :, then u	ü	Ctrl + :, then Shift + u	Ü
Ctrl + &, then s	ß		

Use the following Mac shortcuts:

Option + u, then a	ä	Option + u, then A	Ä
Option + u, then o	ö	Option + u, then O	Ö
Option + u, then u	ü	Option + u, then U	Ü
Option + s	ß		

You can also set your computer to work like a German keyboard. You will need to remember what the characters on your keys now correspond to:

' ➡ ä		@ ➡ Ä	
; ➡ ö		: ➡ Ö	
[➡ ü		{ ➡ Ü	
- ➡ ß			

Also note:

z ➡ y	y ➡ z

If you really can't find the accents you want, use *ae* for *ä*, *oe* for *ö*, *ue* for *ü* and *ss* for *ß*.

Using a dictionary

When looking up new meanings, it's useful to know what type of word (noun, verb etc.) you want to find (see the Glossary of terms, page 173).

Nouns
Your dictionary should tell you each noun's gender (masculine, feminine or neuter). It will do so either by giving the nominative definite article (*der Mann; die Frau; das Kind*) or by giving the initial of the noun's particular gender (*Mann **m**; Frau **f**; Kind **n***).

The dictionary should also give you the noun's **genitive ending** and show you how the **plural** is formed. The genitive form is given first, then the plural:

Kind n (-(e)s, -er)

From the above example you should be able to work out that the genitive form of *Kind* is *Kinds* or *Kindes*, and the plural of *Kind* is *Kinder*.

Verbs
You can also discover whether or not a verb is irregular. This may be indicated by an abbreviation e.g. *essen* **irreg** or *essen* **unreg**, or by the fact that the dictionary also gives you the imperfect second person form and the past participle, e.g. *essen* pret. *aß* ptp. *gegessen*.

The abbreviation **sep** tells you that a verb is separable, e.g. *mitkommen* **sep**. Remember, not all prefixes added to verbs make them separable – for instance, *ankommen* is separable, but *bekommen* is not.

The letters **vt** and **vi** tell you whether a verb is transitive (it takes a direct object) or intransitive (it doesn't take a direct object). Often a verb is both and will have **vti**. Sometimes you will find separate sections on the transitive and intransitive forms of the verb, as these can offer different meanings.

Adjectives and adverbs
Remember that in German, an adjective (e.g. slow) and an adverb (e.g. slowly) are usually translated by the same word (e.g. *langsam*). Sometimes a dictionary will only give the translation from German to English as an adjective, but you can usually work out from context if you need to make this into an adverb. The dictionary abbreviations for adjectives and adverbs are *adj.* and *adv*.

Cases
If you look up a preposition, the dictionary should tell you what case needs to follow it, e.g. *mit* **prep + dat**. If you are looking up a preposition which can take both the dative and the accusative, the dictionary should indicate the differences in meaning e.g. *in* prep. **(+ dat)** in, inside, **(+ acc.)** into.

The abbreviations *jdn* and *jdm* both mean 'somebody (sb)' – *jdn* is accusative, *jdm* is dative. If you find these after a verb, it shows you whether it needs to be followed by a direct (accusative) or indirect (dative) object pronoun:

helfen to help (***jdm*** sb) ➡ Er hilft **mir**.

bitten to ask (***jdn*** *um etw* sb for sth) ➡ *Ich bitte* **dich***!*

1 Try to find the correct German translations for these words. Don't forget that you look up the main word, ignoring little words at the front like 'the' or 'to'.

1 to phone (to ring somebody up)
2 the books
3 to dress (as in to get dressed)
4 the bags
5 light (the opposite of dark)
6 to lie (as in to tell a lie)

2 The sentence below was produced by a person studying German who used the dictionary very badly. See if you can work out:

a what the English sentence he was trying to translate was,

b what the sentence should be in German.
Ich Dose Stück Fußball.

1.1 F Isst du gesund?

Lernziele

Discussing different types of diet

Using the present tense

Making sure that you always give an answer

1 ⓥ Find the odd one out.

Beispiel: 1 *Kaffee*

1 Orangensaft / Limonade / Kaffee
2 Kartoffel / Aprikose / Gurke
3 Pommes / Obst / Salat
4 Kartoffel / Birne / Himbeere
5 Schinken / Hähnchen / Schweinefleisch
6 Tee / Kaffee / Praline
7 Bohne / Zwiebel / Banane
8 Pfirsich / Keks / Pflaume

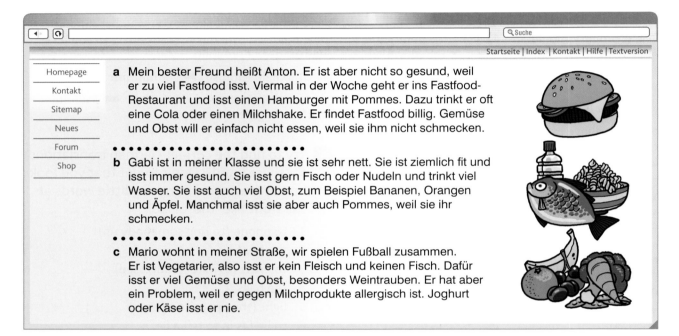

◄ | ⟳ | [   ] | 🔍 Suche

Startseite | Index | Kontakt | Hilfe | Textversion

Homepage
Kontakt
Sitemap
Neues
Forum
Shop

a Mein bester Freund heißt Anton. Er ist aber nicht so gesund, weil er zu viel Fastfood isst. Viermal in der Woche geht er ins Fastfood-Restaurant und isst einen Hamburger mit Pommes. Dazu trinkt er oft eine Cola oder einen Milchshake. Er findet Fastfood billig. Gemüse und Obst will er einfach nicht essen, weil sie ihm nicht schmecken.

• •

b Gabi ist in meiner Klasse und sie ist sehr nett. Sie ist ziemlich fit und isst immer gesund. Sie isst gern Fisch oder Nudeln und trinkt viel Wasser. Sie isst auch viel Obst, zum Beispiel Bananen, Orangen und Äpfel. Manchmal isst sie aber auch Pommes, weil sie ihr schmecken.

• •

c Mario wohnt in meiner Straße, wir spielen Fußball zusammen. Er ist Vegetarier, also isst er kein Fleisch und keinen Fisch. Dafür isst er viel Gemüse und Obst, besonders Weintrauben. Er hat aber ein Problem, weil er gegen Milchprodukte allergisch ist. Joghurt oder Käse isst er nie.

2a 📖 🎧 Read about Kevin's friends' eating habits and choose the correct answers.

Beispiel: 1 *c*

1 Anton eats fast food …
   a once a week **b** never **c** frequently.
2 He dislikes fruit and vegetables because …
   a of the taste **b** they are expensive
   c they are not cooked.
3 Gabi enjoys eating …
   a fish **b** meat **c** pizza.
4 She eats chips …
   a often **b** never **c** occasionally.
5 Mario particularly enjoys eating …
   a pears **b** grapes **c** plums.
6 For medical reasons, he mustn't eat …
   a dairy products **b** sugar **c** meat.

Strategie 2a

Making sure that you always give an answer

When answering multiple choice questions, one of the answers given must be correct. If you are really unsure which is the correct answer, choose one which sounds reasonable. It is always better than not choosing an answer at all. In Activity 2a, for example, there is a 1 in 3 chance of getting the answers right, so you must always have a go.

In question 4, you need to know how often Gabi eats chips. Look at the sentence *Manchmal isst sie Pommes, weil …* and at the choice of answers: 'often' = *oft* (you probably know), 'never' = *nie* (did you spot it in the last line?), so *manchmal* must mean 'sometimes'.

2b 📖 🎧 Read Kevin's descriptions again and match the correct person with these statements.

Beispiel: **1** *Mario*

1 ... avoids fish.
2 ... likes sweet drinks.
3 ... eats healthily.
4 ... thinks fast food is cheap.
5 ... likes vegetables.
6 ... is unhealthy.

3a 🅖 Add the correct endings to the stem to complete the parts of the regular verb *spielen*. Refer to page 180 if you get stuck.

ich spiel_   wir spiel_
du spielst   ihr spielt
er / sie / es spiel_   sie / Sie spielen

3b 🅖 Now do the same for the irregular verbs *essen* and *laufen*.

4a 🎧 Listen to Maria, Christoph, Silke, Jürgen, Daniela and Heiko. Match the person with the correct opinion words.

Beispiel: **1** *Jürgen*

1 fantastic _____
2 terrible _____
3 delicious _____
4 great _____
5 boring _____
6 tasty _____

4b 🎧 Listen again. What do they eat? Is it healthy or not? Note down the foods and say whether their diet is healthy (**H**) or unhealthy (**U**).

Beispiel: **a** *Maria: ham, sausage, (U)*

5 🖊 Write a blog about what your best friend eats and drinks and what you think about it.

Beispiel: *Mein bester Freund / Meine beste Freundin heißt ... .*
Er / Sie isst gern ... und trinkt ... . Das finde ich ...

Zum Frühstück In der Pause Zu Mittag Um drei Uhr Abends	isst er / sie	Müsli / Toast / Schinken / Pizza ... einen Apfel / eine Banane / ein Butterbrot ... viel / nichts.
	trinkt er /sie	Fruchtsaft / Tee / Kaffee / Cola ...
Das	finde ich	gesund / ungesund / lecker ...

Using the present tense

The present tense is used to talk about what you are doing now. To form the present tense for regular verbs, take the -en from the infinitive to find the stem:

Infinitive   **Stem**
spielen   *spiel*

Then add the correct endings for each person (*ich, du, er / sie / es, wir, ihr, sie / Sie*).

With irregular verbs the stem usually changes in the *du* and the *er / sie / es* form, e.g.

*ich **ess**e* but *du **iss**t, er / sie / es **iss**t*
*ich **lauf**e* but *du **läuf**st, er / sie / es **läuf**t*

(Remember that *er / sie **isst*** and *er / sie **ist*** sound exactly the same, so be very careful when listening to German being spoken.)

Also learn how to say 'I eat a / an ...'. For more on this, see page 27. In addition, learn how to say *ich esse kein / e / en.*
See page 28 ➡

🅖 **Grammatik** *Seite 180*

Hinweis
1.1 Groundwork is available in the Foundation Book.

1.1 H — Eine gesunde Ernährung?

Lernziele
Comparing different diets
Using *gern* and *nicht gern*
Keeping conversations going

Tipps zur Ernährung:

1 **Marlene:** Ich esse viele Sachen, aber nicht zu viel. Die richtigen Lebensmittel in der richtigen Menge halten dich schlank und gesund.

2 **Stefan:** Ich esse sehr gern fettarm. Zu viel Fett macht dick und krank. Nicht vergessen: Wurst, Sahne, Pommes frites, Käse, Butter, Kuchen, Schokolade und Nüsse enthalten Fett.

3 **Karola:** Ich esse ziemlich gern würzig, aber nicht salzig. Zu viel Salz kann den Blutdruck erhöhen.

4 **Dirk:** Ich esse nicht gern Süßes. Zucker schadet den Zähnen. Es lohnt sich, nicht zu viele Süßigkeiten zu essen oder süße Getränke (z. B. Limonade und Cola) zu sich zu nehmen.

5 **Ilse:** Ich esse sehr gern Obst und Gemüse. Diese Lebensmittel spenden viel Vitamin C und sind daher gut gegen Infektionen.

6 **Freddy:** Ich esse wenig Eiweiß in Form von Fleisch. Pflanzliches Eiweiß ist gut für deinen Körper und deine Muskeln.

7 **Petra:** Ich esse ganz gern kleinere Mahlzeiten. Das hält dich fit. Genieße das Essen in Ruhe.

1a 📖🎧 Read the article and find the German words for the following:

1 spicy
2 to consume
3 low in fat
4 it's worth it
5 blood pressure
6 protein
7 damages
8 quantity

1b 📖 Your friend has sent you an e-mail about his eating habits. Complete the text using the words from the list below.

| Kuchen | Vitamine | Portionen | Pfeffer |
| Kartoffelchips | Fett | Eiweiß | Salat |

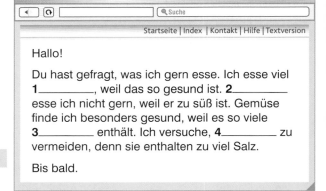

◄ | 🔎 | | 🔍 Suche

Startseite | Index | Kontakt | Hilfe | Textversion

Hallo!

Du hast gefragt, was ich gern esse. Ich esse viel **1**_____, weil das so gesund ist. **2**_____ esse ich nicht gern, weil er zu süß ist. Gemüse finde ich besonders gesund, weil es so viele **3**_____ enthält. Ich versuche, **4**_____ zu vermeiden, denn sie enthalten zu viel Salz.

Bis bald.

2 Ⓖ Answer the following questions in German. Vary your answers so they include *gern, ziemlich / ganz gern, sehr gern, nicht gern, gar / überhaupt nicht gern.*

Beispiel: 1 *Nein, ich esse gar nicht gern Spinat.*

1 Isst du gern Spinat?
2 Trinkst du gern Tee?
3 Isst du gern Pommes frites?
4 Trinkst du gern Mineralwasser?
5 Was isst du gern zum Frühstück?
6 Und zu Mittag?
7 Und zu Abend?
8 Was trinkst du gern in der Pause?

3a 🎧 Listen to Klaus talking about his family and their opinions about certain food and drinks. If the opinion is positive, write **P**, if negative write **N**, if positive and negative write **P + N**.

Beispiel: 1 *P + N*

1   What is Klaus's opinion of fast food?
2   And of grilled fish?
3   What is Monika's attitude towards pasta and rice?
4   What is Sabine's attitude towards eggs?
5   And towards organic food?
6   What is Jochen's opinion of being allergic to certain foods?
7   And of fizzy drinks?
8   What is Hans's attitude towards fast food?

Grammatik   *Seite 186*

Using *gern(e)* and *nicht gern(e)*

To say you (don't) like doing something, put *(nicht) gern* after the verb:

Ich esse Obst. I eat fruit. → *Ich esse gern Obst.* I like eating fruit.

Ich trinke nicht gern Cola. – I don't like drinking cola.

To say how much you like doing something, you can add the following words:

ziemlich / ganz (quite), *sehr* (very much), *überhaupt nicht / gar nicht* (not at all)

Ich esse ganz gern Blumenkohl. – I quite like eating cauliflower.

Mein Vater isst sehr gern Forelle. – My father likes eating trout very much.

Mein Bruder isst gar nicht gern Karotten. – My brother doesn't like eating carrots at all.

Learn more about how to express opinions.

See page 29 ➡

3b 🎧 Listen again and answer the following questions in English.

Beispiel: 1 *Mainly healthy*

1   What does Klaus think about his family's eating habits?
2   How much water do they drink each day?
3   Which **two** types of fish do they eat?
4   What does Monika avoid eating?
5   When does she eat fruit?
6   Which **four** things make up Sabine's favourite salad?
7   Which **three** things is Jochen allergic to?
8   Which **two** things does Hans like to have when watching TV?

4 🗩 Work with a partner to conduct interviews on healthy eating. One partner asks the questions and the other answers. Then swap roles.

Was isst du (zum Frühstück / in der Pause / zu Mittag / zu Abend)?

(Zum Frühstück) esse ich _____ .

Und was trinkst du?

Ich trinke _____ .

Und wie findest du deine Ernährung?

Ich finde meine Ernährung (gesund / lecker / _____ .)

Inferring information when listening

Strategie 3a

A really important skill when listening, especially at Higher Tier, is the ability to infer information, i.e. to work out what the correct answer is based on what is suggested rather than actually said. In this activity, question 3 asks about Monika's attitude to pasta and rice. We are not actually told that she likes them, but because we know that she likes running and that she eats lots of carbohydrates including pasta and rice, it can be deduced that her attitude towards these foods is positive.

Keeping conversations going

Strategie 4

In Speaking activities, don't give up if you don't know the exact word. You can make up an answer using the language you do know. Rather than try to think what the German word is for 'shepherd's pie' (there may be no equivalent!), just give some ingredients: *Fleisch mit Kartoffeln* … etc.

1.2 F Bist du in Form?

1 **V** Separate the words in the word snakes and translate the sentences into English.

Beispiel: 1 *Ich esse kein Fastfood und trinke keinen Alkohol.*
(I don't eat fast food and I don't drink alcohol.)

1 IchessekeinFastfoodundtrinkekeinenAlkohol.
2 NormalerweisegeheichviermalproWocheschwimmen.
3 MeineSchwestersitztjedenAbenddreiStundenvordemFernseher.
4 ManchmaltrinkenmeineFreundeAlkohol.
5 Ummichzuentspannen,leseichgerneineZeitschrift.
6 IchmussmehrfürmeineGesundheittun.
7 LeiderrauchtmeinVaterzwanzigZigarettenproTag.
8 IchtreibevielSport,umfitzubleiben.

2 📖🎧 Read about Andreas's lifestyle and choose the correct answers.

Beispiel: 1 *b*

1 Andreas plays table tennis …
   a occasionally b regularly c rarely.
2 He goes jogging …
   a three times a week
   b in all types of weather
   c in fine weather only.
3 Usually in the evening, he …
   a watches TV b plays computer games
   c likes being active.
4 He sleeps … a less than six hours
   b about six hours c more than six hours.
5 He can't sleep longer because he …
   a has to get up early b studies late c can't relax.
6 He … a stopped smoking two years ago
   b has never smoked c smoked for two years.

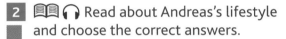

🔍 Suche

Startseite | Index | Kontakt | Hilfe | Textversion

Hallo! Ich heiße Andreas und bin fünfzehn Jahre alt. Ich bin ziemlich gesund, denn dreimal pro Woche spiele ich normalerweise Tischtennis. Samstags gehe ich mit zwei Freunden im Wald joggen – das Wetter ist für uns unwichtig. Abends will ich bestimmt nicht fernsehen oder Computerspiele spielen, weil ich lieber aktiv bin, aber im Augenblick muss ich so viele Hausaufgaben machen.

In der Schule schreiben wir jetzt Klassenarbeiten und mein Leben ist sehr stressig. Pro Nacht schlafe ich etwa sechs Stunden. Ich möchte länger schlafen, aber ich kann mich einfach nicht entspannen!

Ich habe vor zwei Jahren geraucht, aber jetzt nicht mehr.

3 **G** Re-write the following sentences starting each with the underlined word or phrase:

Beispiel: 1 *Am Wochenende spiele ich Tennis.*

1 Ich spiele <u>am Wochenende</u> Tennis.
2 Wir essen Fastfood <u>einmal pro Woche</u>.
3 Mein Bruder sieht <u>jeden Tag</u> vier Stunden fern.
4 Meine Freundin geht <u>dreimal pro Woche</u> ins Hallenbad.
5 Stress ist <u>manchmal</u> ein Problem für mich.
6 Meine Eltern haben <u>leider</u> nicht genug körperliche Bewegung.
7 Mein Onkel und ich gehen <u>am Samstag</u> windsurfen.

Recognising and using near-cognates

Strategie 2

When you are reading, learn to look out for near-cognates to help you understand new vocabulary. These are words which look similar to English, e.g. *Zigaretten* (cigarettes), *Alkohol* (alcohol), *Portionen* (portions). (Beware, though, as they are often pronounced differently from English, so make sure you learn them carefully.)

4a 🎧 Listen to these young people talking about their lifestyles. Choose the appropriate picture for each.

Beispiel: **a** *Katharina – b*

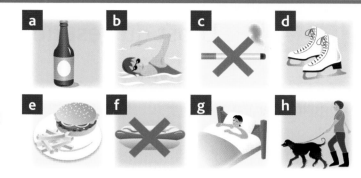

4b 🎧 Listen again. Copy the sentences and fill in the gaps with one of the words given below. Two words are not used.

Beispiel: **1** *Morgen*

1 Katharina geht jeden _____ schwimmen.
2 Leon ist zu dick, weil er_____ isst.
3 Steffi geht mit ihrem Hund _____.
4 Sebastian isst _____.
5 Yvonne treibt _____ Sport.
6 Johann und seine Freunde sind ziemlich _____.
7 Paula kann gut _____.
8 Markus raucht _____.

schlafen	nicht	Abend	spazieren	ungesund
Süßigkeiten	Morgen	gesund	Fastfood	oft

5 📝 Answer the questions on the clipboard, using full sentences and a different time phrase each time (see the language structure box below). Try to add an extra detail each time.

Beispiel: *Wie oft treibst du Sport? Ich treibe oft Sport. Ich spiele Fußball und gehe schwimmen.*

- Wie oft treibst du Sport?
- Wie oft isst du Pommes frites?
- Wie oft trinkst du Mineralwasser?
- Wie oft gehst du zum Arzt?
- Wie oft gehst du kegeln?
- Wie oft hörst du Musik?

> **Grammatik** *Seite 186*
>
> **Using inversion**
>
> In a normal sentence, the subject (the person or thing doing the action) comes before the verb. The verb is the second idea in the sentence:
>
> | **Subject** | **Verb** | |
> |---|---|---|
> | Ich | treibe | manchmal Sport. |
> | Mein Freund | raucht | 10 Zigaretten pro Tag. |
>
> If a sentence does not start with the subject, the verb and subject have to be turned around so that the verb stays as the second idea. This is called inversion.
>
> | **Verb** | **Subject** | |
> |---|---|---|
> | *Manchmal* **treibe** | *ich* | *Sport.* |
> | *Pro Tag* **raucht** | *mein Freund* | *10 Zigaretten.* |
>
> Also learn how to use adverbs of frequency. *See page 28* ➡

Ich treibe	immer	Sport.
Ich spiele	oft	Tennis / Fußball / Golf.
Ich gehe	ab und zu	schwimmen / joggen.
	selten	
	nie	
	täglich	
	einmal pro Woche	
	dreimal pro Monat	

Hinweis

1.2 Groundwork is available in the Foundation Book.

1.2 H Lebst du gesund?

1a 📖 🎧 Read the letter and find the German words for the following:

1 overweight
2 unemployed
3 daily
4 physical
5 lazy bones
6 dies
7 movement
8 lifestyle

1b 📖 🎧 Read the letter again. Answer the following questions in English.

Beispiel: **1** *every day*

How often or when does Beate's father:

1 smoke 20 cigarettes?
2 drink alcohol?
3 watch sport on TV?
4 eat 5 portions of fruit and vegetables?
6 eat fast food?

2 **G** Identify the verbs in the following sentences. Then place the words in the correct order so that they make sense. Start with the underlined word.

Beispiel: **1** *treibe / Einmal pro Woche treibe ich Sport.*

1 ich pro treibe Sport Woche <u>Einmal</u>.
2 einem vor Vater mein langen Fernseher ein <u>Nach</u> schläft Tag dem.
3 ins geht <u>Am</u> Schwester Wochenende meine Tanzstudio.
4 mein Fußballspiel und das Onkel sehen <u>Samstags</u> ich.
5 pro ich Basketball spiele Woche <u>Dreimal</u>.
6 gutem meine ich und <u>Bei</u> Fußball Park spielen Wetter im Brüder.
7 haben Schule der wir viel <u>Im</u> sehr in Stress Moment.
8 acht immer <u>Pro</u> Stunden ich Nacht schlafe.

Liebe Frau Hilgert!

Mein Vater heißt Georg und ist 38 Jahre alt. Er sieht aber älter aus, denn sein Lebensstil ist nicht besonders gesund. Leider ist er arbeitslos. Er hat keinen Stress, findet aber das Leben ziemlich langweilig. Er interessiert sich überhaupt nicht für körperliche Bewegung, da er mindestens zwanzig Zigaretten pro Tag raucht und abends zu viel Bier trinkt. Sport will er nur im Fernsehen sehen, also verbringt er täglich mehrere Stunden vor dem Fernsehapparat. Er ist ein richtiger Faulpelz. Leider ist er auch übergewichtig. Er isst alles, was wir essen (inklusive fünf Portionen Obst und Gemüse fast täglich), aber dazu isst er ab und zu Fastfood oder kleine Snacks beim Fernsehen. Meine Familie und ich wollen nicht, dass unser Vater früh stirbt. Können Sie etwas vorschlagen?

Beate

Inversion and the second idea

Remember that the verb is not necessarily the second word in the sentence, but the **second idea**, e.g.

First idea	Second idea	
Am Samstag	*spielt*	*mein Bruder Squash.*
Nach der Schule	*lese*	*ich eine Zeitschrift.*

Also learn how to use the accusative with definite times.   *See page 29* ➡

Grammatik   Seite 186

3 🎧 Listen to these three people talking about their relatives' lifestyles and choose the correct answers.

Beispiel: 1 *c*

1 For Charlotte, her health is …
   a not important
   b fairly important
   c very important.

2 She eats fast food …
   a occasionally   b regularly
   c never.

3 She …
   a smokes at parties
   b never smokes
   c smokes only with her friends.

4 Michael enjoys …
   a watching sport
   b reading about sport
   c playing sport.

5 He goes jogging …
   a occasionally   b daily   c at weekends.

6 He …
   a eats low fat foods   b is vegetarian   c avoids fast food completely.

7 Aunt Maria works …
   a abroad   b from home
   c in a hotel.

8 During the evening, she …
   a meets lots of people
   b stays in
   c goes out drinking.

4 🗨 Interview your partner to find out how he or she keeps healthy. Use the questions on the clipboard.

Gesundheitsumfrage

1 Was machst du, um fit zu bleiben?
  _____

2 Wie oft machst du das?
  _____

3 Wo machst du das?
  _____

4 Wie entspannst du dich?
  _____

Reading the question carefully — Strategie 3

Reading the question carefully will give you an indication of the sort of vocabulary you are about to hear. It is always an advantage to have an idea of what is going to be said. For example, in question 3, you should know the word for 'smokes' (*raucht*), but you then have a choice of three phrases: try to have the German for these in your mind before you hear the recording (i.e. *auf Partys, nie, mit Freunden*), so you can select the correct answer.

Assessing your partner — Strategie 4

When practising with a partner, it is a good idea if you can help each other to improve by listening to how your partner performs their part. Make a note about whether they have done everything they had to in the task, whether it was accurate (jot down any mistakes), whether they pronounced everything correctly and whether they hesitated with their answers. For fun, you could give a mark out of 5 for each of these points. Discuss what went wrong afterwards (if anything)!

Um fit zu bleiben,	treibe ich esse ich trinke ich	viel / keinen Sport. gesund / Obst / Biokost. Saft / keinen Alkohol …
Manchmal / Oft / Gewöhnlich	spiele ich	Fußball / Tennis mit …
Das mache ich	im in der	Hallenbad / Stadion. Schule / Stadt.
Um mich zu entspannen,	lese / schlafe höre setze	ich. ich Musik. ich meinen Kopfhörer auf.

1.3 F Zigaretten, Alkohol oder Drogen braucht man nicht

Lernziele

Talking about the consequences of smoking, drinking and taking drugs

Using the modal verbs *wollen*, *können* and *sollen*

Using context to predict meanings

1 **V** Match the following German and English words:

a	verboten	1	dangerous
b	süchtig	2	to stop
c	Leber	3	banned
d	Öffentlichkeit	4	to cause
e	gefährlich	5	public
f	Herz	6	addicted
g	verursachen	7	liver
h	aufhören	8	heart

Kirsten, 15 Jahre alt

Ich rauche überhaupt nicht. Es stinkt und es ist auch sehr gefährlich für die Gesundheit. Es verursacht Lungenkrebs und andere Krankheiten. Ich habe nur einmal eine Zigarette probiert, aber sie hat furchtbar geschmeckt. Ich rauche nie wieder!

Stefan, 17 Jahre alt

Wie meine Freunde nehme ich Drogen – normalerweise rauche ich Cannabis, weil es ein tolles Gefühl ist. Meine Eltern finden das aber schrecklich, weil Cannabis Motivationsprobleme verursachen kann.

Jörg, 14 Jahre alt

Meiner Meinung nach ist Alkohol trinken blöd. Mein Vater ist vor drei Jahren an Alkoholismus gestorben. Jeden Tag hat er eine Flasche Whisky und ein paar Flaschen Bier getrunken. Das war für unsere Familie so traurig.

Hannah, 16 Jahre alt

Ich rauche zehn Zigaretten pro Tag. Meine Freundinnen sagen, es macht schlank. Es ist aber so ungesund, ich soll das Rauchen aufgeben, aber ich kann aufhören, wenn ich älter bin.

2 📖🎧 Read what the people say about smoking, drinking and drugs. Match the correct person with the statements.

Beispiel: 1 *Jörg*

1 My father died.
2 I know I should stop smoking.
3 My friends take drugs.
4 I am worried about illnesses caused by smoking.
5 My parents don't like what I do.
6 I think drinking alcohol is stupid.
7 My friends think smoking helps you to stay slim.
8 I hate smoking.

Using context to predict meanings

Strategie 2

Using the context (here it is smoking, drinking and drugs) can help you predict the meaning of new words, e.g. *Mein Onkel ist an **Lungenkrebs** gestorben* (My uncle died of **lung cancer**). Notice that *Lungenkrebs* is a compound word (two words joined together – *Lungen + Krebs*).

3 **G** Copy out the sentences and insert the correct form of the modal verb given in brackets. Then translate the sentences into English.

Beispiel: 1 *Ich will überhaupt nicht rauchen.* (*I don't want to smoke at all.*)

1 Ich _____ überhaupt nicht rauchen. (wollen)
2 Mein Onkel _____ nicht so viel Bier trinken. (sollen)
3 Meine Schwester _____ Drogen nicht leiden. (können)
4 Ich _____ öfter joggen gehen. (sollen)
5 Er _____ nicht so gut schwimmen. (können)
6 _____ du nur Apfelsaft trinken? (wollen)
7 Mein Bruder _____ das Rauchen aufgeben. (sollen)
8 Wir _____ keine Drogen nehmen. (wollen)

> ### Using the modal verbs *wollen*, *können* and *sollen*
>
> Grammatik — Seite 181
>
> Modal verbs are verbs like 'want to', 'can' and 'am supposed to'. There are six in all. Learn each one as you meet it.
>
> | *wollen* – to want to | *können* – to be able to / can | *sollen* – to be supposed to |
> |---|---|---|
> | *ich will* | *ich kann* | *ich soll* |
> | *du willst* | *du kannst* | *du sollst* |
> | *er / sie / es will* | *er / sie / es kann* | *er / sie / es soll* |
> | *wir wollen* | *wir können* | *wir sollen* |
> | *ihr wollt* | *ihr könnt* | *ihr sollt* |
> | *sie / Sie wollen* | *sie / Sie können* | *sie / Sie sollen* |
>
> Modal verbs are often used with another verb which must be in the **infinitive** form **at the end of the sentence or clause**.
>
> *Ich soll das Rauchen aufgeben.*
>
> Also learn how to use the modal verbs *dürfen*, *müssen* and *mögen*. See page 28 ➡

4a 🎧 Listen to the interview about smoking and decide which of these statements are true.

1 25% of adults in Germany smoke.
2 More boys smoke than girls.
3 Smoking causes health problems and damages the brain and liver in particular.
4 Many people find it hard to stop smoking.
5 In Germany there are nicotine plasters and sprays to help people stop.
6 Smoking is not permitted on public transport.
7 Smoking is banned in all pubs and restaurants.

4b 🎧 Listen again. Correct the answers which are false.

5 ✏ Write a blog explaining the possible attractions and dangers of smoking, drinking and drugs.

- Warum rauchen viele Leute?
- Was sind die Nachteile?
- Warum trinkt man Alkohol?
- Welche Probleme gibt es, wenn man zu viel trinkt?
- Warum nimmt man Drogen, wenn sie so gefährlich sind?

> ### Making sentences longer
>
> **Strategie 5**
>
> Try to use *weil* ('because'), *da* ('since / because'), *wenn* ('when') or *obwohl* ('although') to make your sentences longer, more interesting and more impressive! Make sure you use the correct word order (with the verb at the end of the clause / sentence).

> **Hinweis**
>
> 1.3 Groundwork is available in the Foundation Book.

1.3 H Alkohol, Rauchen und Drogen: warum?

Lernziele

Why some people smoke, drink or take drugs

Saying 'must not' / 'don't have to' in German

Understanding word order

■ Alkohol, Drogen und die Schweizer Jugend

Prozent der Jugendlichen in der Schweiz, die . . .

einmal in der Woche Alkohol trinken	**25%** der 15–jährigen Jungen
	18% der 15–jährigen Mädchen
schon zweimal betrunken waren	**28%** der 15–jährigen Jungen
	19% der 15–jährigen Mädchen
schon Erfahrung mit Cannabis haben	**34%** der 15–jährigen Jungen
	27% der 15–jährigen Mädchen

1a 📖 🎧 Two teenagers are discussing the above survey about smoking, alcohol and cannabis use among young people in Switzerland. Read the statistics and the text and list any words used that fit in the categories: Smoking / Alcohol / Drugs / Ailments.

Franz: Das kann ich mir vorstellen. Meine Freunde und ich treffen uns abends hinter dem Bahnhof und wollen schnell betrunken werden. Cannabis rauchen wir auch.

Marion: Mensch, bist du dumm! Kannst du nichts anderes mit deinem Leben anfangen?

Franz: Warum denn? Darf ich keinen Spaß haben? Schule und Eltern machen mir so viel Stress, weil ich immer viel arbeiten muss – Hausaufgaben, im Haushalt helfen und so weiter: ich darf nie machen, was ich will. Ich habe überhaupt keine Freiheit!

Marion: Das stimmt doch nicht. Du weißt, dass Alkohol dich total kaputt machen kann, besonders deine Leber, außerdem kannst du süchtig werden. Und Cannabis ist genauso schädlich wie Zigaretten. Du kriegst bestimmt Motivationsprobleme. Hast du keine Angst?

Franz: Mir ist das egal. Ich bin kein Alkoholiker und ich habe keinen Lungenkrebs. Meine Freunde und ich müssen irgendwie unsere Sorgen vergessen!

Marion: Das ist schade, weil du bestimmt Probleme bekommst, wenn du weiter so trinkst und rauchst.

Franz: Darfst du denn kein Bier trinken?

Marion: Doch, aber ich mag Alkohol und Drogen überhaupt nicht. Für mich ist Abstinenz wichtig, weil ich Sportlerin bin. Ich muss meine Gesundheit schützen, wenn ich erfolgreich sein will.

1b 📖 🎧 Read the statistics and text again and answer the following questions in English:

Beispiel: 1 *19%*

1 How many 15 year old girls have already been drunk twice?
2 How many young people in Switzerland have experience of using cannabis?
3 Where do Franz and his friends meet at night?
4 What do they do there?
5 Why does Franz have so much stress?
6 What could happen if he carries on drinking so much?
7 Why is Marion against drinking and drugs?

2 **G** Translate the following sentences into German:

Beispiel: **1** *Ich darf keinen Kuchen essen.*

1 I mustn't eat cake.
2 She mustn't drink coffee.
3 You (adult speaking to child) don't have to take drugs.
4 My brother mustn't watch TV.
5 I don't have to smoke.
6 We mustn't drink beer.
7 I mustn't meet my friends.

Saying 'must not' / 'don't have to' in German

If you want to say 'must not' in German, i.e. you are not allowed to do something, use the correct form of *dürfen* + *nicht*. If you 'don't have to' do something, i.e. you don't need to do it / there is an alternative,', use the correct form of *müssen* + *nicht* (see page 28), e.g.

Ich darf keinen Alkohol trinken. – I mustn't drink alcohol.

Wir müssen nicht zu Hause bleiben. – We don't have to stay at home.

Also learn how to use *weil*.   *See page 29* ➡

Grammatik   **Seite 181**

3 Watch the interview with the rock star Blitz and choose the correct answers.

Beispiel: **1** *b*

1 Blitz drank heavily …   **a** for a year   **b** after each performance   **c** on stage.
2 He used to indulge in …   **a** smoking and drinking   **b** drinking and drugs   **c** smoking, drinking and drugs.
3 He changed his lifestyle because …   **a** his father died   **b** his friends wanted him to   **c** a band member died.
4 He left the clinic …   **a** after three months   **b** three months ago   **c** after less than three months.
5 He found the treatment …   **a** difficult   **b** straightforward   **c** a waste of time.
6 He is looking forward to starting a new …   **a** family   **b** band   **c** life.

Using *ich sollte*

You may often hear German speakers using *ich sollte* rather than *ich soll*, especially when talking about things they really ought to do (but might not):

Ich sollte gesund essen. – I (really) should eat healthily.

Strategie 3

4   Work with a partner to conduct interviews similar to the one with Blitz. One of you is the interviewer while the other is either a hard-living celebrity or a clean-living sportsperson. Then swap roles.

Understanding word order

Remember that when you are using *weil* with modal verbs, the modal verb will come at the end of the sentence, after the infinitive:

*Ich rauche Cannabis nicht, weil es Motivationsprobleme **verursachen kann**.*

Strategie 4

Ich habe gar keine / viele Probleme mit		Alkohol / Rauchen / Drogen.
Ich habe nie		geraucht / Alkohol getrunken / Drogen genommen.
Ich rauche / trinke / nehme		ab und zu / regelmäßig / oft Drogen.
Um fit zu bleiben,		muss ich täglich trainieren.
Ich vermeide		Zigaretten / Alkohol / Drogen.
Ich rauche nicht, Ich trinke keinen Alkohol,	da / weil	es tödliche Krankheiten verursachen kann. ich nicht früh sterben will. man süchtig werden kann. er zu viele Kalorien enthält.
Ich glaube, Ich bin der Meinung,	dass	Drogen furchtbar / entsetzlich sind.

Health

1 Underline all the indefinite articles in the accusative case. Take care because not every article is in the accusative!

Beispiel: 1 *Ich trinke gern eine Cola, aber ein Orangensaft schmeckt besser.*

1 Ich trinke gern eine Cola, aber ein Orangensaft schmeckt besser.

2 In der Pause isst sie ein Käsebrot oder einen Apfel.

3 Zu Mittag isst sie einen Hamburger mit Pommes und trinkt ein Glas Limonade.

4 Ich esse gern ein Omelett oder eine Pizza, aber mein Lieblingsessen ist ein halbes Hähnchen mit Kartoffelsalat.

5 Zum Abendessen esse ich normalerweise eine Portion Fleisch mit Gemüse.

2a Translate the following sentences into English.

1 Ich gehe ab und zu mit meinen Freunden ins Kino.

2 Meine Familie und ich gehen oft kegeln, weil es Spaß macht.

3 Fleisch esse ich nie, weil ich Vegetarier bin.

2b Now translate these sentences into German. Be careful with the word order!

1 I rarely eat cheese or butter.

2 We play table-tennis now and again.

3 I sometimes go swimming at the weekend.

3 Copy the sentences and fill in the gaps with the correct form of *müssen* or *dürfen*.

Beispiel: 1 *Mein Cousin ist 10 Jahre alt und er darf keinen Alkohol trinken.*

1 Mein Cousin ist 10 Jahre alt und er keinen Alkohol trinken.

2 Du zum Arzt gehen – du bist krank!

3 Ich bestimmt nicht rauchen.

4 Wir nicht in die Disko gehen, weil man dort Drogen verkauft.

5 Meine Mutter versuchen, das Rauchen aufzugeben.

Using the indefinite article and the accusative case

Grammatik — Seite 175

In German, the word you use for 'a' or 'an' depends on the gender of the noun (masculine, feminine or neuter) and the case. You use the nominative case for the subject of a sentence:

***Ein Apfel** ist sehr gesund.*

For the direct object of the sentence, you need the accusative:

*Ich esse **einen Apfel** in der Pause.*

These are the different forms you need to remember:

	masc.	fem.	neut.
(nom.)	*ein*	*eine*	*ein*
(acc.)	*einen*	*eine*	*ein*

As you can see, the only articles which are different depending on whether they are nominative or accusative are masculine.

Using adverbs of frequency

Grammatik — Seite 178

Adverbs are words which qualify the action of the verb, e.g. slowly, loudly, neatly etc. Adverbs of frequency describe how often you do something, e.g. sometimes, often etc. Here are some common ones in German:

immer – always   *ab und zu* – now and again
oft – often   *selten* – rarely
nie – never

In German the adverb comes after the verb (never between the verb and subject, as sometimes happens in English):

*Er geht **manchmal** ins Sportzentrum.* – He **sometimes** goes to the sports centre.

Using the modal verbs *dürfen, müssen, mögen*

Grammatik — Seite 181

There are three more modal verbs to learn:

dürfen – to be allowed to	müssen – to have to	mögen – to like
ich darf	*ich muss*	*ich mag*
du darfst	*du musst*	*du magst*
er / sie / es darf	*er / sie / es muss*	*er / sie / es mag*
wir dürfen	*wir müssen*	*wir mögen*
ihr dürft	*ihr müsst*	*ihr mögt*
sie / Sie dürfen	*sie / Sie müssen*	*sie / Sie mögen*

As with the other modal verbs, remember that the other verb being used must be in the **infinitive** form at the **end of the sentence or clause**.

*Ich **darf** keinen Alkohol **trinken**, weil ich zu jung bin.*

4 Give your opinions of the following items. Use the vocabulary list on pages 30–31. Vary your expressions as much as you can.

Beispiel: 1 *Meiner Meinung nach ist Käse köstlich.*

1 Cheese
2 Tea
3 Garlic
4 Honey
5 Pears
6 Scrambled eggs
7 Fruit
8 Onions

> ### Expressing opinions
> Apart from saying you like or dislike something, there are other ways of expressing your opinion. Learn as many as you can so that you increase your vocabulary and what you say will sound more interesting too. Here are some phrases you can use:
>
> *Meiner Meinung nach sind Kartoffelchips zu salzig.* – **In my opinion**, crisps are too salty.
>
> *Ich denke, Fisch schmeckt gut.* – **I think** fish tastes good.
>
> *Ich finde Obst köstlich.* – **I think** fruit is delicious (lit. I find fruit delicious).
>
> *Ich hasse Senf.* – **I hate** mustard.
>
> *Ich kann Hähnchen nicht leiden.* – **I can't stand** chicken.

5 Using the vocabulary list on pages 30–31, translate these phrases into German.

Beispiel: 1 *nächsten Dienstag*

1 next Tuesday
2 last year
3 every month
4 next summer
5 this Saturday
6 last July
7 next year
8 every morning
9 this March
10 every day

> ### Using the accusative with definite times
> Whenever you are referring to a definite time in German, e.g. 'every Monday', 'next week', 'last year' etc., you must use the accusative form of *jed-, nächst-, letzt- and dies-*.
>
> You add endings to these words as follows:
>
> | | masc. | fem. | neut. |
> |---|---|---|---|
> | **(acc.)** | jeden / nächsten / letzten /diesen (Montag) | jede / nächste / letzte / diese (Woche) | jedes / nächstes / letztes / dieses (Jahr) |

6 Join the pairs of sentences using *weil* to make one sentence each time.

Beispiel: 1 *Mein Vater raucht nicht mehr, weil er nicht krank werden will.*

1 Mein Vater raucht nicht mehr. Er will nicht krank werden.
2 Ich nehme keine Drogen. Sie sind einfach zu gefährlich.
3 Wir wollten nicht auf der Party bleiben. Viele Leute haben im Haus geraucht.
4 Der Junge muss ins Krankenhaus gehen. Er hat zu viel Alkohol getrunken.
5 Das Mädchen ist gestorben. Sie hat eine Überdosis Heroin genommen.
6 Man sollte nicht jeden Tag Alkohol trinken. Zu viel Alkohol kann der Leber schaden.

> ### Word order using *weil* (revision)
> Remember when using *weil*, the finite verb (i.e. the verb whose ending can change), must go **to the end of the sentence or clause**, e.g.
>
> *Ich rauche nicht, **weil** es schlecht für die Gesundheit **ist**.* – I don't smoke because it's bad for your health.
>
> *Meine Freundin trinkt keinen Alkohol, **weil** ihre Mutter an Alkoholismus gestorben **ist**.* – My friend doesn't drink alcohol because her mother died of alcoholism.
>
> *Ich will Cannabis nie probieren, **weil** es Gesundheitssprobleme verursachen **kann**.* – I never want to try cannabis because it can cause health problems.
>
> *Seite 186*

Grammatik

Health

Topic 1.1 You are what you eat

1.1 F Isst du gesund? ➡ pages 16–17

	allergisch (gegen)	allergic (to)
die	Ananas	pineapple
	billig	cheap
die	Birne	pear
der	Blumenkohl	cauliflower
	dazu	with it, in addition
	furchtbar	terrible
das	Gemüse	vegetables
	gesund	healthy / healthily
der	Käse	cheese
der	Keks	biscuit
	köstlich	delicious
	lecker	delicious
	manchmal	sometimes
	nie	never
die	Pflaume	plum
die	Praline	chocolate sweet
der	Schinken	ham
die	Weintraube	grape
die	Zwiebel	onion

1.1 H Eine gesunde Ernährung ➡ pages 18–19

das	Eiweiß	protein
	enthalten	to contain
die	Ernährung	diet
	fettarm	low fat
die	Forelle	trout
	genießen	to enjoy
der	Honig	honey
der	Knoblauch	garlic
der	Körper	body
der	Lachs	salmon
die	Lebensmittel (pl)	food items, groceries
die	Mahlzeit	meal
die	Menge	quantity

> ## Learning new vocabulary
>
> As you work through Topic 1, refer to these vocabulary pages to help you find out what new words mean. There is one list for each sub-topic. To help you to learn the words, try covering the English words and testing yourself, or asking a friend to test you. You might like to download the audio file to help you with pronunciation. Find ways of learning that work for you, such as spotting connections with English: *das Fleisch* is like 'flesh'. How many other connections can you find?

das	Rührei	scrambled egg
das	Salz	salt
die	Sache	thing
	schaden	to harm, damage
die	Süßigkeit	sweet
	vermeiden	to avoid
	versuchen	to try

Topic 1.2 How healthy are you?

1.2 F Bist du in Form? ➡ pages 20–21

der	Alkohol	alcohol
	einfach	simple, simply
	(sich) entspannen	to relax
	etwa	about, roughly
der	Fernseher	TV set
	fettig	fatty
die	Gesundheit	health
	halten	to keep
	jetzt	now
das	Leben	life
	leider	unfortunately
	rauchen	to smoke
	schlafen	to sleep
	Schlittschuh laufen	to go ice-skating
der	Spaß	fun
	spazieren gehen	to go for walks
die	Stunde	hour
	treiben	to drive, to do
	vor	in front of, before, ago
die	Zigarette	cigarette

1.2 H Lebst du gesund? ➡ *pages 22–23*

	alles	everything
	aussehen	to look (appearance)
die	Bewegung	movement, exercise
	fast	almost
der	Faulpelz	lazybones
der	Geruch	smell
	körperlich	physical
der	Lebensstil	lifestyle
	leiden	to stand, to suffer, to bear
	mehrere	several
	mindestens	at least
der	Monat	month
	reisen	to travel
der	Schwimmverein	swimming club
	sowohl … als auch …	both … and …
	sterben	to die
	übergewichtig	overweight
	verbringen	to spend (time)
	vorschlagen	to suggest
	zurzeit	at present

Topic 1.3 Tobacco, alcohol and drugs

1.3 F Zigaretten, Alkohol oder Drogen braucht man nicht ➡ *pages 24–25*

	atmen	to breathe
	aufgeben	to give up
	aufhören	to stop
der	Drogenhändler	drug dealer
der / die	Erwachsene	adult
	(sich) fühlen	to feel
	gefährlich	dangerous
	gering	low
die	Gewohnheit	habit
das	Herz	heart
die	Leber	liver
der	Lungenkrebs	lung cancer
die	Öffentlichkeit	public (noun)
	probieren	to try

	regelmäßig	regularly
	riechen	to smell
die	Spritze	syringe
	süchtig	addicted
	verbieten	to forbid, to ban
	verursachen	to cause

1.3 H Alkohol, Rauchen und Drogen: warum? ➡ *pages 26–27*

	außerdem	besides
	betrunken	drunk
die	Drogenberatungsstelle	drug addiction centre
der / die	Drogensüchtige	drug addict
die	Entziehungskur	withdrawal treatment
die	Erfahrung	experience
der	Erfolg	success
	erfolgreich	successful(ly)
	Mir ist das egal	I don't care about that
die	Freiheit	freedom
das	Gehirn	brain
	kaputt machen	to ruin, wear out
	kriegen	to get
	Recht haben	to be right
	schädlich	damaging
	schützen	to protect
die	Sorge	worry
	spritzen	to inject
	tot	dead
die	Überdosis	overdose

2.1 F

Wie ist es in deiner Familie?

Lernziele

Family relationships

Using the present tense of *haben* and *sein*

Identifying patterns between German and English

1 ⓥ Using the vocabulary list on page 46, solve these anagrams. Then translate them into English.

Beispiel: 1 *ledig (single)*

1 digle
2 threetevair
3 tentreng
4 fredrubstie
5 trolbev
6 teesborng
7 skinue
8 chinseedge
9 grachwes

2 📖 🎧 Read about Thomas's family and choose the correct answers.

> Hallo. Mein Name ist Thomas und ich bin fünfzehn Jahre alt. Ich möchte meine Familie vorstellen. Ich habe zwei Zwillingsbrüder, Ernst und Rudi. Sie sind zwölf Jahre alt. Ich habe auch eine Stiefschwester, Tanja. Wir wohnen in Bamberg mit meiner Mutter Helga und meinem Stiefvater Kai. Leider ist mein Vater gestorben, aber meine Mutter hat letztes Jahr wieder geheiratet. Mit meinem Stiefvater kommen wir alle ganz gut aus. Tanja ist zwei Jahre älter als meine Brüder, aber ein Jahr jünger als ich. Sie ist immer nett und auch lustig.
>
> Ich habe Verwandte in Norddeutschland: mein Onkel Heinrich und meine Tante Elisabeth wohnen in Kiel. Sie haben einen Sohn, Peter. Er ist siebzehn Jahre alt und schon verlobt. Meine Großmutter wohnt allein in Bremerhaven, weil sie und mein Opa getrennt sind. Zurzeit wohnt er in Frankreich. Also sehen wir uns selten. Ab und zu besuchen wir meine Oma, aber nicht sehr oft. Ich habe ein gutes Verhältnis zu ihr, weil sie so nett ist.

Beispiel: 1 *c*

1 Compared with Thomas, his brothers are …
   a older   b the same age   c younger.
2 Thomas has …   a twin sisters   b a step-sister   c a half sister.
3 His mother …   a is divorced   b has re-married   c is separated.
4 Kai and Thomas …   a don't see each other   b argue a lot
   c get on quite well.
5 Tanja is …   a 14   b 15   c 16.
6 His uncle and aunt live in …   a Bamberg   b North Germany
   c France.
7 His cousin is …   a separated   b married   c engaged.
8 He sees his gran …   a sometimes   b regularly   c never.

Identifying patterns between German and English

Strategie 2

Watch out for near-cognates (words which are not exactly the same as in English but easy to recognise), e.g. *Vater* ('father') and *Bruder* ('brother'). However, do be careful when you meet 'false friends'. These are words which look the same in both languages but have very different meanings, e.g. *bald* ('soon'), *Stern* ('star'), *Chef* ('boss').

3 ⓖ Complete the sentences with the correct form of *haben* or *sein*.

1 Ich _____ drei Schwestern und einen Halbbruder. (haben)
2 Meine ältere Schwester _____ verheiratet. (sein)
3 Leider _____ unsere Eltern geschieden. (sein)
4 Meine Freundin _____ keine Geschwister. (haben)
5 _____ du ein Einzelkind? (sein)
6 In unserer Familie _____ sechs Personen. (sein)
7 Meine Tante und mein Onkel _____ keine Kinder. (haben)
8 Sven _____ mein bester Freund. (sein)

4a 🎧 Listen to Paul, Michael and Julia. Match the correct person with these statements.

Beispiel: **1** *Michael*

1 My parents are divorced.
2 My mother died.
3 I have three brothers.
4 I have a half-brother.
5 I don't live in Germany.
6 I have a grandparent at home.
7 I didn't mention my age.
8 My family all share in the housework.

Grammatik *Seite 181*

Using the present tense of *haben* and *sein*

The German verbs for 'to have' and 'to be' are irregular so you need to learn them by heart.

haben – 'to have' **sein** – 'to be'

ich habe	*ich bin*
du hast	*du bist*
er / sie / es hat	*er / sie / es ist*
wir haben	*wir sind*
ihr habt	*ihr seid*
sie / Sie haben	*sie / Sie sind*

Also learn how to use possessive adjectives. *See page 44* ➡

4b 🎧 Listen again. Answer these questions in English.

Beispiel: **1** *None*

1 How many sisters does Paul have?
2 Whereabouts in the country does Paul live?
3 Who is 68 years old?
4 Who is engaged?
5 Why does the family help at home?
6 How old is Michael?
7 And Tobias?

5 🖊 Imagine your ideal / nightmare family. Write answers to the questions giving as much detail as you can.

- Name? / Alter? / Wohnort?
- Wie viele Personen gibt es in deiner Familie?
- Wer sind sie? (Namen? / Alter?)
- Leben deine Großeltern? (Namen? / Alter?) (Wo wohnen sie?)
- Sind die Familienmitglieder ledig / verheiratet / verlobt?

Hinweis

2.1 Groundwork is available in the Foundation Book.

In meiner Familie gibt es	meinen Vater / Bruder / Stiefbruder / Halbbruder / Opa / Onkel.	
	meine Mutter / Schwester / Stiefschwester / Halbschwester / Oma / Tante.	
Ich habe	(k)einen (jüngeren / älteren) Bruder. (k)eine (jüngere / ältere) Schwester. zwei Brüder / Schwestern.	
Mein Vater Meine Mutter	ist lebt	gestorben / geschieden. getrennt.
Meine Eltern Meine Großeltern	sind leben	
Mein Bruder Meine Schwester	ist	ledig / verheiratet / verlobt.

2.1 H Ich komme mit meiner Familie ganz gut aus

Lernziele

Talking about relationships in more detail

Using *ihr* to mean 'you'

Using your knowledge of grammatical categories

■ Probleme zu Hause

Startseite | Index | Hilfe | Kontakt | Textversion

Jasmin (14)

Meine Familie wohnt in Köln in einem Zweifamilienhaus. Ich verstehe mich sehr gut mit meinem Vater und meiner Stiefmutter. Ich habe eine Stiefschwester. Sie heißt Sara und ist auch vierzehn, aber ich kann sie nicht leiden, weil sie immer meine Sachen nimmt. Sie ist so eifersüchtig und eingebildet. Außerdem bringt sie ihre Freundinnen mit nach Hause und sie schwatzen die ganze Zeit. Wir streiten uns oft.

Lutz (15)

Ich wohne mit meiner Mutter und meiner jüngeren Schwester in einem Wohnblock. Leider hat meine Mutter Gesundheitsprobleme, also kann sie nicht arbeiten. Sie ist sehr sympathisch und wir verstehen uns gut. Nach der Schule muss ich viel in der Wohnung helfen oder babysitten. Mein Leben ist nicht gerade einfach, aber ich bin zufrieden.

Natascha (16)

Meine beste Freundin heißt Laura und sie ist sehr nett. Sie ist ein Jahr älter als ich. Abends treffen wir unsere Freunde im Park und manchmal trinkt Laura Alkohol, aber ich mag das nicht. Normalerweise kommen wir spät nach Hause und mein Vater ist böse. Meine Eltern mögen Laura nicht und glauben, dass sie einen schlechten Einfluss auf mich hat. Ich finde das so gemein!

1a 📖 🎧 Read about the three people's problems and find the German words for the following:

1 jealous
2 mean
3 angry
4 influence
5 health problems
6 things
7 conceited
8 chatter

1b 📖 🎧 Read about the problems again and look at these statements. Write **T** (true), **F** (false) or **?** (not in the text).

Beispiel: 1 *F*

1 Jasmin has problems with her parents.
2 Her step-sister isn't very nice.
3 Her step-sister plays loud music in her bedroom.
4 Lutz gets on well with his mother.
5 They live at the top of a block of flats.
6 He thinks his life is hard sometimes.
7 Natascha's friend is 17.
8 She doesn't get on with her very well.
9 They both smoke.
10 Natascha's parents don't have a problem with Laura.

2 **G** Complete the following questions using the correct word for 'you' (*du, Sie, ihr*) and the appropriate form of the verb given in brackets.

Beispiel: **1** *Wie kommt ihr miteinander aus, Alexa und Tom?*

1 Wie ____ ____ miteinander aus, Alexa und Tom? (kommen)
2 Paul, ____ ____ keine Geschwister? (haben)
3 Frau Braun, ____ ____ Verwandte in der Schweiz? (haben)
4 Andrea und Petra, ____ ____ euch manchmal? (streiten)
5 ____ ____ ein gutes Verhältnis zu deinem Stiefvater, Timo? (haben)
6 Herr Bachstein, ____ ____ immer so streng mit Ihrer Tochter? (sein)
7 Uwe, ____ ____ einen schlechten Einfluss auf meinen Sohn! (haben)

3 🎧 Listen to Matthias talking about his family. Answer the following questions in English.

1 How many people are in Matthias's family?
2 What is the problem for his step-father?
3 What does his mother have to do?
4 How often?
5 Why do his brother's friends annoy him?
6 How often does he visit his father?
7 How does he feel about seeing him?
8 Why?

4 🗨 Prepare a presentation on your family (or an imaginary family, e.g. in a soap opera). Say who is in it, who you get on well with / don't get on with. Make sure that you include some reasons.

Strategie 1a

Using your knowledge of grammatical categories

If you can recognise whether a word is a noun, a verb or an adjective, this will help you to choose an answer which sounds reasonable.

In German, all nouns have capital letters.

Learn to recognise verbs with their different endings and position in the sentence.

Adjectives can go immediately before a noun or often after *ist* and *sind*.

Verb	Adjective	Noun
Deswegen **habe** *ich*	*ein sehr* **gutes**	**Verhältnis** *zu ihnen.*

Grammatik Seite 179

Using *ihr* to mean 'you'

Ihr is the plural form of *du*, so you use it when talking to more than one person you know.
So, for example, you might ask:

Wo wohnst du?

when talking to a friend, but

Wo wohnt ihr?

when talking to more than one friend. The verb is usually formed by adding -*t* to the stem, e.g. *geh* + *t* = *geht*, *komm* + *t* = *kommt*. However, if the stem already ends in -*t* or -*d*, you must add -*et*, e.g. *arbeit* + *et* = *arbeitet*.

Also learn how to use the word 'it'. *See page 45* ➡

In meiner Familie gibt es					… Personen	
Ich habe					einen Bruder, eine Schwester. zwei Brüder / Schwestern.	
Ich verstehe mich (nicht) gut mit	meinem Bruder meiner Stiefmutter		weil er / sie		immer nett / freundlich / hilfsbereit ist. mich ärgert / mich nervt / zu laut ist.	
Ich streite mich oft mit	meiner Mutter meinen Eltern		weil		sie immer so streng ist / sind. ich bis 22 Uhr zu Hause sein muss. ich überhaupt keine Freiheiten habe.	
			denn		sie beschwert sich immer über mein Aussehen.	
Ich komme mit	meinem Vater meiner Halbschwester	(nicht) gut aus,	da er / sie		mit meinen Hausaufgaben hilft. Alkoholiker(in) ist.	

2.2 F Wie findest du Heiraten?

1 **V** Sort these words into three categories:
Marital status / Person / Object

ledig   Mann   verlobt   Schwiegersohn   getrennt

Familienmitglied   Trauring   Verlobte   Gast   verheiratet

Schwägerin   Verlobungsring   geschieden   Frau

Gisela (16)

Mein Freund und ich heiraten nächstes Jahr. Ich kann es kaum erwarten. Ich habe schon den Verlobungsring und ich möchte eine traditionelle Hochzeit. Dann will ich zwei oder drei Kinder. Für mich ist Familie das Wichtigste. Meiner Meinung nach sollen der Mann und die Frau verheiratet sein und nicht einfach nur zusammenleben. Ein Kind muss Stabilität haben.

Meine Eltern streiten sich so viel und sind immer unglücklich – ich heirate nie! Ich möchte mit einer Freundin zusammenleben und alles teilen – den Haushalt, das Geld und die Verantwortung. Heutzutage kann ein Kind auch bei unverheirateten Eltern glücklich sein.

Dominic (14)

2a 📖 🎧 Read what Gisela and Dominic say about getting married and choose the correct answers.

Beispiel: 1 *b*

1   Next year, Gisela is getting …   a engaged   b married   c divorced.
2   She wants …   a no children   b a lot of children   c a few children.
3   She thinks children need …   a both parents   b a stable home-life   c friends.
4   Dominic's parents …   a usually get on   b are planning to marry   c are never happy.
5   He …   a is against marriage   b hopes to marry one day   c wants to marry soon.
6   He wants to …   a let his partner do the housework   b do the housework himself   c share the housework.

2b 📖 🎧 Read the texts again and look at these statements.
Write **T** (true), **F** (false) or **?** (not in the text).

Beispiel: 1 *F*

1   Gisela is anxious about getting married.
2   She already has the engagement ring.
3   She wants to get married in the summer.
4   Family is important to her.
5   She thinks a couple should live together before marrying.
6   Dominic wants to live with a girlfriend.
7   He thinks a man should be in charge of running the home.
8   He thinks it is better for the child if the parents are married.

3 **G** Unscramble the statements about the future so that they make sense. Start with the underlined word. Remember that the verb should be the second idea.

Beispiel: **1** *Nächstes Jahr ziehen meine Freundin und ich zusammen.*

1 Jahr ich ziehen meine zusammen <u>Nächstes</u> Freundin und
2 heirate Jahren <u>In</u> ich fünf
3 meinen kaufen <u>Am</u> wir Verlobungsring Samstag
4 ich sind zusammen Verlobter glücklich mein <u>Hoffentlich</u> und
5 Kinder drei haben oder wir <u>Später</u> vier
6 wir <u>Nach</u> fliegen Hawaii Hochzeit nach unserer
7 ich ledig <u>Hoffentlich</u> nicht bleibe

4 🎧 Listen to Björn, Diana, Günther, Melanie and Samuel talking about whether they are going to get married and what they think about it. If the opinion is positive, write **P**, if negative write **N**, if positive and negative write **P + N**.

5 🖊 Write about whether you want to get married and what you think about it. Then write about a famous person, saying whether they want to get married, and their opinions. (Make up the opinions if you like.)

Ich heirate Er / Sie heiratet	eines Tages / nicht.	
Ich will heiraten,		weil ich eine traditionelle Hochzeit will. da mir Heiraten wichtig ist. weil ich nicht unverheiratet zusammenleben will.
Ich will nicht heiraten,		weil meine Eltern immer traurig waren. denn mein Freund / meine Freundin und ich wollen unverheiratet zusammenleben. da meine Karriere wichtiger ist.
Das finde ich Das findet er / sie		romantisch / toll / wunderbar. altmodisch / sinnlos / unnötig.
Meiner / Seiner / Ihrer Meinung nach	ist das	

Grammatik

Discussing the future with the present tense

In English, you don't always have to use 'will' or 'shall' when talking about the future. Provided you have a **future indicator**, you can just use the present tense. For example, 'I am getting married **in 20 years' time**' refers to what you are going to do in the future. It is the same in German:

Ich heirate in 20 Jahren.

Nächstes Jahr gehe ich auf die Uni. ('I am going to university next year.')

Also learn about adverbial phrases of time. *See page 44* ➡

Strategie 4

Remembering opinion words

Make sure that you know the 'opinion words' e.g. *toll*, *furchtbar*, etc. Even if you do not understand fully what the person is saying, knowing just the one opinion word may well give you the right answer on this kind of question!

Hinweis

2.2 Groundwork is available in the Foundation Book.

2.2 H Warum soll ich denn heiraten?

Lernziele

Reasons for and against getting married

Using *um … zu …*

Reading the questions before you listen

◄ | ◐ | | 🔍 Suche

Startseite | Index | Kontakt | Hilfe | Textversion

Homepage
Kontakt
Sitemap
Neues
Forum
Shop

Nach der Uni möchte ich einen guten Job, um viel Geld zu verdienen. Eines Tages möchte ich im Ausland arbeiten, vielleicht in Asien oder in den USA. Weil ich in Zukunft wahrscheinlich viel reise, werde ich einfach keine Zeit für eine Beziehung oder Kinder haben. Erst wenn ich ein erfolgreicher Geschäftsmann mit einem Luxushaus bin, möchte ich eine Partnerin finden. Ich weiß aber nicht, ob ich heiraten muss, um glücklich zu sein. **Ralf**

• •

Meine Familie kommt aus der Türkei, aber wir wohnen zurzeit in Deutschland. Ich brauche keinen Freund, denn meine Eltern haben meinen Bräutigam schon gefunden! Er ist drei Jahre älter als ich und wohnt in der Türkei. Ich habe ihn nur einmal getroffen und kenne ihn kaum, aber meine Eltern wissen, dass er aus einer guten Familie kommt. Im Sommer besuche ich seine Familie, um sie alle besser kennen zu lernen. Meine deutschen Freundinnen können diese Situation gar nicht verstehen, aber ich freue mich darauf. Wahrscheinlich heiraten wir in zwei Jahren. **Ceylan**

• •

Ich bin der Meinung, dass Heiraten unnötig und altmodisch ist. Meine Freundin und ich leben seit sechs Monaten zusammen und wir sind sehr zufrieden. Meistens haben wir ein schönes Leben, weil wir ähnliche Interessen haben. Wir streiten uns ab und zu, aber das ist in einer Beziehung normal. Ich habe aber ein paar Freunde im selben Alter, die schon geschieden sind. Am Anfang war für sie alles toll, aber jetzt ist alles zu Ende. So was will ich nicht für uns. **Erich**

1a 📖 🎧 Read the three people's views on marriage and find the following sentences or phrases:

Beispiel: 1 *Ich bin der Meinung, dass Heiraten unnötig und altmodisch ist.*

1 I think that getting married is unnecessary and old-fashioned.
2 no time for a relationship
3 (I) hardly know him
4 We argue
5 to get to know them all better
6 We'll probably get married in two years' time.
7 My girlfriend and I have been living together for six months.

1b 📖 🎧 Read the views on marriage again and decide which of these statements are true.

1 Ralf wants to be successful in his career.
2 He doesn't want a relationship.
3 Ceylan is looking for a boyfriend.
4 She is happy about getting married.
5 Erich thinks couples shouldn't argue.
6 He doesn't want his relationship to end like his friends'.

2 **Ⓖ** Match the pictures below to the sentences. Then rewrite each pair of sentences as one sentence, using *um … zu …*

Beispiel: 1 *Ich fahre nach Frankreich, um meine Freundin zu besuchen.*

1   Ich fahre nach Frankreich. Ich besuche meine Freundin.
2   Sie hat keine Zeit. Sie findet einen Freund.
3   Wir leben zusammen. Wir sparen Geld.
4   Sie fliegen nicht ins Ausland. Sie feiern ihre Hochzeit.
5   Meine Freunde wollen nicht heiraten. Sie haben eine Familie.

> ### Using *um … zu …*   *Grammatik*   *Seite 185*
>
> *Um … zu …* means 'in order to' and is always used with the infinitive at the end of the clause. Make sure you separate the *um … zu …* clause from the rest of the sentence with a comma.
>
> *Sie fährt in die Stadtmitte, um ihren Freund zu treffen.*
>
> *Nur um Kinder zu haben, wollen wir nicht heiraten.*
>
> Also learn about using adjectives after nouns and quantifiers / intensifiers.   *See page 45* ➡

3 🎧 Listen to Petra, Lars, Sophie, Achim and Elke talking about whether they want to get married. Read the following statements and decide which five are true.

1   Petra wants to get married.
2   She doesn't like children.
3   Lars doesn't want to get married.
4   He doesn't want to work abroad.
5   Sophie wants to have a traditional wedding.
6   She would like to have two children.
7   Achim doesn't want to get married.
8   He doesn't want to go out with his friends every night.
9   Elke wants to stay single.
10   Her parents are no longer living together.

> ### Reading the questions before you listen   *Strategie 3*
>
> It is important that you read all the questions carefully before you listen to the recording. In this way, you can anticipate what you should be listening out for when you come to hear it. Aim to read and think ahead whenever possible. Because you hear the recording twice only, you need every advantage you can get!

4 🗨 Class survey. Using the questions on the right, find out people's views on marriage. Use the box below to help you give your own responses. When you have completed the survey, you can write up people's different viewpoints (but remember to use the third person!).

> • Willst du heiraten oder Single bleiben?
> • Und warum?
> • Wann willst du heiraten?
> • Möchtest du Kinder haben?
> • Warum (nicht)?

Ich heirate,		weil	ich einen Partner / eine Partnerin will.
Ich will nicht ledig bleiben,		da	ich eine Familie möchte.
Ich bleibe Single,		denn	meine Karriere ist mir wichtiger.
Ich heirate noch nicht,			ich will reisen.
Ich heirate	in zehn Jahren, irgendwann, erst mit 25 Jahren,	weil da	ich erst einmal Spaß haben will. ich im Moment keine Verantwortung will.
Ich möchte (keine) Kinder haben,		denn	ich mag sie (nicht).

2.3 F Gleichheit für alle – ist das möglich?

■ Hat Ahmet keine Chance?

Interviewer: Guten Tag, Ahmet. Woher kommst du?

Ahmet: Ich komme aus Berlin in Deutschland. Ich bin hier geboren, aber meine Eltern kommen aus der Türkei. Wir wohnen in einer Wohnung im sozialen Wohnungsbau.

Interviewer: Wie findest du das?

Ahmet: Dort ist es nicht so schön, denn es gibt Probleme mit Vandalismus und Gewaltkriminalität.

Interviewer: Was für eine Schule besuchst du?

Ahmet: Ich besuche eine Hauptschule am Stadtrand.

Interviewer: Und bist du in der Schule glücklich?

Ahmet: Eigentlich nicht. Die meisten Schüler hier sind Türken, also sind fast alle meine Freunde Türken. Im Klassenzimmer müssen wir Deutsch reden, aber auf dem Schulhof sprechen wir nie Deutsch, nur Türkisch. Am Anfang habe ich Deutsch schwierig gefunden, aber jetzt geht's besser.

Interviewer: Und wie ist es zu Hause?

Ahmet: Meine Eltern können wenig Deutsch sprechen und zu Hause spricht niemand Deutsch. Jeden Tag sehen wir nur Sendungen aus der Türkei im Satellitenfernsehen. Das finde ich schade.

Interviewer: Hast du denn keine deutschen Freunde?

Ahmet: Doch, ich kenne ein paar Leute in der Schule, aber wir sind keine richtigen Freunde. Ich bleibe normalerweise in der Gegend und war noch nie in der Stadtmitte.

Interviewer: Und wie sind deine Noten in der Schule?

Ahmet: Nicht besonders gut – ich bin sehr schwach in Mathe. Ich möchte auf die Uni gehen, aber ich habe keine Chance!

1 ⓥ Using the vocabulary list on page 47, solve these anagrams connected with social problems. Then translate them into English.

Beispiel: **1** *reden (to speak)*

1	dreen	4	trimakitinäl
2	danimen	5	zaislo
3	asmalsidnuv	6	rusasisms

7 badschool

8 neecilight

9 tulee

2a 📖 🎧 Read about Ahmet's problems. Choose the correct answers.

Beispiel: **1** *a*

1 Ahmet was born in … **a** Germany **b** Turkey **c** Switzerland.
2 His parents live in … **a** Turkey **b** Berlin **c** Bern.
3 Where he lives, there are problems with … **a** Turks **b** the flat **c** crime.
4 His school is … **a** on the outskirts of the city **b** in the city centre **c** in the next town.
5 He speaks German … **a** with his parents **b** in the classroom **c** in the school yard.
6 With his German friends, he … **a** goes into the city centre **b** watches TV **c** does nothing – he meets them only at school.

2b 📖 🎧 Read the text again and answer the following questions in English.

Beispiel: 1 *In a social housing flat*

1 What type of accommodation does Ahmet's family live in?
2 How is his German now?
3 What do we know about his family's TV habits?
4 How does he feel about the situation at home?
5 Where does he usually spend his time?
6 How is he getting on at school?
7 What does he regret about the future?

3 Ⓖ Join the two sentences together to form one new sentence by using the correct conjunction from the two given in brackets. Then translate the new sentences into English.

1 Ich kenne ein paar Leute in der Schule.
   Wir sind keine richtigen Freunde. (aber/denn)
2 Dort ist es nicht so schön.
   Es gibt Probleme mit Rassismus. (aber/denn)
3 Wir besuchen eine Schule am Stadtrand.
   Sie ist nicht sehr groß. (und/denn)
4 Meine Eltern bleiben meistens zu Hause.
   Sie haben Probleme mit der Sprache. (aber/denn)

4 🎧 Listen to the radio report about a project in Germany called „Schule ohne Rassismus – Schule mit Courage". Choose the three correct statements.

1 It is a project for students who are against all forms of discrimination.
2 Religion and skin colour are of no importance to those taking part in the project.
3 The project began in Germany in 1988.
4 To gain the title, 80% of students and teachers must show that they are against discrimination.
5 Unfortunately, the school doesn't organise enough events to support the project.
6 There is less fear now among immigrants and German people.

5 💬 Taking it in turns, interview each other playing the role of an immigrant. In your answers, make sure that you include examples of *seit* + present tense, *aber*, *denn*, *weil* and *obwohl*.

- Woher kommst du?
- Seit wann lebst du in ...?
- Welche Probleme hast du?
- Wie findest du das?

Grammatik · *Seite 187*

Using coordinating conjunctions

Coordinating conjunctions are words which join sentences together. The most common ones are *und* ('and'), *aber* ('but') and *denn* ('for', 'because'). They are easy to use because **they do not affect the word order**.

Ich habe wenig Geld. + Ich kann die Leute nicht verstehen.

Ich habe wenig Geld und ich kann die Leute nicht verstehen.

If you use *aber* and *denn* as conjunctions, put a comma before them.

Ich mag die Leute, aber es gibt Probleme mit dem Essen.

Also learn how to use *seit* + present tense.   *See page 44* ➡

Strategie 5

Gaining thinking time when speaking

During a Speaking task, it is important to respond fairly promptly to a question and to avoid long silences. To help you do this, it will help to learn a few phrases which you can use to give you 'thinking time', e.g. *das stimmt* ('That's right'), *ich glaube schon* ('I think so'), *naja / tja / also* ('well'), *im Großen und Ganzen* ('on the whole'), *meinetwegen* ('as far as I am concerned / I don't mind').

Hinweis

2.3 Groundwork is available in the Foundation Book.

2.3 H Armut

■ Zwei junge Leute, zwei verschiedene Lebensstile

Claudia

Hallo, ich heiße Claudia und bin 19 Jahre alt. Mein Vater ist der Inhaber einer internationalen Firma, die Markenkleidung produziert. Wir haben ein wunderschönes Haus in der Schweiz an einem See. Hier befindet sich unsere Jacht. Zu meinem letzten Geburtstag habe ich einen roten Lamborghini bekommen. Meine Freundinnen sind total neidisch! Normalerweise stehe ich gegen zehn Uhr auf, ziehe mich an und schminke mich. Dann rufe ich ein paar Freundinnen an. Manchmal treffen wir uns zu Mittag und dann gehen wir einkaufen. Nach so einem Tag bin ich sehr müde, aber ich muss mich für die Party bei meiner besten Freundin zurechtmachen. Das ist ganz schön anstrengend!

Bodo

Ich heiße Bodo und bin siebzehn Jahre alt. Meine Eltern haben mich vor drei Jahren rausgeschmissen, weil sie drogensüchtig sind. Jetzt bin ich obdachlos und mein „Schlafzimmer" ist der Eingang von einem Supermarkt. Abends finde ich oft alte Butterbrote in der Mülltonne, da ihr Mindesthaltbarkeitsdatum überschritten ist. Nachts kann ich aber nicht gut schlafen, weil ich Angst habe. Um Geld zu bekommen, sitze ich tagsüber mit meinem Hund vor dem Bahnhof. Wenn ich Glück habe, geben mir die Leute etwas. Ich habe wenige Freunde, weil so viele Obdachlose Alkoholiker sind. Ich finde mein Leben so langweilig, aber was kann ich tun? Ich bin schmutzig und meine Kleider riechen. Ich habe keine Aussicht auf einen Job, aber ich weiß, dass ich Hilfe brauche.

1a 📖 🎧 List the adjectives and nouns which suggest a) a well-off lifestyle, and b) a poor lifestyle.

1b 📖 🎧 Read about Bodo again. Complete the sentences using words from the list below.

Beispiel: 1 *seit*

Bodo lebt **1**＿＿＿＿ drei Jahren auf der Straße, weil seine Eltern Drogen **2**＿＿＿＿. Er isst nur alte Butterbrote, die er findet. Nachts schläft er nicht so **3**＿＿＿＿, da er Angst hat. Tagsüber sitzt er vor dem Bahnhof und bekommt **4**＿＿＿＿ von Leuten, die vorbeigehen. Er kennt viele Obdachlose, die Alkoholiker sind. Also **5**＿＿＿＿ er sie. Leider hat er keine Chance auf einen Job, **6**＿＿＿＿ er sieht so schmutzig aus.

lange	bitten	denn	meidet	seit
Butterbrote	nehmen	Geld		

Identifying compound words

Strategie 1a

German sometimes uses long words, but these don't have to be daunting. Learn how to break them up to understand the meaning,

e.g. *Mindesthaltbarkeitsdatum = Mindest + haltbarkeits + datum*

= minimum keep-ability date, in other words, 'best-before date'.

2a **G** Join the sentences together to form one new sentence by using the subordinating conjunction given in brackets.

Beispiel: 1 *Nachts kann ich nicht gut schlafen, weil ich Angst habe.*

1   Nachts kann ich nicht gut schlafen. Ich habe Angst. (weil)
2   Die Dame hat sich ein neues Auto gekauft. Sie hat schon zwei andere Autos. (obwohl)
3   Ich fühle mich sehr einsam. Ich schlafe hinter dem Supermarkt. (wenn)
4   Das Mädchen kann täglich viel Geld ausgeben. Ihr Freund ist einfach so reich. (da)
5   Ich kann etwas zu essen kaufen. Ich bekomme genug Geld. (wenn)
6   Heiko geht heute Abend auf eine Party. Er hat gestern zu viel getrunken. (obwohl)
7   Meine Freundin arbeitet oft ehrenamtlich. Sie findet das sehr wichtig. (weil)

2b **G** After you have had your answers checked, rewrite the sentences so that they start with the subordinate clause.

Beispiel: 1 *Weil ich Angst habe, kann ich nachts nicht gut schlafen.*

3a 🎧 Listen to these three young people being interviewed about their voluntary work for the homeless. Choose the correct answers.

Beispiel: 1 *a*

1   Renate helps the homeless by …   a cooking for them
    b donating money   c buying them food.
2   She …   a thinks she should do more   b enjoys the work
    c helps in a supermarket too.
3   Benjamin's school has a charity event …   a once a week
    b three times a month   c weekly.
4   He helps by …   a selling cakes
    b collecting nearly-new clothes   c helping with the cooking.
5   He and his friends …   a raise lots of money
    b don't raise money   c raise a little money.
6   For the homeless, Bettina's school organises …
    a charity events   b practical help   c a bed for the night.
7   At the school, the homeless can …   a make friends
    b find work   c get a haircut.

> **Grammatik** Seite 188
>
> ### Using subordinating conjunctions
> Conjunctions join clauses together. Subordinating conjunctions make the main verb go to the end of the clause. The most common ones are *weil* ('because'), *wenn* ('if' / 'when'), *obwohl* ('although'), *dass* ('that') and *da* ('since' / 'because').
>
> *Ich will Karriere machen.* + *Meine Eltern sind sehr reich.*
>
> main clause
>
> subordinate clause
>
> *Ich will Karriere machen, obwohl meine Eltern sehr reich sind.*
>
> Also learn how to use *um … zu ….*   *See page 39* ➡

3b 🎧 Listen again. Answer the following questions in English.

1   How often does Renate help the homeless?
2   How do supermarkets help?
3   What does she say about society?
4   Why does Benjamin help?
5   Which three things does Bettina say are luxuries for homeless people?
6   How often does her school organise what it does for the homeless?

4 ✏ Imagine that you are either very rich or very poor. Write about your lifestyle – *Ein Tag in meinem Leben*. Mention:

■ your daily routine
■ what you wear
■ where you live
■ any problems you face

Relationships and choices

1 Copy out the sentences and fill in the missing possessive adjective. For questions 1–4, you will need the nominative case, and for 5–7 the accusative.

Beispiel: **1** *Mein bester Freund heißt Felix.*

1 _____ bester Freund heißt Felix. (mein / meine / meinen)

2 _____ Familie wohnt in Köln. (mein / meine / meinen)

3 Am Wochenende gehen _____ Freunde einkaufen. (ihr / ihre / ihren)

4 Hat _____ Vater ein deutsches Auto? (dein / deine / deinen)

5 Ich treffe _____ Bruder in der Stadtmitte. (sein / seine / seinen)

6 Karl und ich besuchen am Samstag _____ Onkel. (unser / unsere / unseren)

7 Beate muss _____ Hausaufgaben machen. (ihr / ihre / ihren)

Using possessive adjectives

These are words which tell you who something belongs to, e.g. 'my', 'your' etc. The basic words are:

mein – my

dein – your (familiar singular)

sein – his, its (masc. or neut. nouns)

ihr – her, its (fem. nouns)

unser – our

euer – your (familiar plural)

ihr – their

Ihr – your (polite, sing./pl.)

They often add endings and this depends on the gender and case of the noun which follows:

	Masc.	**Fem.**	**Neuter**	**Plural**
Nominative	*mein*	*meine*	*mein*	*meine*
Accusative	*meinen*	*meine*	*mein*	*meine*

Mein Vater ist 40 Jahre alt. – My father is 40 years old.

Unsere Oma wohnt in Süddeutschland. – Our grandmother lives in Southern Germany.

For a reminder about cases and gender, see pages 174–175.

Grammatik Seite 175

---

2 Note down the adverbial time phrases in the following sentences. Then translate the sentences into English:

1 Ich heirate in fünf Jahren.

2 Wir kaufen am Samstag unsere Trauringe.

3 Ich will mit dreißig Jahren verheiratet sein und Kinder haben.

4 Meine Freundin und ich suchen am Wochenende eine Wohnung.

5 Seine Schwester will eines Tages heiraten, aber jetzt noch nicht.

Adverbial phrases of time

These are phrases such as:

in zwei Jahren – in two years / in two years' time

nächstes Jahr – next year

eines Tages – one day

in den Ferien – in the holidays

Often these phrases can help you to talk about the future while using the present tense:

In den Ferien fahre ich nach Schottland.

(Note that the verb comes next if you begin a sentence with one of these phrases.)

Grammatik Seite 179

---

3 Answer the following questions in German using complete sentences.

1 Seit wann lernst du Deutsch? Ich lerne seit … Deutsch

2 Seit wann wohnst du in …? ich wohne seit … in …

3 Seit wann besuchst du diese Schule? Ich besuche diese Schule seit …

4 Seit wann kennst du deinen besten Freund / deine beste Freundin? Ich kenne ihn / sie seit …

Using *seit* and the present tense

To say you have been doing something for a certain length of time, you must use *seit* and the present tense, e.g.

Ich lerne seit zwei Jahren Deutsch. – I have been learning German for two years.

Here is a list of useful phrases:

seit vier Tagen – for four days

seit einer Woche – for a week

seit zwei Wochen – for two weeks

seit einem Monat – for a month

seit einem Jahr – for a year

seit fünf Jahren – for five years

Grammatik Seite 186

4 Complete the following sentences using the correct word for 'it'. Use a dictionary to check the gender of the word that 'it' refers to.

Beispiel: 1 *Ich habe ein schweres Leben. Es ist furchtbar!*

1   Ich habe ein schweres Leben. _____ ist furchtbar!

2   Meine Beziehung zu meinem Stiefvater? _____ ist sehr gut.

3   Hast du ein gutes Verhältnis zu deinen Eltern? Ja, _____ ist toll.

4   Wir wohnen in einem sehr großen Wohnblock. _____ ist so hässlich.

5   Jeden Tag kauft ihre Stiefmutter Alkohol. _____ ist ganz teuer.

6   Mein Onkel wohnt in einer Wohnung. _____ ist sehr gemütlich.

> **Grammatik** Seite 179
>
> ### Using the word 'it'
> The German word for 'it' is not always *es*! It depends on the gender of the noun 'it' refers to. For the nominative case, you use *er* (masc.), *sie* (fem.) and *es* (neut.) So *das Buch* is *es*, but *die Banane* is *sie*. Don't be put off by the fact that *er* and *sie* also mean 'he' and 'she' – it should be clear from the context what the particular meaning is.

5 Read the following sentences and note down all the adjectives and quantifiers / intensifiers. Write 'A' or 'Q' above each one.

                  Q   A   Q   A
Beispiel: 1 *sehr böse ziemlich jung*

1   Mein Vater ist sehr böse, weil ich heirate, obwohl ich noch ziemlich jung bin.

2   Martina ist ziemlich eifersüchtig, weil ihre Schwester schon verlobt ist.

3   Seine Kusine will eine große Hochzeit, die ganz traditionell ist.

4   Ottos Eltern sind wirklich traurig, dass er jetzt getrennt ist.

5   Ihr Freund ist normalerweise nett, aber er kann ab und zu etwas eingebildet sein.

> **Grammatik** Seite 177
>
> ### Adjectives after nouns
> Adjectives are words which describe nouns. When they come after the noun, they work the same way as in English and do not have to be changed in any way:
> *Mein Bruder ist groß.*
> *Meine Schwester ist klein.*
>
> ### Quantifiers / intensifiers
> Quantifiers or intensifiers are a type of adverb (words which describe verbs or adjectives – these often end in 'ly' in English.) Quantifiers indicate the extent of something:
> *Mein Bruder ist **sehr** groß.*
> *Meine Schwester ist **ziemlich** klein.*

6a Add the correct definite article for each of these nouns.

1   _____ Enkelin
2   _____ Rassismus
3   _____ Diskriminierung
4   _____ Freundschaft
5   _____ Rentner
6   _____ Kriminalität
7   _____ Humor
8   _____ Geschlecht
9   _____ Käfig
10 _____ Formular

> **Grammatik** Seite 174
>
> ### Understanding nouns and gender
> Deciding whether a noun is masculine, feminine or neuter can be tricky, but here are some ways to help. (There are some exceptions, though.)
>
> **Masculine**
> Usually words ending in -ich, -ig, -us, -or
> Many words ending in -er
>
> **Feminine**
> Words ending in -ei, -heit, -ie, -in, -keit, -schaft, -tät, -tion, -ung, -ur
>
> Most words ending in -e (but *der Käse, der Name, das Auge, das Interesse, das Ende*)
>
> **Neuter**
> Most words starting with Ge- (but *die Geschichte, die Gesundheit*)
> Many words ending in -al, -ar, -ier, -o

6b Using the German you know, find further examples of each type of ending.

Relationships and choices

Topic 2.1 Relationships with family and friends

2.1 F Wie ist es in deiner Familie?
➡ *pages 32–33*

das	Alter	age
	auskommen mit	to get on with
	geschieden	divorced
	gestorben	dead, died
	getrennt	separated
die	Großeltern	grandparents
	heiraten	to marry, get married
	leben	to live
	ledig	single
	lustig	fun, cheerful
	nett	nice
der	Schwager	brother-in-law
	Stief-	step-
	sympathisch	nice, kind
das	Verhältnis	relationship
	verheiratet	married
	verlobt	engaged
der / die	Verwandte	relation
	vorstellen	to introduce
	Zwillings-	twin (adj)

2.1 H Ich komme mit meiner Familie ganz gut aus ➡ *pages 34–35*

	ärgern	to annoy, irritate
die	Beziehung	relationship
	böse	angry
	deswegen	because of this / that
	eifersüchtig	jealous
der	Einfluss	influence
	eingebildet	conceited
die	Feier	celebration

	gemein	mean
	Halb-	half-
	hilfsbereit	helpful
das	Leben	life
	nerven	to annoy, irritate
die	Sache	thing
	schwatzen	to gossip, chatter
	Schwieger...	-in-law
	(sich) streiten	to argue
	streng	strict
	(sich) verstehen mit	to get on with
	zufrieden	content, satisfied

Topic 2.2 Future plans regarding marriage / partnership

2.2 F Wie findest du Heiraten? ➡ *pages 36–37*

	bestimmt	definitely
	einfach	simple, simply
	erwarten	to wait (for)
	(sich auf etw.) freuen	to look forward to sth.
der	Gast	guest
	heutzutage	these days
	hoffentlich	hopefully
die	Hochzeit	wedding
	kaum	hardly
die	Meinung	opinion
der	Moment	moment
das	Mitglied	member
	ohne	without
	(sich) scheiden (lassen)	to get divorced
	teilen	to share
der	Trauring	wedding ring
die	Verantwortung	responsibility
der / die	Verlobte	fiancé(e)

	wenig	little, not much
die	*Zeit*	time

2.2 H Warum soll ich denn heiraten?
➡ *pages 38–39*

	ähnlich	similar
	altmodisch	old-fashioned
der	*Anfang*	beginning
die	*Braut*	bride
der	*Bräutigam*	bridegroom
	der / die / dasselbe	the same
die	*Einladung*	invitation
	erfolgreich	successful(ly)
	feiern	to celebrate
	jedoch	yet, however
der	*Junggeselle*	bachelor
die	*Karriere*	career
	kennen lernen	to get to know
die	*Kusine*	cousin (f)
	küssen	to kiss
	miteinander	with one another
	ein paar	a couple, few
die	*Trauung*	wedding ceremony
	unnötig	unnecessary
	wahrscheinlich	probably

Topic 2.3 Social issues and equality

2.3 F Gleichheit für alle – ist das möglich?
➡ *pages 40–41*

die	*Angst*	fear
der	*Ausländer*	foreigner
die	*Diskriminierung*	discrimination
	eigentlich	actually, really
der	*Einwanderer*	immigrant
die	*Gegend*	area
die	*Gesellschaft*	society
die	*Gewalt*	violence
die	*Hautfarbe*	skin colour
die	*Kriminalität*	crime
die	*Leute (pl)*	people

	niemand	no one
	obdachlos	homeless
	ohne	without
der	*Rassismus*	racism
	reden	to speak
der	*soziale Wohnungsbau*	social housing
die	*Sprache*	language
der	*Vandalismus*	vandalism
	weniger	less

2.3 H Armut ➡ *pages 42–43*

	anstrengend	demanding
die	*Armut*	poverty
	ausgeben	to spend (money)
(keine)	*Aussicht auf Arbeit*	(no) prospect of work
der / die	*Bedürftige*	person in need
	ehrenamtlich	voluntary, voluntarily
	einsam	lonely
	ermüdend	tiring
die	*Gelegenheit*	opportunity
das	*Mindesthaltbarkeitsdatum*	best-before date
	notwendig	necessary
	nützlich	useful
	passieren	to happen
	sammeln	to collect
	spenden	to donate
die	*Veranstaltung*	event
	verbringen	to spend (time)
	verkaufen	to sell
die	*Wohltätigkeit*	charity
	wunderschön	gorgeous, very beautiful

Higher – Exam practice

ⓘnfo

These pages give you the chance to try GCSE-style practice exam questions at grades B-A* based on the AQA Context of Lifestyle.

Hinweis

Foundation practice exam questions (grades D-C) are available at the end of this Context in the Foundation book.

1 📖 Christian has written about his lifestyle. Read the letter and choose the correct word from the list below for each gap.

gehen	gefahren	fahre	sitze
gegessen	fit	Restaurants	habe
Training	soll		

(**Total = 7 marks**)

2a 📖 Andrei has written about his family life. Read the email and decide whether the statements are true (**T**), false (**F**) or not in the text (**?**).

1 Andrei and his family have a pleasant lifestyle.
2 His mother works in a suburb of Bremerhaven.
3 Andrei's mother likes her job.
4 Andrei gets on well with his brother.
5 Andrei's brother works in a homeless shelter every weekend.

(**Total = 5 marks**)

Als ich jünger war, **A** *ich immer sehr gesund gelebt. Jedes Wochenende bin ich schwimmen gegangen und unter der Woche bin ich immer mit dem Rad in die Schule* **B** *. Ich habe mich auch immer gesund ernährt, weil meine Mutter immer gesagt hat, dass ich Obst und Gemüse essen* **C** *.*

Heutzutage ist das leider etwas anders, weil ich und meine Freunde oft in Fastfood **D** *essen. Ich bin auch nicht mehr so aktiv und* **E** *meistens vor dem Fernseher oder mache irgendwelche Spiele am Computer.*

Ich muss etwas dagegen machen, weil ich mich nicht mehr wohl fühle. Ich werde ab nächster Woche in einen Sportverein **F** *und zweimal in der Woche trainieren, um wieder* **G** *zu werden.*

Christian

Guten Tag. Mein Name ist Andrei und ich wohne in Bremerhaven in Norddeutschland. Meine Familie und ich haben einen sehr angenehmen Lebensstil. Mein Vater ist Firmenchef und meine Mutter hat eine Boutique im Stadtzentrum. Ich liebe meine Eltern sehr, aber mein Bruder, Petru, geht mir auf den Wecker. Obwohl er erst siebzehn Jahre alt ist, hat er ein Auto und er ist so angeberisch. Er geht drei- oder viermal pro Woche auf Partys, er trinkt zu viel und er arbeitet nicht! Er bekommt das Geld dafür von unseren Eltern. Ich finde das furchtbar. Ich glaube, man sollte anderen Leuten helfen und kein Geld verschwenden. Deswegen arbeite ich jedes Wochenende mit den Obdachlosen neben dem Busbahnhof. Mein Bruder findet das blöd, aber ich finde ihn blöd. Wir haben Glück, dass wir viel Geld haben und uns ein schönes Leben machen können. Das sollen wir nicht vergessen.

2b 📖 Read the email again. Answer the questions in English.

1 What exactly does Petru do three or four times a week? (2)
2 Where does Petru get money from?
3 Where is the homeless shelter?
4 What does Petru think about Andrei's work?
5 What is Andrei's attitude towards his family's lifestyle?

Total = 6 marks

3 🎧 Kurt is talking about drugs. Listen and answer the questions in English.

Part 1
a How old was Kurt when he started smoking cannabis?
b What did his parents make him do?
c What happened most days?

Part 2
d How old was he when he met Sonja?
e What did Kurt want to do?
f What happened after six months?

Part 3
g How do Kurt and Sonja make money?
h What do they think is awful?
i What is Kurt afraid of?

Total = 9 marks

4a 🎧 Anna is talking about her family. Listen and choose the correct answer for each statement.

Part 1
1 Anna's parents
  a live together
  b are divorced
  c both have a step-brother.

Part 2
2 Anna can get into trouble when she
  a is home late
  b doesn't do her homework
  c plays music too loudly.

Part 3
3 Anna is
  a 15
  b 17
  c 19.

Total = 3 marks

4b 🎧 Listen to Anna again and answer the questions in English.

1 Who does Anna live with? (3)
2 What does Anna do at the weekend?
3 What is most important to Anna?
4 What does Anna find unfair?
5 How does Anna's step-father react when her step-brother comes home drunk? (2)

Total = 8 marks

Total for Reading and Listening = 38 marks

Strategie 1

Tackling gap fill tasks

Understanding grammar can help you fill in gaps. Particular structures require certain types of words. If you use a modal verb such as *sollen* or *wollen*, for example, you need to have another verb in the sentence which is in the infinitive and therefore ends in *-en*. If you see a past participle (which often starts with *ge-*), remember that the sentence also needs a form of *haben* or *sein*.

Strategie 2a

Searching for clues

Occasionally you may not find exactly the words or phrases you have learned. Try and find other clues and expressions to lead you to the answer. Instead of 'I get on with' or 'I don't get on with' you may find an adjective in the text which expresses likes and dislikes.

Strategie 4b

Getting maximum marks

Always check how many marks are awarded to a question. You will find this in brackets after the question. If the bracket includes (2) you will have to mention two things; if the bracket includes (3), make sure you mention three points.

Higher – Speaking

Meine Familie: heute und in der Zukunft

You are talking to a German friend about your family and your future plans.

Your teacher will play the role of the friend. He or she could ask you the following:

1. Who is in your family?
2. What are they like?
3. Who do you get on with?
4. Who don't you get on with?
5. What problems do you have at home?
6. What are your future family and relationship plans?
7. !

! Remember, you will have to respond to something that you have not yet prepared.

> **info**
>
> **Important information:**
> This sample task is for practice purposes only and should not be used as an actual assessment task. Study it to find out how to plan your Controlled Assessment efficiently to gain maximum marks and / or work through it as a mock exam task before the actual Controlled Assessment.

---

1 Who is in your family?
- say how many people there are in your family and which family members live with you
- introduce two of the family members and give details about their age and when they were born
- talk about your relationship with them
- explain why you have a good or bad relationship with them

> **Strategie**
>
> Start your plan. Write a maximum of six words for each bullet point. Here are some suggested words for the first bullet point: *Familienmitglieder, bei uns, Grund, verwandt sein*. Remember that the maximum number of words allowed in your plan is 40.
>
> Use *wir verstehen uns* to say that you all get on well with each other. Use conjunctions such as *weil, da, denn, obwohl* to explain why you get on with someone.

---

2 What are they like?
- describe at least two of your family members and compare them
- talk about the personality of one or two of your family members
- give an account of what one of the family members likes doing
- give details of why they enjoy doing the activity

> **Strategie**
>
> Suggested words for your plan: *freundlicher als, nicht so nett wie*.
>
> Show initiative when you describe your family, e.g. say what a person looks like now and how they used to look. Show initiative by extending your answers. You could, for example, mention what one person used to be like by adding *früher war er / sie … aber jetzt …* . See Exam technique S10.

---

3 Who do you get on with?
- say who you get on with in your family and why this person is special to you
- say for how long you have known the person
- describe the person's character
- mention things you like doing together, how often you do them and where

> **Strategie**
>
> Suggested words for your plan: *auskommen, besonders, wichtig sein*. Add two or three more words to the list.
>
> Show that you can use the perfect tense, for example for the last sub-division. Although it only asks you to talk about things you like doing together, give an example of something you did together recently: *Wir sind zusammen in die Stadt gegangen und haben einen Film gesehen. Der Film war super*. This shows that you can use a variety of tenses and show initiative.

4 Who don't you get on with?

- say who you don't get on with in your family
- give at least three reasons why you don't get on with this person
- give a description of the person's character
- give an account of an occasion recently when the person did something you didn't like

Suggested words for your plan: *nerven, kürzlich, Persönlichkeit.* Add three more words to this list.

Use an advanced structure such as *Als wir kürzlich im Kino waren, hat er / sie …* By doing so you show that you can use complex structures. Remember that the word **when** in the past tense is *als* in German.

For the last sub-division it is important that you tell a story in order to have access to the highest grades.

5 What problems do you have at home?

- describe your home life
- mention one problem you have at home and who it is with
- mention how you feel about the problem
- say how you could be solving the problem

Suggested words for your plan: *im Allgemeinen, Alltagsleben, täglich.* Add a maximum of three words to this list.

This is a good opportunity for you to be creative as the first sub-division is very open ended. You could decide to talk about helping at home or your daily routine and add as much information and detail as you can.

Use the conditional tense to say how you could solve the problem. *Ich könnte, ich sollte, ich müsste* + verb in the infinitive at the end of the sentence are all useful phrases for this.

6 What are your future family and relationship plans?

- say whether you want to get married or stay single
- say why
- say whether you want to live on your own or with someone else
- give a reason

Suggested words for your plan: *ledig, geschieden, Vorteil, Nachteil.* Add two more words to this list.

Use a variety of starter phrases to introduce your plans. *Wenn ich älter bin, möchte ich …; In Zukunft wenn ich erwachsen bin, werde ich … .* All of these phrases need a verb in the infinitive at the end of the sentence, e.g. *Ich werde einmal heiraten.*

Improve your speaking by adding a comparison:

Auf der einen Seite … auf der anderen Seite … . Add the verb after *Seite* to make sure that the word order is correct.

7 **!** At this point, you may be asked to …

- describe your best friend
- say who your favourite family member is
- say who you get on with the least in your family
- say whether being an only child is an advantage or a disadvantage.

Think about what the surprise question could be. There are some suggestions in the sub-divisions. Then work out what your answer would be to each of those and any other questions you think might be asked.

You should have four words left to add to your list, so choose carefully. For the second sub-division, you might choose *Lieblingsfamilienmitglied. Nicht leiden* could be useful for answering the third sub-division.

Pick words that you haven't already used in your preparation, as you're more likely to need help remembering these. Remember to check the total number of words you have used. It must be 40 or fewer.

Hinweis

Foundation sample assessment tasks for this Context can be found in the Foundation book.

Higher – Writing

Ich will gesund leben

You are entering a competition and have to write an article in German about what you do to stay healthy. You could include:

1. how healthy you are at the moment
2. your diet
3. whether you exercise at the moment
4. your view on smoking
5. your view on drinking alcohol / taking drugs
6. an example of someone with an unhealthy lifestyle
7. how you intend to stay healthy in future.

> **info**
>
> **Important information:**
> This sample task is for practice purposes only and should not be used as an actual assessment task. Study it to find out how to plan your Controlled Assessment efficiently to gain maximum marks and / or work through it as a mock exam task before the actual Controlled Assessment.

---

1 How healthy you are at the moment

– introduce yourself and say whether you think you have a healthy or unhealthy lifestyle
– give reasons for your answer
– give a physical description of yourself and say how you feel about that
– mention how much sleep you get, how stressed you feel and give reasons

Strategie

Start your plan. Write five or six words for each bullet point. Here are some suggested words for the first bullet point: *Lebensstil, Schlaf, Schulstress, spät, aufstehen, wiegen.*

Look at the sub-divisions in the later bullet points to avoid an overlap and repeating yourself.

Avoid giving too much basic information when describing yourself. Use more advanced phrases such as *Ich wiege … und ich denke, dass das … ist.* This allows you to describe yourself and give an opinion at the same time.

---

2 Your diet

– say what you consider to be a healthy diet and give reasons
– say whether you consider your own diet to be healthy and explain why
– give your view about fast food and how often you eat fast food
– say how you could improve your diet

Strategie

Suggested words for your plan: *Nahrungsmittel, Kohlenhydrate, Eiweiß, vor kurzem.* Add one more word.

Try not to write down long lists of food and drink in your plan, which are relatively easy to remember. You can still mention them but try putting them into a more advanced context by explaining which food category they fall in to and whether that makes your diet healthy or unhealthy.

Ich esse viel Brot, Pasta und Pizza, was viele Kohlenhydrate enthält. Meiner Meinung nach ist das …

For the last bullet point use the future or conditional forms: *ich werde / möchte / könnte + infinitive.*

---

3 Whether you exercise at the moment

– say what exercise you do at the moment and where and how often you exercise
– mention why you think that exercise is beneficial to your health
– give an account of an activity you did recently
– say whether you enjoyed it or not and whether you will do it again

Strategie

Suggested words for your plan: *Leichtathletik, Mannschaft, letzte Woche, gefallen.* Add one more word.

Think of various ways of expressing your opinion, e.g. *ich glaube, dass …, ich denke, dass …, ich bin der Meinung, dass …* . Remember to put the verb to the end after *dass*.

When you use the past tense, make sure you remember to use *haben* or *sein* for the perfect tense, e.g. *ich bin in den Sportverein gegangen* but *ich habe dort Kricket gespielt.*

You can write down past participles in your plan such as the word *gefallen.* Remember to say *es hat mir (nicht) gefallen* to say whether you liked or didn't like an activity.

4 Your view on smoking
- say whether you have tried smoking already and what you thought about it
- mention a variety of reasons why people smoke
- mention at least three disadvantages and risks of smoking
- give some advice about how people could stop smoking

Suggested words for your plan: *schon, geraucht, entspannend*. Add three more words to this list.

Remember that the bullet points allow for some flexibility. You may say that you have not smoked before and give reasons for it rather than say that you have tried smoking and what you thought about it.

Try and link the three disadvantages and risks of smoking together, for example by saying *erstens, zweitens, drittens, außerdem,* etc. This will add some flow to your writing.

5 Your view on drinking alcohol / taking drugs
- say whether you have tried alcohol and what the effects were
- say what you think about alcohol and what the consequences of drinking are
- say why you think people take drugs
- give your opinion about drugs and their consequences

Suggested words for your plan: *probiert, betrunken, Gewalt*. Add three more words to this list.

Put together a list of consequences and risks of drinking too much and taking drugs. Make sure you don't use the same reasons for the second and the fourth bullet point to avoid repetition. This is important to gain more points for content.

If you talk about risks and consequences in general you are likely to use *man*, e.g. *Man kann die Kontrolle verlieren*. Remember to use the 3rd person singular for *man*.

6 An example of someone with an unhealthy lifestyle
- talk about someone you know who has an unhealthy lifestyle
- describe their diet and lifestyle
- give reasons why you think their lifestyle is unhealthy
- say what advice you would give them to change their lifestyle

Suggested words for your plan: *fettig, salzig, Vorschlag*. Add three more words to this list.

You are writing about someone else, so make sure you use the correct form of the verbs. *Essen* is particularly tricky as it is an irregular verb. Remember to say *er / sie isst*. Use a number of irregular verbs to show the examiner that you can master those, e.g. *er / sie fährt immer mit dem Auto, er / sie sieht immer fern* etc.

7 How you intend to stay healthy in future
- mention changes to your diet in order to live more healthily
- say what changes you will make to get more sleep, feel less stressed and get more exercise
- mention one bad thing you won't do any more and why
- say what positive impact your lifestyle changes will have on you

Suggested words for your plan: *ändern, Computer*. Add four more words to the list.

This bullet point gives you the opportunity to use the future tense. Don't forget that there are a number of ways to express the future tense, e.g. *ich werde, ich will, ich möchte*.

Try to add other phrases which express the future tense such as *ich habe vor … zu …, ich habe mir vorgenommen … zu …,ich plane … zu …* .Vary the way you talk about the future to increase the range of structures you use.

You could extend your answer by saying what might happen if you don't make any changes to your lifestyle. *Wenn ich mein Leben nicht ändere, werde ich …*

Hinweis

Foundation sample assessment tasks for this Context can be found in the Foundation book.

Exam technique – Speaking

S1 Responding to the bullet points

In a Speaking task, there are likely to be between three and seven bullet points on the task you are given to prepare. One of the bullet points will be the unpredictable element and will appear as an exclamation mark. The teacher will ask you questions based on these bullet points. You could break down the bullet points into sub-divisions, as in this course book, to help you find interesting details to talk about, if your teacher has not already done it for you. It is important that you respond to every question / bullet point in the exam to gain as many marks as possible.

S2 The Speaking plan

You are allowed to write a maximum of 40 words in your plan. Those words can be in German or English. Choose them carefully so that your plan works well as a reminder of what you want to say. Try to use a maximum of six words per bullet point. Remember that you are not allowed to use conjugated verbs (i.e. verbs with an ending other than the infinitive or the past participle) in your plan. Visuals, codes, letters or initialled words, e.g. *i … b … g …* for *ich bin gegangen*, are not allowed.

S3 Preparing for the !

The exclamation mark (often the last bullet point) is there to test you on something that you have not prepared. As you cannot predict exactly what you are going to be asked, it is often referred to as 'the unpredictable element'. However, the unpredictable is often predictable! Ask yourself: what question would logically follow the questions I have already answered? Practise guessing what the unpredictable bullet point might be about. You are likely to come up with two or three possibilities. Prepare answers to cover those possibilities. Practise your possible responses. When you are asked the question, focus on the meaning of the question itself to make sure you understand it and then give your full answer.

Grade booster

To reach grade B, you need to …

- Give a good amount of information for every bullet point and answer generally without hesitation, e.g. bullet point 2. Give many details about two members of your family (physical description) and use a variety of structures to compare them, for example *so groß wie, kleiner als, nicht so schlank wie* etc.

- Include some complex structures, a variety of tenses and ideas and communicate these clearly, e.g. bullet point 5. Although most of the answer will be in the present tense, you should try to include different tenses whenever you can. You could, for example, mention something that happened at home recently. *Mein Leben zu Hause ist normalerweise in Ordnung, aber gestern habe ich mit meiner Schwester gestritten, weil sie mich genervt hat …*

To reach grade A, you need to …

- Develop nearly all your answers and show initiative. For example, bullet point 6 is very open-ended, which gives you an opportunity to show initiative and be creative. Mention, for example, what you definitely want to do in the future but also what you don't want to do. Link your plans and reasons together. *Ich will in Zukunft Karriere machen, aber ich will auf keinen Fall in einem Büro arbeiten, weil ich etwas Kreatives machen möchte.*

- Have a good range of vocabulary and your pronunciation must generally be good. Think, for example, about the *ch* sound in German words. Try not to repeat the same words and phrases but think of synonyms to use, for example *ich komme (nicht) mit … . aus / ich verstehe mich (nicht) mit … / Ich habe (keine) Probleme mit …*

To reach grade A*, you need to …

- Present your ideas and points of view with confidence and sustain a conversation at a reasonable speed, e.g. bullet point 3. Give a number of examples of why the person is special to you, refer to events in the past and say what the person has done to help you by giving a thorough account.

- Use a variety of verb tenses and other structures with accuracy even in more complex sentences, for example after conjunctions. Verb endings and the position of verbs are particularly important in all tenses. *Obwohl ich mich mit allen Familienmitgliedern verstehe, komme ich am besten mit meiner Tante aus, da sie mir immer hilft und ich oft bei ihr war, als ich noch kleiner war.*

Exam technique – Writing

W1 Help available

Your teacher is allowed to discuss each task with you in English, including the kind of language you may need and how to use your preparatory work. You can have access to a dictionary, your German books, Kerboodle and internet resources. This is the stage when you will prepare your plan using the Task Planning Form.

When you actually perform the task, you can have access to a dictionary. You will also have the task itself, your plan and your teacher's feedback on your plan, i.e. the Task Planning Form. You cannot use your exercise book, course book or any drafts you may have written to help you practise.

W2 The Writing plan

In your Writing plan you can write a maximum of 40 words. Visuals, conjugated verbs or codes are not allowed.

Use your plan to remind yourself of what you should be writing next. Although it is more helpful to you to write German words in your plan, you can also use English words. Try to divide the 40 words equally between the six to eight bullet points of the task. Don't go over your 40 words allowance.

W3 AQA Administration

For the writing part of your exam, you have to do two different tasks (at two different times). When your teacher has taught you the necessary language for you to complete a task, you will be given the task to prepare. You may be asked to prepare a plan using the Task Planning Form. You will get some feedback on your plan from your teacher at that point. You will then complete your final version, under the direct supervision of your teacher.

You will have 60 minutes to complete each task. You will work in exam conditions and will not be allowed to communicate with others.

Grade booster

To reach grade B, you need to ...

- Have a good variety of vocabulary and structures, e.g. bullet point 2. All the bullet points ask you to use the present tense. Make sure you can use it accurately for a variety of pronouns, e.g. *Ich esse normalerweise … / Viele Menschen essen zu oft Fastfood. / Es ist nicht so gut, wenn man fettiges Essen isst.*

- Convey a lot of information clearly, e.g. bullet point 2. As the language needed for the task is fairly simple, try to write 40 to 50 words for this bullet point but make sure that you write simple sentences with accuracy. Also try to use some more complex structures such as modal verbs and subordinate clauses, to show that you can also use more difficult language.

To reach grade A, you need to ...

- Express and explain ideas and points of view with clarity, e.g. bullet point 4. Explain your views about smoking and its risks and effects clearly. Use a variety of expressions to give your opinion, e.g. *Ich bin der Meinung, dass Rauchen nicht gut ist, da es erstens sehr teuer und zweitens schlecht für die Gesundheit ist.*

- Develop the majority of the points you make, e.g. bullet point 4. In addition to giving advice on how people could stop smoking, you should also give examples of how these changes could affect people positively, e.g. *Man könnte mehr Sport treiben und dadurch fitter und gesünder werden.*

To reach grade A*, you need to ...

- Give a fully relevant and detailed response to the task which is largely accurate, e.g. bullet point 7. Give a lot of information about your lifestyle changes and how you will benefit from them and link all the information together.

- Handle complex sentences with confidence, making very few errors in the process, e.g. bullet point 7. Include the future tense with *werden* as you are talking about what you will do but also try to use additional tenses such as the present tense, for example when you give reasons why you won't do certain things any more. Use complex phrases to talk about the positive consequences of your lifestyle changes, e.g. *Aus diesem Grund werde ich … / Wenn ich mein Leben geändert habe, werde ich …*

3.1 F   Was hast du gestern gemacht?

Lernziele

Talking about free time activities in the past

Using the perfect tense in the singular

Recognising past participles

1 **Ⓥ** These words are all associated with activities you might do in your free time. Put them into three groups: music, sport or other activities.

Geige   Klavier   Kino   Schach   reiten   kegeln   fernsehen

turnen   Trompete   Handball   bergsteigen   lesen

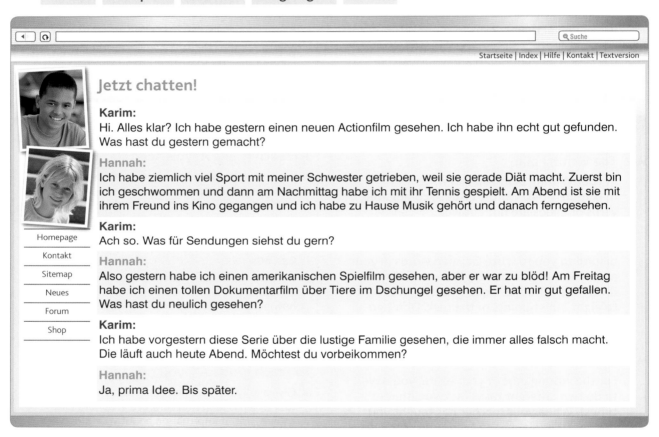

Startseite | Index | Hilfe | Kontakt | Textversion

Jetzt chatten!

Karim:
Hi. Alles klar? Ich habe gestern einen neuen Actionfilm gesehen. Ich habe ihn echt gut gefunden. Was hast du gestern gemacht?

Hannah:
Ich habe ziemlich viel Sport mit meiner Schwester getrieben, weil sie gerade Diät macht. Zuerst bin ich geschwommen und dann am Nachmittag habe ich mit ihr Tennis gespielt. Am Abend ist sie mit ihrem Freund ins Kino gegangen und ich habe zu Hause Musik gehört und danach ferngesehen.

Karim:
Ach so. Was für Sendungen siehst du gern?

Hannah:
Also gestern habe ich einen amerikanischen Spielfilm gesehen, aber er war zu blöd! Am Freitag habe ich einen tollen Dokumentarfilm über Tiere im Dschungel gesehen. Er hat mir gut gefallen. Was hast du neulich gesehen?

Karim:
Ich habe vorgestern diese Serie über die lustige Familie gesehen, die immer alles falsch macht. Die läuft auch heute Abend. Möchtest du vorbeikommen?

Hannah:
Ja, prima Idee. Bis später.

Homepage
Kontakt
Sitemap
Neues
Forum
Shop

2 📖 🎧 Copy the sentences and fill in the gaps with one of the words on the right.

1 Karim war gestern im _____.

2 Der Actionfilm hat ihm gut _____.

3 Hannah ist mit ihrer Schwester ins _____ gegangen.

4 Am Abend hat sie einen _____ aus Amerika gesehen.

5 Hannah fand die Sendung über Tiere viel _____.

6 Die Sendung über die _____ Familie hat Karim gefallen.

7 Karim möchte, dass Hannah zu ihm nach _____ kommt.

8 Hannah findet, dass Karims Plan für heute Abend eine gute _____ ist.

Hause

Hallenbad

Kino

besser

gefallen

Idee

komische

Film

3 **ⓖ** Copy the sentences and fill in the gaps with the correct form of *haben* or *sein*.

1   Ich _____ gestern nach der Schule Schach gespielt.
2   Wann _____ du Musik gehört?
3   Er _____ sehr spät nach Hause gekommen.
4   Meine Freundin _____ ferngesehen.
5   Ich _____ ins Fitnesszentrum gegangen.
6   Andrea _____ Pizza gegessen und Cola getrunken.

4a 🎧 What did these people do last week? Match the names to the activities.

- Anna
- Stefan
- Michaela
- Nuri
- Maik

4b 🎧 Listen again, return to your answers to 4a and put a tick or a cross to show if they enjoyed the activity or not.

5 🖊 You are describing last weekend to friends. Write down what you did following the prompts:

- what you did last weekend
- who else took part in the activity
- how you found the weekend

Now describe what someone else did.

Ich habe / Er hat / Sie hat	letztes Wochenende dann später danach	Sport ... Musik ... einen Film ... Freunde ... Pizza ...	getrieben. gemacht. gesehen. getroffen. gegessen. eingekauft. ferngesehen.
Ich bin / Er ist / Sie ist		ins Kino / ins Schwimmbad / einkaufen / nach London	gegangen. gefahren.
Ich habe	das	mit meinen Freunden / mit meiner Familie / allein	gemacht.
	das Wochenende	gut / schlecht / interessant	gefunden.

Grammatik   *Seite 182*

Using the perfect tense in the singular

The perfect tense is used to talk about the past. It is made up of two parts – an auxiliary verb (*haben* or *sein*) and a past participle. Verbs that involve movement from one place to another take *sein*. Here are the forms you need in the singular:

ich habe	*gemacht*
du hast	*gespielt*
er / sie / es hat	*gehört*
ich bin	*geschwommen*
du bist	*gegangen*
er / sie / es ist	*gefahren*

Also learn how to use separable verbs with the perfect tense.

See page 68 ➡

Strategie 4a–4b

Recognising past participles

You may meet past participles you have not encountered before, but with weak verbs you can work them out from the stem:

gespielt, gemacht etc.

Many verbs have *ge-* in their past participle. Watch or listen out for past participles of separable verbs, where the *ge-* comes in the middle of the word, after the separable prefix:

an*ge***sehen an***ge***rufen** etc.

Note: The verb *gefallen* starts with *ge-* in its infinitive form so take care when you meet it. It might not be in a past tense.

ⅭⅭⅭ Hinweis

3.1 Groundwork is available in the Foundation Book.

3.1 H Ich bin in die Stadt gegangen

Ich bin in die Stadt gefahren

Kornelia
Ich bin in die Stadt gefahren. Ich wohne außerhalb des Zentrums und bin deshalb mit dem Zug gefahren. In der Stadt bin ich einkaufen gegangen. Ich bin mit dem Zug um 17 Uhr wieder nach Hause gefahren.

Natascha
Am Wochenende bin ich zu Hause geblieben, weil am Freitag Feiertag war und ich am Donnerstagabend mit Freunden in die Disko gegangen bin. Wir sind nach der Disko mit dem Taxi nach Hause gefahren. Ich hatte deshalb am Wochenende kein Geld.

Erika
Ich mache gern Sport im Freien. Vorgestern bin ich in den Skatepark gegangen und bin mit ein paar Freunden Skateboard gefahren. Ich bin zum ersten Mal in einer Halfpipe gefahren und über Hindernisse gesprungen und bin ein paar Mal vom Skateboard gefallen. Und dann ist es passiert – ich habe mein Bein gebrochen.

Andreas
Ich bin Mitglied im Schwimmverein. Ich gehe also sehr oft schwimmen. Ich bin schon um halb sechs aufgestanden und mit Freunden zu einem Wettkampf gefahren, wo wir geschwommen sind. Ich habe schon an vielen Wettkämpfen teilgenommen und oft gewonnen.

Kai
Ich bin am Wochenende mit meinen Freunden in die Stadt gegangen. Wir haben uns den neuen James-Bond Film angesehen. Nach dem Film sind ein paar meiner Freunde nach Hause gegangen, und mit den anderen bin ich noch ein bisschen in der Stadt herumgelaufen.

---

1 📖🎧 Read what the teenagers say about their weekends then answer the following questions:

1 Who didn't go out at the weekend?
2 Who likes doing sport outdoors?
3 Who doesn't live in the town centre?
4 Who got up very early?
5 Who went to the cinema?
6 Who came back at 5 p.m.?
7 Who has been very successful in sporting competitions?
8 Who has been out dancing during the week?
9 Who has had an accident?

2 **G** Copy and complete each sentence, using the correct form of *haben* or *sein*.

1 Wir _____ an einem Wettkampf teilgenommen.
2 Am Samstag _____ wir in die Stadt gefahren.
3 Anke und Fabian_____ ins Kino gegangen.

> **Grammatik** Seite 182
>
> **Using the perfect tense in the plural**
>
> Remember the perfect tense is made up of two parts – an auxiliary verb (*haben* or *sein*) and a past participle. The singular forms are shown on page 33. Here are the forms you need in the plural:
>
> | | |
> |---|---|
> | wir haben | gespielt |
> | ihr habt | teilgenommen |
> | Sie / sie haben | gehabt |
> | wir sind | gekommen |
> | ihr seid | gelaufen |
> | Sie / sie sind | gefallen |
>
> You should learn whether to use *haben* or *sein* in the perfect tense.
> See page 69 ➡

4 Frau Schiller, _____ Sie einkaufen gegangen?
5 Die Kinder _____ Musik gehört.
6 Armin und Peter, _____ ihr heute früh aufgestanden?

Reusing questions when giving answers

When giving an answer work out how you can reuse the question you were asked.

*Wohin bist du **gestern gegangen**?*
***Gestern** bin ich ins Kino **gegangen**.*

3a 🎧 Listen to the following interviews and write down the correct letters for Fabian, Max, Charlotte and Denise. You need to listen for where they went, when, with whom and, for three of them, how they got there.

3b 🎧 Listen again and for each person write **P** if their experience was positive, **N** if it was negative and **P+N** if it was both.

4 💬 Work with a partner: one partner asks questions and the other answers. Then swap roles. Use the pictures in Activity 3.

> Wohin bist du am Wochenende gegangen? *(points to picture l)*

> Ich bin in den Park gegangen.

> Was hast du gemacht? *(points to picture k)*

> Ich bin im Schwimmbad geschwommen.

> Wie bist du dorthin gefahren? *(points to _____)*

> Ich bin _____ gegangen / gefahren.

> Mit wem bist du gefahren? *(points to _____)*

> Ich _____

Understanding questions

It is important that you understand questions fully in order to be able to answer them correctly. *Wo, wohin* and *woher* all contain the word *wo* but mean different things. Learn the meanings of question words thoroughly.

Was? – 'what?' *Wie?* – 'how?'
Wer? – 'who?' *Warum?* – 'why?'
Wann? – 'when?' *Wo?* – 'where?'
Mit wem? – 'with whom?'
Was für … ? – 'what sort / type of … ?'
Wohin? – 'where to?'
Welche/r/s? – 'which?'
Woher? – 'where from?'

Ich bin		mit dem Bus / Auto / Zug / Fahrrad	in die Stadt /	gefahren.
Du bist	am Wochenende		in die Schule /	gegangen.
Er / Sie ist	gestern	mit der Straßenbahn / U-Bahn	nach Hause	
Wir sind	letzte Woche			
Ihr seid		zu Fuß	im Schwimmbad	geschwommen.
Sie sind			zu Hause	geblieben.

3.2 F Wir bekommen nicht genug Taschengeld!

Lernziele

Talking about money and shopping

Using the perfect tense of irregular verbs

Checking your written work for accuracy

1 ⓥ Identify the items below. Match them up with the correct shop.

a Obst- und Gemüseladen
b Juweliergeschäft
c Schreibwarengeschäft
d Elektrogeschäft
e Metzgerei
f Konditorei

Mein Geld

Ich bekomme 10 Euro pro Woche und dazu gibt man mir oft Geld zum Geburtstag oder Weihnachten. Ich habe ziemlich viel Geld gespart. Am Wochenende bin ich zum Kaufhaus gegangen und habe mir eine schicke Jacke gekauft. Meine Mutter hat die Hälfte bezahlt.

Nina

Im Moment habe ich nur ein 2-Euro-Stück in meinem Portemonnaie. Das ist nicht viel. Am Samstag habe ich 15 Euro Taschengeld von meinen Eltern bekommen. Dann habe ich aber eine CD und einige Süßigkeiten gekauft. Da bleibt nicht viel übrig! Ich finde es unfair, dass alles so teuer ist!

Saed

Meine Mutter gibt mir kein Taschengeld, aber wenn ich etwas brauche, gibt sie mir genug Geld. Zum Beispiel bin ich letzte Woche mit meiner Freundin ins Kino gegangen. Ich hatte einen 50-Euro-Schein von meiner Mutter und nach dem Film haben wir noch eine Pizza gegessen und eine Cola getrunken. Das Kleingeld habe ich ihr nicht zurückgegeben. Meiner Meinung nach ist das viel besser als Taschengeld!

Christian

2 📖 🎧 Read the texts above and decide whether the statements are true (**T**), false (**F**) or not in the text (**?**).

1 Saed has spent most of last week's pocket money.
2 Christian wishes his mother would give him regular pocket money.
3 Nina has been saving up her pocket money.
4 Christian's mother asked him for the change from a €50 note.
5 Nina's mother made a contribution towards the cost of her jacket.
6 Saed thinks it's unfair that he gets so little pocket money.

Hinweis

3.2 Groundwork is available in the Foundation Book.

3 **G** Copy out the sentences and add the correct past participle in the gaps.

1 Ich bin in die Stadtmitte _____. (gehen)
2 Mein Bruder ist mit dem Bus _____. (fahren)
3 Ich habe zu viel Geld _____. (ausgeben)
4 Hast du Pommes _____? (essen)
5 Katrin hat 12 Euro Taschengeld _____. (bekommen)
6 Saed hat einen 10-Euro-Schein _____. (finden)

4a 🎧 Listen to the interviews with Ahmet, Serena, Ralf, Patrick and Anja and answer the questions in English.

1 Who gets €15 a week?
2 Who says they must buy everything with their pocket money?
3 Who has saved up and bought some trainers?
4 Who gets extra money when they need it?
5 Who has bought some fashion magazines?
6 Who is saving up to travel?

4b 🎧 Listen again and fill in the gaps in these sentences.

1 Ahmet hat neue _____ gekauft.
2 Serena bekommt _____ Taschengeld.
3 Ralf war vor drei Jahren in _____.
4 Patrick muss auch seine _____ kaufen.
5 Anja hat Geld von ihrer _____ bekommen.

Stiefel	Amerika	Mutter	genug	Turnschuhe
kein	Kanada	Essen	Vater	Kleidung

5 🗨️✏️ Carry out a pocket money survey in class. Make up an amount that you would like to get and talk about your dream spending / saving habits! Ask the questions below and use the box to help you with your answers. Then write up the results of your survey, using the worksheet to help you (you will need to use verbs in the third person!).

Ich bekomme	... Euro / Pfund / kein Taschengeld	pro Woche / Monat.
Ich kaufe	Makeup / Zeitschriften / CDs / DVDs / Guthaben fürs Handy / Schmuck / Kleidung / Klamotten	.
Ich gebe mein Geld für		aus.
Ich habe		gekauft.
Ich habe mein Geld für		ausgegeben.
Ich spare für	die Ferien / ein Geschenk für meinen Freund / einen MP3-Spieler / einen Laptop / ein Handy / Konzertkarten / Stiefel.	

Grammatik Seite 182

Using the perfect tense of irregular verbs

Some verbs in the perfect tense don't follow the normal pattern. Very often the vowels in the middle change, e.g. *schreiben* → *geschrieben*, *trinken* → *getrunken*. Sometimes an additional letter is added, e.g. *essen* → *ge**g**essen*. Occasionally the vowel changes and an additional letter is added, e.g. *nehmen* → *ge**n**o**mmen*. Some even look the same as the infinitive, e.g. *bekommen* → *bekommen*. Irregular past participles always end in -*en*. You need to learn them off by heart.

Also learn about recognising the imperfect tense. See page 68 ➡

Strategie 5

Checking your written work for accuracy

As well as using the right auxiliary verb (*haben* or *sein*) in the perfect tense, you need to make sure that the auxiliary verb has the right ending for the person you are talking about (the subject). A very frequent error is to use a singular subject with a plural verb, or a plural subject with a singular verb. Make sure you check for this in your written work.

Taschengeldumfrage:
• Wie viel Taschengeld bekommst du?
• Was machst du mit deinem Taschengeld?
• Was hast du kürzlich mit deinem Taschengeld gemacht / gekauft?
• Wofür sparst du?

3.2 H Wir waren im Einkaufszentrum

Ich kaufte Klamotten

Katharina, 16

Ich war im KaDeWe. Das ist ein großes Kaufhaus in Berlin. Gestern war mein Geburtstag und ich hatte etwas Geld. Ich habe eine neue Jeans und ein grünes Top dazu gekauft. Ich bin ganz zufrieden, obwohl es keine Jacke gab, die mir passte. Ich muss morgen noch einmal schauen.

Selima, 17

Ich hatte kein Glück. Ich war in einer Boutique. Ich habe nichts gefunden, was mir gefallen hat. Es war Sommerschlussverkauf, aber die Qualität der Klamotten war echt schlecht. Ich wollte einen Rock kaufen, aber die waren wirklich alle ätzend.

Lars, 16

Ich war mit ein paar Freunden in der Stadt unterwegs. Wir waren in ein paar Sportgeschäften. Ich wollte eigentlich nichts kaufen, aber ich schaute mich ein bisschen um und habe diese tollen Turnschuhe gesehen. OK, sie waren ein bisschen teuer, aber ich kaufte sie dann doch, nur darf ich das nicht meinen Eltern sagen.

Uli, 16

Ich stehe auf Markenwaren und gehe normalerweise in Designerläden. Da weiß ich, dass die Qualität gut ist. Meine letzte Hose war aus dem Billigladen. Einmal und nie wieder. Die war sofort kaputt und passte nach dem ersten Waschen nicht mehr. Ich muss sie jetzt umtauschen.

Frau Peters, 56

Ich kaufe jetzt nicht mehr so viel Kleidung, aber als ich jünger war, kaufte ich sehr viel. Ich investierte mein ganzes Geld in Hüte, Kleider und Schuhe. Ich kann mir das jetzt nicht mehr leisten. Ich bestelle jetzt meistens aus dem Katalog.

1a 📖🎧 Read the texts above and find the German for these words and phrases.

1 which fitted me
2 from a cut-price store
3 summer sales
4 I now order mostly
5 I looked round for a bit.
6 designer goods
7 I can't afford it any longer.

1b 📖🎧 Put the correct name in each of the gaps.

1 _____ only really went to town to do some window shopping.
2 _____ couldn't find anything worth buying.
3 _____ prefers to buy designer labels.
4 _____ doesn't buy as much now as in the past.
5 _____ bought something although it wasn't cheap.
6 _____ bought two items of clothing.

2 **G** Fill in the gaps with the correct form of the imperfect.

1 Ich _____ (*saved*) zweihundert Euro.

2 Der Pulli _____ (*fitted*) mir gut.

3 Wir _____ (*bought*) neue Schuhe.

4 Meine Freundin _____ (*noticed*), dass die Hose zu lang war.

5 Ihre Mutter _____ (*said*), sie sollte Geld sparen.

6 Du _____ (*bought*) einen schwarzen Mantel.

3a 🎧 Listen to the recordings about 4 people who went shopping. For each one say if their attitude towards their purchases was positive (**P**), negative (**N**) or both positive and negative (**P+N**).

3b 🎧 If their experiences were negative, what were the problems with the purchases?

4 ✏ Write an email to a friend about a shopping trip. Mention:

- ▪ where you went and what you bought
- ▪ what the item looked like
- ▪ whether the item was expensive or cheap
- ▪ any problems with the item

If you're able to work on a computer, find pictures of the items you bought to send as attachments. Refer to page 14 to find the correct German characters (ß, ä, ö, ü) on your keyboard.

> **Grammatik** | **Seite 183**
>
> ## Using the imperfect tense of weak verbs
>
> The imperfect of weak verbs (e.g. *kaufen*) is formed by taking the stem (*kauf-*) and adding endings as follows:
>
> | | |
> |---|---|
> | *ich kauf**te*** | *wir kauf**ten*** |
> | *du kauf**test*** | *ihr kauf**tet*** |
> | *er / sie / es kauf**te*** | *Sie/sie kauf**ten*** |
>
> Other weak verbs which you will find useful are: *sparen* (to save), *bemerken* (to notice), *passen* (to fit).
>
> Also learn about the imperfect of strong verbs.   *See page 69* ➡

> **Strategie 4**
>
> ## Paraphrasing
>
> If you don't remember a particular phrase or word you can use alternatives. For example, if you can't remember *es passte mir nicht*, you can say *es war zu groß / klein / eng / weit* etc.

Ich war / Wir waren	gestern / letzten Samstag / am Wochenende	in der Stadt / im Einkaufszentrum.		
Es gab	eine große Auswahl / wenig Auswahl.			
Ich kaufte / Wir kauften	einen Pulli / eine Jacke / ein T-Shirt / Schuhe.			
Er / Sie / Es / Sie	war / waren	neu / blau / billig.		
		zu teuer / zu klein / zu altmodisch.		
Er / Sie / Es / Sie	kostete / kosteten	... Euro / Pfund.		
Er / Sie / Es / Sie	passte / passten stand / standen	mir gut. mir nicht.		
Ich musste	ihn / sie / es	umtauschen,	weil er / sie / es	die falsche Farbe / Größe zu eng / weit / lang / kurz	hatte / hatten war / waren.

3.3 F Handy, MP3, Computer – wie wichtig sind sie?

Lernziele

Comparing new and traditional media

Using modal verbs (revision)

Saying how many times a week / month

1 **Ⓥ** Which of these items might you have used 30 years ago, and which would not have existed then? Sort the words into two groups.

MP3-Spieler   Schallplatte   Laptop   Handy

Kassettenrekorder   E-Book Reader   Schreibmaschine

Bücher   Tablet-PC   Kopfhörer

	jeden Tag	zwei- bis dreimal pro Woche	alle zwei Wochen
Ich schreibe E-Mails.	62%	20%	15%
Ich chatte im Internet.	65%	15%	7%
Ich lade Fotos hoch.	14%	38%	22%
Ich kaufe im Internet ein.	6%	18%	43%
Ich simse.	92%	6%	1%
Ich lade Musik herunter.	43%	26%	10%
Ich spiele Wii.	28%	35%	16%
Ich höre Musik auf einem MP3-Spieler.	85%	7%	5%
Ich lese E-Books.	16%	11%	12%

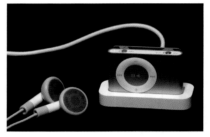

2 📖 A class of students were asked questions about how often they use different technologies. Their answers are represented in this table.

1   What percentage of students listen to their MP3 player every day?
2   What percentage of students text 2–3 times a week?
3   What percentage of students upload photos every 2 weeks?
4   What percentage of students email every day?
5   What percentage of students shop on the internet less than 3 times a week?
6   What percentage of students download music more than once a week but not every day?

Saying how many times a week / month

Strategie 2

There are different ways of saying the same thing:

einmal / zweimal / dreimal die Woche

einmal / zweimal / dreimal in der Woche

einmal / zweimal / dreimal pro Woche

All of these are correct.

You can also say

einmal / zweimal / dreimal im Monat

einmal / zweimal / dreimal pro Monat

3a 🎧 Four young people are talking about their use of new media compared to traditional media. Which of these things do they mention?

a   social networking sites
b   making music
c   listening to music
d   playing computer games
e   watching films
f   using a mobile
g   watching TV on computer
h   reading books

3b 🎧 Do they prefer new or traditional media? Listen again. Is each speaker positive (**P**), negative (**N**) or both positive and negative (**P+N**) about new media?

4 **G** Translate these sentences into English.

1   Ich muss mein Geld für einen MP3-Spieler sparen.
2   Du darfst nicht auf diese Website gehen!
3   Wir können uns später simsen.
4   Man darf das Handy nicht im Unterricht benutzen.
5   Ich soll nur einmal in der Woche im Internet chatten.
6   Wir mögen unseren E-Book-Reader.

5 🖊 How often do you use new technology? Write a short paragraph in response to the question: *Wie oft benutzt du die neuen Medien?* Make use of the sentences from activity 2.

Ich simse / Ich schreibe	einmal die Woche / zweimal die Woche / jeden Tag / jede Woche / jeden Abend / am Wochenende	E-Mails.
Ich lade		Musik herunter.

Grammatik   *Seite 184*

Using modal verbs (revision)

Modal verbs are *können* (can, to be able to), *mögen* (to like), *sollen* (should, to be supposed to), *dürfen* (may, to be allowed to), *wollen* (to want to) and *müssen* (must, to have to). They usually go together with a second verb in the infinitive, which goes at the end of the sentence or clause, e.g. *Ich darf heute in die Stadt gehen*.

Note: take care when using negatives.

du darfst nicht = you must not

du musst nicht = you don't have to

Also learn more about mixing the perfect and imperfect tenses.

See page 68 ➡

Hinweis

3.3 Groundwork is available in the Foundation Book.

3.3 H Neue Medien: Vor- und Nachteile

Lernziele

The advantages and disadvantages of new technologies

Using different tenses (past and present)

Dealing with the unpredictable question in Speaking (!)

Surfen, chatten und SMSen

Ich simse gern. Es ist praktisch, schnell und billig.

Benny

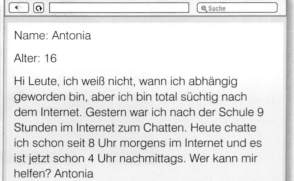

Name: Antonia

Alter: 16

Hi Leute, ich weiß nicht, wann ich abhängig geworden bin, aber ich bin total süchtig nach dem Internet. Gestern war ich nach der Schule 9 Stunden im Internet zum Chatten. Heute chatte ich schon seit 8 Uhr morgens im Internet und es ist jetzt schon 4 Uhr nachmittags. Wer kann mir helfen? Antonia

Thema: Wie findest du soziale Netzwerke?

Ich hatte eine Seite bei Nettheadz. Als ich sie zum ersten Mal ausprobierte, fand ich soziale Netzwerke positiv und glaubte, dass man dort viele Freunde findet. Dann haben meine „Freunde" begonnen, über mich negativ zu chatten. Sie haben mich total gemobbt. Später dann auch mit dem Handy. Ich weiß nicht warum, aber jetzt finde ich die neue Technologie ziemlich gefährlich.

Simon

Von: Martina@gcsegerman.de

An: EmailfreundeInternational

Hallo, ich heiße Martina. Ich finde das Internet und E-Mail super. Ich habe viele E-Mail-Freunde in anderen Ländern und auf verschiedenen Kontinenten, zum Beispiel Afrika und Südamerika. Ich kann schnell etwas recherchieren und wenn man zum Beispiel Freunde in anderen Ländern hat, kann man kostenlos Bilder schicken. Ich habe zum Beispiel gestern meine Ferienbilder gemailt. Ich suche jetzt einen Freund oder eine Freundin in Griechenland.

Ich habe schon lange keine CDs mehr gekauft. Als ich noch CDs kaufte, fand ich sie immer sehr teuer. Ich lade jetzt immer Musik runter. Das kostet weniger und ich kann sie auf CD brennen, wenn ich will, oder mit meinem i-Pod synchronisieren. **Karina**

1a 📖 🎧 Find these phrases in the text and write them out.

1 I am completely addicted.
2 Who can help me?
3 They totally bullied me.
4 quite dangerous
5 I emailed my holiday photos.
6 to burn onto CD

1b 📖 🎧 For each statement write **T** (true), **F** (false) or **?** (not in the text).

1 Antonia has been on the internet for 9 hours today.
2 Simon has stopped using social networking sites.
3 Martina has an email penfriend in Greece.
4 Karina downloads music more often than she buys CDs.
5 Simon thinks modern technology has its downsides.
6 Martina has been sending her holiday photos to friends in Africa.

2 **G** Reread the texts on page 66 and, for each person, identify and note down the verbs and tenses he or she uses.

Beispiel:

	Present	Imperfect	Perfect	Infinitive
Benny	simse, ist			

3 🎧 Listen to the conversation between Norbert and his grandmother and answer the questions in English. In places you will have to infer meaning, i.e. work something out rather than just translate what you hear.

1 Why is Norbert's grandmother annoyed with him? (2)
2 How did she make phone calls when she was younger? (1)
3 What is she worried about? (2)
4 What criticism does she make of his parents? (1)
5 Give two arguments Norbert uses to try to persuade his grandmother that all is well. (2)
6 What does Norbert offer to do at the end of the conversation? (1)

4 💬 What are the advantages and disadvantages of new technologies? Work with a partner. Take 10 minutes to prepare 3 questions each, but do not tell your partner what your questions are. Think about what they might ask you and prepare possible answers. Then take it in turns to put the questions to each other. You might find it helpful to revise question words on page 188.

Grammatik · *Seite 181*

Using different tenses (past and present)

Aim to use at least 2 tenses in every point you make in speaking and writing as in this response to a question in the present tense:

Wie oft benutzt du einen Computer?

Ich surfe (present) *jeden Tag im Internet und gestern habe ich ein paar E-Mails geschickt* (past).

You could even go further and aim to use a future too: *… und später werde ich Recherchen für meine Hausaufgaben anstellen.*

Also learn about how to use *wann*, *wenn* and *als*. See page 69 ➡

Strategie 4

Dealing with the unpredictable question in Speaking (!)

The exclamation mark will test you on something which you have not prepared. It is called 'the unpredictable question', but you need to think about and predict what might come up – and so make sure that you are as prepared as you can be! Look at what you have covered already in the bullet points and make a sensible guess about two or three things that have been left out, then prepare some German that would fit and practise some possible responses. Don't forget, however, to listen out for the actual question and make sure that you understand it before you respond.

Ich finde	das Internet / E-Mails / soziale Netzwerke / MP3-Spieler / chatten / simsen	lehrreich / praktisch / langweilig / doof / nützlich / teuer / gefährlich,	weil man so viel Zeit spart / weil man so viel Zeit verschwendet / weil man schnell Informationen findet / weil man neue Freunde kennenlernt.
Meiner Meinung nach ist / sind			
Das Internet / Chatten	macht	süchtig / abhängig / Spaß.	
E-Mails / Soziale Netzwerke	machen		
Es gibt sowohl Vorteile (des Internets / der sozialen Netzwerke …) als auch Nachteile. Ein Vorteil / Nachteil ist, dass … Ich mache mir Sorgen, dass … Ich bin sicher, dass …			

(G) Free time and the media

1a These jumbled sentences contain separable verbs in the perfect tense. Underline both verbs in each one.

1 Ich mein zugemacht habe Buch.
2 aufgemacht Sie hat ihr Geschenk.
3 hat richtig zugehört selten Er.
4 Er hat Spielen mitgemacht bei nie.
5 im Kaufhaus eingekauft Sie hat.
6 die ganze Nacht Ich ferngesehen habe.

1b Unjumble the sentences and write them out using correct word order.

Separable verbs in the perfect tense

Some verbs in German are in two parts. They consist of the normal verb and a separable prefix. Some common examples are **fern**sehen (to watch television), **aus**geben (to spend), **auf**machen (to open) and **an**sehen (to look at).

When you use separable verbs in the perfect tense the prefix comes before ge:

ausgeben Ich habe viel Geld **aus**gegeben. – I spent a lot of money.

fernsehen Ich habe gestern **fern**gesehen. – I watched TV yesterday.

Grammatik · Seite 182

---

2 Identify whether these sentences are in the present or imperfect (past) tense.

1 Ich kaufe CDs und Bücher.
2 Er kaufte neue Schuhe.
3 Sie ging in den Supermarkt.
4 Es gibt viele Geschäfte in meiner Stadt.
5 Was musstest du umtauschen?
6 Es gab ein Problem.

Recognising the imperfect tense

You need to recognise forms of this past tense, and also use them to achieve higher levels. In weak verbs, listen or look out for a -t added to the stem of a verb. This is the only difference between the present and imperfect tenses in regular verbs.

Present:	Imperfect:
ich spiele – I play	*ich / er / sie spielte* – I / he / she played
er macht – he does / makes	*ich / er / sie machte* – I / he / she did / made
Common irregular forms are:	
es gab – there was / were	*ich konnte* – I could, I was able to
ich war – I was	*ich musste* – I had to
ich hatte – I had	*ich sollte* – I was supposed to
	ich wollte – I wanted

Grammatik · Seite 183

---

3 Insert the correct imperfect form of the verb in brackets into the gaps in the sentences.

1 Ich _____ ein neues Handy. (haben)
2 Dieser Tablet-PC _____ billiger im Internet. (sein)
3 Es _____ viele elektronische Bücher. (geben)
4 Mein Vater _____ früher nur Schallplatten kaufen. (können)
5 Ich _____ nicht zu lang am Computer bleiben. (sollen)
6 Man _____ früher ins Kino gehen, um einen Film zu sehen. (müssen)

Past tenses: mixing the perfect and imperfect

In German both tenses can be used to express actions in the past and you can use either. There are some regional differences, for example the perfect tense is used more in Southern Germany and Austria and generally more in speech than in writing. Many people, however, still use the imperfect of common verbs (*ich hatte, ich war, es gab, ich konnte, ich sollte*) when otherwise using the perfect.

Grammatik

4a Would you use *haben* or *sein* in these sentences?

1 I had a birthday. (*haben*)
2 He swam in the sea. (*schwimmen*)
3 The dog disappeared. (*verschwinden*)
4 My grandmother died. (*sterben*)
5 Our Dad telephoned. (*anrufen*)
6 His ice-cream melted. (*schmelzen*)

4b Put the sentences into German using the perfect tense and the verbs in brackets.

Grammatik — Seite 182

Using the perfect tense with *haben* or *sein*

Remember that some past participles take *haben* as the auxiliary in the perfect tense and some take *sein*. Normally verbs of motion take the auxiliary verb *sein*, but you need to be aware that verbs showing a change of state also take *sein*.

Examples of verbs with a change of state are:

sterben	to die	*Er ist gestorben.*	He died.
verschwinden	to disappear	*Wir sind verschwunden.*	We disappeared.
schmelzen	to melt	*Das Eis ist geschmolzen.*	The ice melted.

Make sure you know which past participles take which and learn the different forms of *haben* and *sein*. Use pages 190–193 to check which verbs take *haben* and which verbs take *sein*.

---

5 Rewrite this paragraph in the imperfect.

Heute fahre ich mit meiner Freundin in die Stadt. Wir sehen uns die Geschäfte an. Es gibt so viele schöne Kleider, aber wir haben nicht genug Geld! Wir wissen, dass wir nicht alles kaufen können. Ich finde aber neue Jeans und ich bin überrascht, dass sie mir auch passen. Nach dem Einkaufen gehen wir in ein Café. Wir essen Kuchen und trinken Kaffee.

Grammatik — Seite 183

Imperfect tense of strong verbs

Learn to recognise and use the imperfect of commonly used strong verbs such as:

essen – ich aß

trinken – ich trank

fahren – ich fuhr

You will find others in the verb tables on pages 190–193. This is how you conjugate a strong verb in the imperfect:

ich fuhr	*wir fuhren*
du fuhrst	*ihr fuhrt*
er / sie / es fuhr	*Sie / sie fuhren*

---

6 Read the sentences and fill in the gaps with *wann*, *wenn* or *als*.

1 _____ kaufst du einen neuen Computer?
2 Ich surfe jeden Tag im Internet, _____ ich nach Hause komme.
3 _____ du deine Hausaufgaben nicht machst, bekommst du kein Taschengeld.
4 Mein Vater hatte einen Kassettenrekorder, _____ er jünger war.
5 Er weiß nicht, _____ er ein neues Handy bekommt.
6 Es war alles viel schwieriger, _____ es noch keine Computer gab.

Grammatik

Using *wann*, *wenn* and *als*

The words *wann*, *wenn* and *als* all translate as 'when' in English. However, they are not interchangeable.

Wann means 'at what time':

Wann surfst du im Internet?

Ich weiß nicht, wann ich ankommen werde.

Wenn is a conjunction like *dass* and *weil* and sends the verb to the end. It can also be translated as 'whenever' or 'if':

Ich chatte gern im Internet, wenn mir langweilig ist.

Als refers to the past (either single points in time or uninterrupted periods):

Ich war noch nicht fertig, als er ankam.

Ich habe oft im Internet gespielt, als ich jünger war.

Free time and the media

Topic 3.1 Free time activities

3.1 F Was hast du gestern gemacht?
➡ *pages 56–57*

	anrufen	to telephone
	anstrengend	exhausting
	blöd	stupid
	chatten	to chat (on the internet)
der	Dokumentarfilm	documentary
	gefallen (+ dat)	to please
die	Geige	violin
	kegeln	to bowl
das	Klavier	piano
das	Konzert	concert
	neulich	recently
	nützlich	useful
	quatschen	to chat
	reiten	to ride
das	Schach	chess
die	Sendung	TV programme
die	Serie	TV series
	(sich) treffen (mit)	to meet (with)
die	Trompete	trumpet
	turnen	to do gymnastics

3.1 H Ich bin in die Stadt gegangen
➡ *pages 58–59*

	außerhalb (+ gen)	outside of
die	Disko(thek)	disco
der	Feiertag	public holiday (one day)
das	Freibad	open-air swimming pool
im	Freien	out in the open
	gewinnen	to win
	herumlaufen	to walk about
das	Hindernis	obstacle
	klettern	to climb

die	Mannschaft	team
	mitgehen	to go with someone
das	Mitglied	member
	nirgendwo	nowhere
das	Schwimmbad	swimming pool
	segeln	to go sailing
die	Skateanlage	skateboarding park
	tanzen	to dance
	teilnehmen	to participate
der	Verein	club
der	Wettkampf	competition

Topic 3.2 Shopping, money, fashion and trends

3.2 F Wir bekommen nicht genug Taschengeld! ➡ *pages 60–61*

	ausgeben	to spend
der	(Geld-)schein	note (money)
das	(Geld-)stück	coin
das	Geschenk	present
das	Juweliergeschäft	jeweller's shop
	kaufen	to buy
die	Klamotten (pl)	clothes
das	Kleingeld	change (money)
die	Konditorei	cake shop
die	Metzgerei	butcher's
das	Portemonnaie	wallet, purse
	reichen	to be enough
	reisen	to travel
	sparen	to save
die	Süßigkeit	sweet
der	Tante-Emma-Laden	corner shop
das	Taschengeld	pocket money
	teuer	expensive
der	Turnschuh	trainer (shoe)
die	Zeitschrift	magazine

3.2 H Wir waren im Einkaufszentrum
➡ *pages 62–63*

	anprobieren	to try on
	ätzend	*lousy, rubbish*
die	Auswahl	selection, choice
	bemerken	*to notice*
	bestellen	to order
die	*Kappe*	*baseball cap*
das	Kleid	dress
die	Kleidung	clothes
der	Laden	shop
	(sich) leisten	*to afford*
die	Marke	brand
	passen	to fit
die	Qualität	quality
die	Quittung	receipt, bill
der	Schal	scarf
	schauen	*to look*
	schick	smart, chic
der	Sommerschlussverkauf	end of summer sales
	umtauschen	*to exchange*
	unterwegs	on the move

Topic 3.3 Advantages and disadvantages of new technology

3.3 F Handy, MP3, Computer – wie wichtig sind sie? ➡ *pages 64–65*

	benutzen	to use
der	Computerprogrammierer	computer programmer
	echt	*real*
	einfach	*simple*
	gefährlich	*dangerous*
	hochladen	*to upload*
	informativ	*informative*
die	*Internetseite*	*internet site*
der	*Kassettenrekorder*	*cassette recorder*
der	*Kopfhörer*	*headphones*
	lehrreich	*educational*
	praktisch	*practical*

die	Schallplatte	record
die	Schreibmaschine	typewriter
	simsen	to text
das	soziale Netzwerk	social networking site
	später	later
die	Technologie	technology
der	Virus	virus
die	Webseite	website

3.3 H Neue Medien: Vor- und Nachteile
➡ *pages 66–67*

	abhängig	dependent
im	Ausland	abroad
	ausprobieren	*to try out*
	(sich) beruhigen	*to calm down*
	brennen	*to burn*
	fertig	*finished*
	kennen lernen	*to get to know*
	kostenlos	*free*
	mailen	*to send via e-mail*
	mobben	*to bully*
der	Nachteil	disadvantage
	recherchieren	*to research*
	schnell	*fast, quick*
die	Sorge	worry
	süchtig	*addicted*
	üben	*to practise*
	verschieden	*different*
	verschwenden	*to waste*
der	Vorteil	advantage
die	*Zeitverschwendung*	*waste of time*

4.1 F Wohin fährst du?

Lernziele

Talking about holiday preferences

Using correct word order (time – manner – place)

Listening carefully to German pronunciation

1 ❶ Read these statements about where people go on holiday. Match each one to the season when they are most likely to go there.

1 Wir gehen gern Ski fahren und Schlittschuh laufen.
2 Ich möchte Marokko besuchen und die Sahara entdecken. Aber nur nach dem Hochsommer, wenn es nicht mehr so heiß ist.
3 Es ist die beste Jahreszeit für eine Rundfahrt durch die holländischen Blumenfelder.
4 Ich nehme Sonnencreme und meinen Badeanzug und bleibe den ganzen Tag am Strand.

| im Winter | im Sommer |
| im Frühling | im Herbst |

2a 📖 🎧 Read this quiz from a magazine which is suggesting different types of holiday for different people. Decide which of the holidays mentioned in the introduction would appeal to someone who had chosen mostly (a), mostly (b) or mostly (c).

Welcher Urlaub ist richtig für dich?

Du weißt nicht, wo du nächstes Jahr Urlaub machen willst? Vielleicht eine Klassenfahrt nach Wien? Oder Familienurlaub in der Türkei? Wie wär's mit einem Skiurlaub in den Alpen mit Freunden? Mach unser Quiz, dann wird es dir vielleicht klar!

1 Wann fährst du am liebsten in Urlaub?

a) im Winter
b) im Sommer
c) in den Herbstferien

2 Wo machst du gern Urlaub?

a) in den Bergen
b) am Strand
c) in einer Großstadt

3 Mit wem möchtest du fahren?

a) mit Freunden
b) mit meiner Familie
c) mit einer Gruppe

4 Was willst du im Urlaub machen?

a) aktiv sein und Spaß haben
b) mich entspannen
c) Kunstgalerien besichtigen

5 Wie lange möchtest du Urlaub machen?

a) eine Woche
b) zwei Wochen
c) zehn Tage

2b ✏ Do the quiz yourself! Write a sentence in answer to each question, then copy and complete this sentence with your ideal holiday destination: *Am liebsten fahre ich nach / in die / ans …*

3 ⓖ Put the words in each sentence in the correct order.

Beispiel: **1** *In den Ferien fahre ich mit dem Auto nach Spanien.*

1   fahre ich In den Ferien nach Spanien mit dem Auto
2   Meine Eltern im Sommer reisen alleine nach Italien
3   in die Schweiz möchte ich Nächstes Jahr fliegen mit Freunden
4   mit dem Zug Mein Bruder und ich möchten im Winter nach Holland fahren
5   im Sommer Er ist mit seiner Schulklasse gefahren nach Deutschland

---

Using correct word order (time – manner – place)

When you mention when (time), how (manner) and where (place) you do something, you give the time first, then the manner and then the place. This is called the Time, Manner, Place rule and it applies in all tenses. The conjugated verb still remains the second idea.

Example:

Ich fahre jedes Jahr mit dem Zug nach Frankreich.

Jedes Jahr fahre ich mit dem Zug nach Frankreich.

Also learn the use of the different forms of *ich möchte* etc.   *See page 84* ➡

ⓖ Grammatik   Seite 187

4a 🎧 Listen to the five people discussing holidays. For each person, choose three pictures to illustrate any of the following: destination, season, length of stay, transport, which people he or she went with. Each person will only mention three of the five things.

Beispiel: *Felix i, k, …*

4b 🎧 Listen again and note down any additional details that are mentioned.

5 🖊 Write responses to the questions below. Aim to get in as much detail as possible using the time – manner – place rule.

■ Wo möchtest du Urlaub machen?
■ Was möchtest du dort tun?

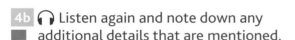

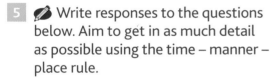

Ich möchte	in den nächsten Ferien / nächstes Wochenende / so bald wie möglich	mit dem Auto / mit dem Zug	in die Berge / ans Meer / irgendwohin	fahren.
	jeden Tag / abends / regelmäßig	mit meiner Familie / mit einer Gruppe / mit meinen Freunden / alleine	im Meer	schwimmen.
			im Restaurant	essen.
			in den Bergen	Ski fahren.

Listening carefully to German pronunciation

Listen out for words which sound similar as they can have very different meanings, e.g. the prepositions *für* and *vor*. Compare:

*Ich war in Paris **für** eine Woche.*
I was in Paris **for** a week.

*Ich war in Paris **vor** einer Woche.*
I was in Paris a week **ago**.

Strategie 4a–4b

🔗 **Hinweis**

4.1 Groundwork is available in the Foundation Book.

4.1 H Schönen Gruß aus dem Urlaub!

Urlaubsgrüße

Liebe Karina,

ich bin im Moment in Österreich in den Alpen. Ich bin hier mit Mutti, Vati und Erik, meinem Bruder. Wir haben eigentlich mit dem Wetter ziemlich viel Glück, aber gestern war es sehr windig und viel zu kalt. Heute scheint die Sonne und meine Eltern und ich waren beim Ski fahren. Erik ist zu Hause geblieben, weil er nicht Ski fahren wollte. Er sagt, sein Bein tut weh, aber meistens ist er nur zu faul. Ich fahre sehr gern Ski und morgen möchte ich einen Snowboardingkurs beginnen. Du weißt ja, dass ich in den Ferien gern aktiv bin. Deshalb ist im Winter ein Skiurlaub in den Alpen für mich ideal. Ich möchte in den nächsten Ferien nach Amerika zum Ski fahren gehen, weil der Schnee in Kalifornien so toll ist. Was machst du in diesen Ferien?

Deine Katja

Lieber Matthew,

hallo aus Sylt. Du fragst dich vielleicht, wo Sylt ist. Also, Sylt ist eine Insel im Norden von Deutschland in der Nordsee. Ich komme jeden Sommer hierher und ich liebe es. Meistens fahre ich mit einer Jugendgruppe und wir übernachten auf einem Zeltplatz. Wir haben meistens Glück mit dem Wetter und können im Meer schwimmen. Ab und zu regnet es aber, und dann ist es relativ kühl. Im Allgemeinen finde ich Sylt aber toll. Nächstes Jahr möchte ich aber woanders hinfahren, zum Beispiel nach Afrika auf eine Safari. Wo bist du dieses Jahr?

Dein Knut

Matthew Simmonds
24 New Street
Aberdeen
AB6 3AK
Scotland

---

1 📖 🎧 Read the postcards. Are the statements true (**T**), false (**F**) or not in the text (**?**) ?

1. The weather in Austria has been bad every day.
2. Erik hurt himself in a fall when he was skiing.
3. Katja has been snowboarding as well as skiing.
4. Katja would like to pursue her interest in skiing much further afield.
5. Sylt is an island in the Baltic Sea.
6. Sylt attracts a lot of tourists.
7. There are opportunities to go camping in Sylt.
8. The weather in Sylt has been changeable during Knut's stay.

> **Recognising information presented in different ways**
> **Strategie 1**
>
> Remember that the same pieces of information may be presented in different ways:
>
> *Es ist nicht warm genug zum Schwimmen. = Es ist zu kalt, um schwimmen zu gehen.*

2 **G** Match up the German and English sentences. Use the grammar box below to help.

1 Wir fahren morgen hin.	a On the way over here we didn't see anything.
2 Auf dem Weg hierher sahen wir nichts.	b We drove here from the North.
3 Wir sind viel hin und her gefahren.	c We're going there tomorrow.
4 Wir kamen dorther und fahren jetzt weiter.	d We drove around a lot.
5 Ich weiß nicht, wo wir hinfahren.	e I don't know where he is from.
6 Ich weiß nicht, wo er herkommt.	f We came from there and now we're continuing our journey.
7 Wir sind von Norden hierhergefahren.	g I don't know where we're going.

3a 🎧 Listen to Nico and Jasmin talking about past holidays and then choose the right answers.

1   Nico
   a likes sunbathing   b doesn't like sunbathing   c enjoys all sorts of holidays.

2   Nico went on
   a a cycling holiday in Holland   b a cycling tour of the Lake District   c a cycling tour of Switzerland.

3   Nico found the holiday
   a tiring because he was unfit   b tiring but enjoyable   c tiring and he never wants to do it again.

4   Jasmin went to England because she wanted to
   a see the beautiful countryside   b see the sights of the capital   c practise her English.

5   Jasmin travelled by
   a budget coach and train   b train and bus   c low-cost airline and bus.

6   Jasmin
   a ate in restaurants every day   b ate in restaurants now and again   c never ate in restaurants.

3b 🎧 Listen again and answer these questions in English. In places, you may have to infer the information, i.e. you won't always hear the exact words that correspond to the answers.

1   Why did Nico's parents disagree at first about where to go on holiday? (3)

2   Why do you think Nico was a bit anxious before they went? (2)

3   What does Jasmin say about expensive holidays? (2)

4   How did she and her friend save money? (2)

5   What does she say about the weather? (2)

4 🗨 Prepare answers to these questions about a holiday in the past (you can make it up) and then practise the questions and answers with a partner.

- Beschreib' mir deinen letzten Urlaub.
- Wie hat er dir gefallen?

Applying rules in new situations

Strategie 4

When you're working with new topics and tenses, it's easy to forget the grammar rules you've already learnt. For instance, when talking about a holiday in the past, don't forget to apply the time – manner – place rule if you want to say when, how and where you did something.

Using hin and her

Grammatik   Seite 188

The suffixes *hin* and *her* are used to show direction.

Wohin fährst du? – Where are you going to?

Woher kommst du? – Where do you come from?

Ich fahre dorthin. – I'm going there.

Ich komme daher. – I come / I am coming from there.

Note that in questions the *hin* / *her* can come at the end, e.g. *Wo gehst du hin?*

As an idiom, *hin und her* can mean 'to and fro' or 'back and forth', e.g. *Ich bin hin und her gelaufen.* I went all over the place.

Also learn how to use adjectives after *etwas, nichts, …*

See page 85 ➡

4.2 F Los geht's!

Lernziele

Talking about getting around and what to do on holiday

Using different tenses

Listening for different tenses

1 **V** You see the following signs while travelling and around town. Which one would you find if you wanted to … ?

1 leave your suitcase
2 drive into a car-park
3 leave the motorway
4 get some information
5 leave a building in an emergency
6 have a snack
7 enter a shop

| Einfahrt | Auskunft |

| Ausfahrt | Imbiss | Eingang |

| Gepäckaufbewahrung | Notausgang |

2a These signs contain important information for travellers. Read them and answer the questions in English.

1 What do you have to do if the ticket machine is out of order? (2)
2 What do you have to do if you want to get to the airport? (1)
3 What do you need to do before you get on an Interregio train? (1)
4 What information is given to people who want to hire a bike? (3)
5 What is available for 1st class passengers? (1)
6 What do you need to do if you want to buy tickets for abroad? (1)

Zug hält. Endstation. Bitte aussteigen.

Wichtige Informationen!

Wartesaal für Reisende erster Klasse.

Fahrradverleih – Ermäßigung für Kinder und Rentner.

Wenn Sie internationale Fahrkarten kaufen wollen, zeigen Sie bitte Ihren Reisepass.

Für die Verbindung zum Flughafen steigen Sie bitte hier um.

Für den Interregio-Zug müssen Sie Zuschlag bezahlen, bevor Sie einsteigen.

Automat außer Betrieb. Bitte benutzen Sie den Fahrkartenschalter neben dem Zeitungskiosk.

2b Find and write out the German for:

1 to get on the train
2 to get off the train
3 to change trains
4 passport
5 ticket
6 connection
7 passenger
8 airport

3 **G** Where do the sentences start and finish? Are the sentences in the perfect tense, present tense or future tense?

ichfahreindenFerienoftnachAmerikaletztesJahrbinichauch nachAmerikagefahrenwirsindnachOrlandogeflogenichliebe OrlandomeinBruderundichliebendieVergnügungsparksund Wasserparkswirsindvielschwimmengegangenundhabenoftin Fastfood-RestaurantsgegessenwirwerdennächstesJahrnicht nachAmerikafliegenichwerdemeinenBrieffreundinder TürkeibesuchenundmeineElternwerdenhierbleiben.

4 🎧 Five teenagers are being interviewed on holiday. They each mention what they are doing, what they have done and what they are going to do. Copy and complete the table.

	macht	schon gemacht	wird machen
Jutta	b	d, f	d

a   go on a boat trip   b   visit a museum

c   eat in a restaurant   d   go shopping

e   see the sights   f   sunbathe   g   swim in the sea

5 ✏ Write six sentences, two each in the present, past and future tense, describing the holiday activities shown in activity 4.

Ich mache		
Ich habe	eine Bootsfahrt	gemacht.
Ich werde		machen.
Ich gehe		
Ich bin	einkaufen / schwimmen ins Museum / in ein Restaurant	gegangen.
Ich werde		gehen.

Grammatik **Seite 180**

Using different tenses (past, present and future)

When speaking and writing, remember to include different tenses, e.g.

Present: *Normalerweise fliege ich in den Urlaub.*   See page 180 ➡

Perfect: *Letztes Jahr bin ich mit dem Auto nach Frankreich gefahren.*   See page 182 ➡

Imperfect: *Der Urlaub war toll.*   See page 183 ➡

Future: *Ich werde nächstes Jahr mit meinem Freund fahren.*   See page 184 ➡

Also learn how to use question words.   See page 84 ➡

Strategie 4

Listening for different tenses

Listen out for clues to the tense as this doesn't only come in the verb forms. In activity 4 there are clues such as *im Moment* which can only be present, *gestern* can only be past and both *morgen* and *in ein paar Minuten* suggest a future. But watch out for *heute Nachmittag / Abend* as this depends on when the person is speaking. This afternoon or evening could have happened, or be about to happen. Listen out for past or future in verbs to confirm what you are thinking.

Hinweis

4.2 Groundwork is available in the Foundation Book.

4.2 H Unterwegs

1a 📖 🎧 Read what these people have to say about different modes of transport. Find the German for the following words or phrases:

1 We hired a car.
2 to get to know the area
3 I'd like to avoid flying.
4 environmental protection group
5 never again
6 driving licence
7 for a good cause

Olaf
Ich war letztes Jahr in Südamerika mit meiner Familie. Wir wollten zuerst ein Auto mieten, aber dann haben wir uns entschlossen drei Wochen mit dem Reisebus zu fahren. Einmal und nie wieder. Wir haben das viel zu anstrengend gefunden. Ich bleibe nächstes Jahr zu Hause und gehe an den See.

Herr und Frau Schiller
Wir haben letztes Jahr im Urlaub einen Leihwagen gemietet, weil wir die Umgebung erkunden wollten. Wir haben das ausgezeichnet gefunden, weil wir unabhängig waren. Wir wollen das in Zukunft wieder machen.

Esther
Ich werde dieses Jahr mit meiner Schwester ein paar Länder in Osteuropa bereisen. Weil wir beide keinen Führerschein haben, werden wir uns eine Interrailkarte kaufen und mit dem Zug fahren. Das ist relativ billig für Jugendliche.

Tatjana
Ich will nächstes Jahr in Europa herumreisen, aber ich möchte Fliegen vermeiden, weil ich die Umwelt schützen möchte und der CO_2-Ausstoß so hoch ist. Ich bin ziemlich aktiv in meiner Umweltschutzgruppe in der Schule.

Karsten
Ich sammle dieses Jahr Geld für einen guten Zweck. Deshalb werde ich eine gesponserte Radtour in den Alpen machen. Ich muss dafür 500 Euro sammeln. Ich trainiere viel und bin schon ziemlich fit. Gesund bleiben und gleichzeitig etwas für einen guten Zweck tun finde ich prima.

1b 📖 🎧 Which mode of transport does each speaker mention and are their views positive (**P**), negative (**N**) or positive and negative (**P+N**)?

2 **G** Choose the correct accusative article in each of the sentences below.

Beispiel: **1** *den*

1 Er hat den / die / das Bus genommen.
2 Es gibt einen / eine / ein tolles Museum in der Stadt.
3 Wir haben keinen / keine / kein Plan für nächstes Jahr.
4 Ich hatte einen / eine / ein tolle Woche in Berlin.
5 Wir möchten bald einen / eine / ein Ausflug aufs Land machen.
6 Es gab einen / eine / ein langsamen Zug.
7 Wir hatten keinen / keine / kein Geld.
8 Sie will den / die / das Umwelt schützen.

Grammatik — **Seite 175**

The nominative and accusative cases (revision)

In German you need to be aware of the different cases because these affect how words are spelled and spoken (for instance articles and adjective endings). A noun is in the nominative case if it is the subject or 'doer' of an action, for example with the word 'is':

Der Bahnhof ist groß.

A noun is in the accusative case if it is on the receiving end of an action:

*Ich sehe **den Bahnhof**.*

Endings for definite and indefinite articles in the nominative and accusative cases are as follows:

	masc.	fem.	neut.	pl.
nom.	der / (k)ein	die / (k)eine	das / (k)ein	die / keine
acc.	den / (k)einen	die / (k)eine	das / (k)ein	die / keine

You will notice that only masculine singular articles change their spelling.

Also learn about more complex question words.

See page 85 ➡

---

3 🎥 Watch and listen to the dialogues. Where do Katja, Lorenz, Anja and Frank want to go? How will they get there? Note down two extra details for each person.

Beispiel: Katja – main railway station, walk, only five minutes away …

4 🗨 Work with a partner to plan your ideal future trip. Where will you go? How will you get there? Why this destination? Who can think of the most unusual ideas? Use a dictionary to help you express your ideas.

Strategie 4

Using more interesting vocabulary

Use creative tasks as an opportunity to expand your vocabulary. Make a list of five nouns, five verbs and five adjectives that will come in useful. Start by thinking of more unusual English words and then use a dictionary to find their equivalent in German.

Wir	werden	nach Südamerika / Australien / Marokko / auf eine karibische Insel	fliegen,	weil es dort total anders ist. weil ich schon immer dorthinfahren wollte. weil das ein Traum von mir ist.
		mit dem Bus / mit dem Flugzeug / mit dem Schiff	fahren / fliegen.	
		in einem Fünf-Sterne Hotel / in einer Jugendherberge / in der Wüste	übernachten.	
		wilde Tiere sehen / jeden Abend ausgehen / am Strand liegen / mit Kamelen trekken.		
Die Reise	wird	in zwei Tagen / nach den Prüfungen	beginnen.	
		eine Stunde / zwei Tagen / eine Woche	dauern.	
		600 Pfund / 3000 Euro	kosten.	

4.3 F Urlaubspläne

1 **V** Work with a partner and take it in turns to say that you would like to do the things in the pictures, using *ich möchte*. Make something up for the **?**

a

b

c

d

e

f

2a 📖 🎧 Read the holiday plans. Match what each person says to the pictures above.

Das werde ich machen

Klaus
Wenn ich Ferien habe, dann werde ich nach England fahren, um mein Englisch zu verbessern.

Dorit
Ich werde in den Ferien zu Hause bleiben, weil ich kein Geld habe. Ich werde vielleicht in einem Supermarkt oder einer Boutique arbeiten.

Jens
Meine Freunde und ich werden nach Ibiza fliegen. Wir werden abends in die Disko gehen, um zu tanzen und uns tagsüber am Strand entspannen.

Julia
Wir werden nächstes Jahr getrennt Ferien machen. Meine Eltern werden zu Hause am See Urlaub machen, mein Bruder wird zu meinen Großeltern nach Köln fahren und ich werde mit meiner Schule nach Italien fliegen. Es ist eine Klassenfahrt und wir werden Museen, Galerien und natürlich das Kolosseum besuchen.

Paul
In den nächsten Ferien werde ich nach Australien fliegen. Ich werde das mit einer Jugendgruppe machen. Am meisten stört mich, dass der Flug so lange dauern wird. 20 Stunden im Flugzeug sitzen ist einfach schrecklich.

Gabi
Ich weiß noch nicht, was ich machen werde. Wenn ich Geld habe, dann werde ich in Urlaub fahren. Vielleicht werde ich hier bleiben, um mich mit Freunden zu treffen. Ich habe noch keine Ahnung.

2b 📖 🎧 Are the following statements **T** (true), **F** (false) or **?** (not in the text)?

1 Klaus wants to learn to speak a foreign language better next year.
2 Dorit wants to earn some money.
3 Jens is going to fly to Ibiza.
4 Julia is going to go on holiday with her parents next year.
5 Julia is going to go to Italy with other students.
6 Paul has been to Australia before.
7 Paul enjoys long aeroplane flights.
8 Gabi has made plans for her holiday.

3 🅖 Write the correct form of *werden* and add the infinitive in German of the word in brackets.

Beispiel: **1** *Ich werde nach Frankreich reisen.*

1 Ich _____ nach Frankreich _____. (*travel*)
2 Wir _____ meine Oma und meinen Opa _____. (*visit*)
3 Lara und Tobias _____ mit dem Flugzeug _____. (*fly*)
4 Du _____ mit mir nach Amerika _____. (*come*)
5 Sie (she) _____ sich am Strand _____. (*relax*)

4 🎧 Listen to Lukas talking about his holiday plans. Which three of these things does Lukas plan to do?

1 Visit his grandparents
2 Go caravanning with his parents
3 Stay in a tent
4 Cross the Channel in a boat
5 Swim in the sea
6 Go on a tour of Rome

5 ✏ Plan an adventure for your next holiday. Where will you go and who with? Include what you plan to do on holiday.

Ich werde	nächstes Jahr /	mit meinen Eltern /	in die Schweiz /	fahren.
	in den Sommerferien	mit meinen Freunden /	nach Österreich	
Dort werde ich	jeden Tag /	allein	im Meer	baden.
	morgens /		am Strand	Eis essen.
	abends		in den Alpen	Skifahren.

Grammatik **Seite 184**

Using the future tense with *werden*

The future tense is formed with the present tense of *werden* plus the infinitive at the end of the clause:

*Ich **werde** nach Berlin **fahren**.*

*Wir **werden** die Sehenswürdigkeiten besichtigen*.

ich werde	I will
du wirst	you will
er / sie / es wird	he / she / it will
wir werden	we will
ihr werdet	you will (plural)
sie werden	they will
Sie werden	you will (formal)
+ infinitive	

Find out about using prepositions in time phrases.   *See page 84* ➡

Strategie 4

Dealing with false friends

False friends are words which seem similar in different languages but have completely different meanings. You need to watch out for them. Here are some examples:

ich will means 'I want to' and not 'I will'

fast means 'almost', not 'quickly'

der Chef is the boss, not a cook

Not means emergency, so *der Notausgang* is an emergency exit.

Hinweis

4.3 Groundwork is available in the Foundation Book.

4.3 H Berlin ist cool!

Daniels Urlaub

das Bundestagsgebäude

Berlin Zoo

Checkpoint Charlie

Ich heiße Daniel. Ich bin ein richtiger Stadtmensch und möchte nie auf dem Land wohnen. Ich wohne in Berlin und finde es einfach total klasse. Es ist jetzt August und, obwohl ich auch gerne in andere Länder reise, bin ich diese Ferien in Berlin, weil ich auf einen großen Urlaub nächstes Jahr spare. Man kann in Berlin viel unternehmen, es gibt überall etwas Interessantes zu sehen. Wenn das Wetter gut ist, kann man nach Wannsee fahren. Das ist ein Stadtteil von Berlin und dort gibt es auch Seen, wo man schwimmen, surfen und segeln kann. Meine Freunde und ich sind schon mindestens 8 Mal dorthin gefahren, weil das Wetter bis jetzt wirklich super war. Aber in Berlin kann man auch viel unternehmen, wenn die Sonne nicht scheint. Es gibt viele Kinos, wo man die neuesten deutschen und internationalen Filme sehen kann. Natürlich kann man auch gut einkaufen in großen Kaufhäusern, aber auch kleineren Boutiquen. Am Dienstag waren wir im Berliner Zoo. Er ist sehr berühmt und liegt im Zentrum Berlins. Leider hat es an diesem Tag geregnet und viele Tiere haben sich deshalb versteckt. Dieses Jahr habe ich mich auch entschlossen, mal das „touristische Berlin" zu sehen – etwas Kulturelles. Ich bin zum Beispiel letzten Freitag zum Bundestagsgebäude gegangen. Dort kann man manchmal Politiker bei Sitzungen sehen. Morgen werde ich dann zum Museum am Checkpoint Charlie gehen. Dort kann man sehen, wo bis 1989 die Berliner Mauer war, und am Mittwochabend werden ich und ein paar Freunde grillen. Das wird bestimmt Spaß machen.

---

1 📖 Look at this list of words and sort them into a) nouns and b) verbs. For nouns, say if they are singular or plural and anything else you can tell about them; for verbs say which tense they are in or if they are infinitives.

| besucht | wird | mag | bleibt | Geschäften | besichtigen |
| entspannen | gefällt | werde | Freunde | verbringt | Spaß |

2 📖🎧 Read Daniel's article. The text below is a summary of the article. Choose a word from the list in activity 1 to fill the gaps.

Daniel wohnt in Berlin und diese Stadt **1**_____ ihm sehr gut. Dieses Jahr **2**_____ er in den Ferien zu Hause, um Geld zu sparen. Mit seinen Freunden fährt er gern nach Wannsee, wenn sie sich **3**_____ wollen, aber Berlin hat auch historische Sehenswürdigkeiten und eine gute Auswahl an **4**_____. Die Hauptstadt ist auch kulturell sehr interessant und Daniel hat neulich das Bundestagsgebäude **5**_____. Er **6**_____ bald zum Museum über die Berliner Mauer gehen.

3 🎧 Listen to Kai and Nicole talking about their most recent holidays and what they would like to do in future. Answer the questions in English.

1 Who did Kai travel with?
2 Where did he spend his holidays?
3 Why did he not enjoy the coach journey? (Give 2 reasons.)
4 What type of accommodation did he stay in?
5 What did he enjoy the least during his stay and why?
6 Why did he enjoy his stay overall? (Give 2 reasons.)
7 Where does he want to go next year?
8 Where is Nicole's aunt's and uncle's holiday flat?
9 What does she say about the weather?
10 Which country does she want to go to next year?
11 What does she want to do there? (Give 2 details.)
12 What does she have to do first?

> **Tackling longer texts**
>
> In Listening and Reading tasks, don't just focus on the words you don't know. Look or listen out for words you do know and try to work out the unfamiliar ones from the context.
>
> Remember that you don't need to understand every single word to get the gist of a text.

4 **G** Translate these sentences into German using the correct time phrase. Remember to use the correct word order (Time – Manner – Place).

1 We are going to Berlin next summer.
2 This month I am staying at home.
3 He flew to Germany last week.
4 Did you go to Italy last year?
5 Next weekend she is flying to Zürich.
6 We came home last Saturday.

Grammatik Seite 179

> **Using time phrases accurately**
>
> Remember that *letztes* and *nächstes* are adjectives and so need to have the correct ending. Note the gender of the noun they go with. The case used for time phrases with no preposition is the accusative. You need to use the adjective ending for when there is no article, e.g.
>
> *letzten Monat* (masc.)
> *diese Woche* (fem.)
> *nächstes Jahr* (neut.)
>
> Also learn how to use *um … zu, ohne … zu* and *anstatt … zu.*
> *See page 85* ➡

5 🗨 Work in groups and make up some complex sentences about your holiday experiences. Rise to the challenges!

Challenge 1: Use all three tenses in every sentence.
Challenge 2: Choose only three words to write on a card (no conjugated verbs) as a memory aid.

Say your sentences out loud to each other. Judge whose sentence is the best and why. Look at the example sentence below.

Past tense	Present tense	Future tense
Dieses Jahr bin ich zu Hause geblieben, anstatt ins Ausland zu fahren, …	*… weil ich mein Geld spare, …*	*… aber nächstes Jahr werde ich mit meiner Familie nach Portugal fahren.*

Evaluation:
• complex sentence ☆
• 3 tenses used ☆
• *anstatt … zu* clause ☆
• accurate word order ☆
• extra detail (*mit meiner Familie*) ☆
• time phrases ☆

Prompt card
1 anstatt
2 sparen
3 Portugal

Holidays

1 Work with a partner. Ask him or her the following questions about a future holiday. He or she answers. Then swap roles. You could include the key words in brackets in your answers, or use your own ideas.

Beispiel:

> Wohin möchtest du fahren?

> Ich möchte nach Spanien fahren.

- ■ Wohin möchtest du fahren? (Spanien)
- ■ Mit wem möchtest du fahren? (mit Freunden)
- ■ Wie möchtet ihr fahren? (fliegen)
- ■ Wo möchtet ihr übernachten? (Hotel)
- ■ Was möchtest du machen? (surfen)
- ■ Was möchte deine Freundin / dein Freund machen? (sich sonnen)
- ■ Wie viel Geld möchtest du ausgeben? (nicht viel)

> **Grammatik** *Seite 184*
>
> **Saying 'I would like to ...'**
> *Ich möchte* is a very useful expression for saying 'I would like'. It can either be followed by a noun in the accusative, e.g. *Ich möchte ein Eis* (I would like an ice cream), or by a verb, e.g. *Ich möchte Wien besuchen* (I would like to visit Vienna). If using a verb, it needs to go to the end.

2 These statements are answers to questions. Which question word would have been used for each one?

1 Mein Bruder.
2 In Italien.
3 Um vier Uhr.
4 Zwei Stunden.
5 Das ist ein Hund.
6 Weil ich Spanien liebe.
7 Mit dem Zug.

> **Grammatik** *Seite 188*
>
> **Asking questions using simple interrogatives**
> Question words or interrogatives go at the start of a question. German interrogatives start with *w*. Here are the most common ones:
>
> | *Wann?* | When? | *Wer?* | Who? |
> |---|---|---|---|
> | *Wie?* | How? | *Was?* | What? |
> | *Wo?* | Where? | *Wie lange?* | How long? |
> | *Warum?* | Why? | | |

3 Insert the preposition *in*, *nach*, *vor* or *während* to match the English meanings.

1 after lunch: _____ dem Mittagessen
2 in three years: _____ drei Jahren
3 two months ago: _____ zwei Monaten
4 before Easter: _____ Ostern
5 during the summer: _____ des Sommers
6 after our holiday: _____ unserem Urlaub

> **Grammatik** *Seite 176*
>
> **Prepositions in time phrases**
> *In, nach* and *vor* are all useful prepositions for expressing when things happen. They all take the dative case.
>
> *in den Ferien* – in the holidays
>
> *nach den Sommerferien* – after the summer holidays
>
> *vor dem Winter* – before the winter
>
> Note that *vor* can also have the sense of 'ago'.
> *vor einem Jahr* – a year ago
>
> You should also recognise the preposition *während* which means 'during' and is followed by the genitive:
>
> *während der Herbstferien* – during the autumn holidays

4a Translate the following phrases into German.

1 something big
2 something small
3 nothing interesting
4 nothing blue
5 little of interest ('little interesting')
6 much good
7 everything modern

4b Once your teacher has checked your work on the previous activity, write six sentences, each one containing one of the phrases you have translated.

Beispiel: Ich habe diese Stadt besucht, aber es gab nichts Interessantes dort.

5 Choose the correct interrogative in each sentence.

1 Mit wer / wen / wem bist du gefahren?
2 Wohin / woher wirst du nächstes Jahr fahren?
3 Welcher / welchen / welches Urlaub gefällt dir am besten?
4 An wer / wen / wem hast du die Postkarten geschickt?
5 Bei wer / wen / wem hast du übernachtet?
6 Welcher / welche / welches Hotel hast du gebucht?

6a Put the second half of the following sentences into the right order.

Beispiel: 1 Ich werde nach Italien fahren, um Italienisch zu lernen.

1 Ich werde nach Italien fahren, zu um Italienisch lernen.
2 Ich werde nach Paris fahren, ohne zu den Eiffelturm sehen.
3 Wir werden meine Großmutter besuchen, ihren Geburtstag zu feiern um.
4 Sie wird dieses Jahr ans Meer fahren, in die Berge zu anstatt gehen.
5 Sie werden eine Weltreise machen, das Geld anstatt sparen zu.

6b Now complete the following sentences, using *um … zu … , ohne … zu …* or *anstatt … zu …* . Use as many words as possible from below (but you can also add your own ideas!).

essen	besuchen	Chinesisch	Dublin	eine DVD
eine Pizza	im Meer	kaufen	lernen	schwimmen
		sehen		

1 Ich werde nach Irland fahren, …
2 Ich werde zu Hause bleiben, …
3 Wir werden in ein italienisches Restaurant gehen, …
4 Wir werden nach China fliegen, …
5 Sie werden ins Geschäft gehen, …

Grammatik — Seite 178

Using adjectives after *etwas, nichts, viel, wenig* and *alles*

When you add an adjective after *etwas* (something), *nichts* (nothing), *viel* (much) or *wenig* (little) the adjective gains a capital letter (becomes a noun) and you add *-es* to the end of it:

etwas Interessantes

After *alles* (everything) you just add an *-e*:

alles Interessante

Grammatik — Seite 188

More complex interrogatives

Take care when using the question words *Wo?, Wer?* and *Welche(r/s)?*:

Wo? – Where? Sometimes you need to imply direction:

Wohin? – Where to?

Woher? – Where from?

Wer? – Who? This declines in different cases:

Wen kennst du? – Whom do you know?

Mit wem fährst du? – With whom are you going?

Welche(r/s)? – Which? also declines according to gender and case:

Welcher Bus ist das? – Which bus is that?

Welchen Bus nimmst du? – Which bus are you taking?

Grammatik — Seite 185

Using *um … zu … , ohne … zu …* and *anstatt … zu …*

You have already encountered the use of *um … zu …* ('in order to do something' – see page 39). *Ohne … zu …* ('without doing something') and *anstatt … zu …* ('instead of doing something') work in a similar way. You need to put the object after *um* and the verb in the infinitive after *zu*:

Ich werde nach Deutschland fahren, um Deutsch zu lernen.

Ich werde in den Osterferien Ski fahren, anstatt für meine Prüfungen zu lernen.

When you have a separable verb the *zu* goes after the prefix:

Ich werde nach Amerika fliegen, ohne viel Geld auszugeben.

Holidays

Topic 4.1 Holiday possibilities and preferences

4.1 F Wohin fährst du? ➡ *pages 72–73*

die	Alpen	the Alps
der	Berg	mountain
	besichtigen	to see (while sightseeing)
	bleiben	to stay
	dauern	to last (time)
	(sich) entspannen	to relax
	fliegen	to fly
der	Frühling	spring
der	Herbst	autumn
die	Jahreszeit	season
die	Kunstgalerie	art gallery
das	Meer	sea
	normalerweise	usually
	reisen	to travel
	Schlittschuh laufen	to go iceskating
die	Schweiz	Switzerland
der	Sommer	summer
der	Strand	beach
	verbringen	to spend
der	Winter	winter

4.1 H Schönen Gruß aus dem Urlaub!
➡ *pages 74–75*

	anders	different
	beschreiben	to describe
das	Butterbrot	sandwich
	einfach	easy
	einmalig	once in a lifetime
die	Erfahrung	experience
das	Erlebnis	experience
	flach	flat
das	Gebiet	district

die	Insel	island
die	Jugendherberge	youth hostel
die	Landschaft	landscape
	möglich	possible
die	Nordsee	the North Sea
	Österreich	Austria
der	See	lake
	übernachten	to stay the night
	unternehmen	to undertake, to do
	woanders	somewhere else
	zelten	to camp

Topic 4.2 What to see and getting around

4.2 F Los geht's! ➡ *pages 76–77*

die	Ausfahrt	exit (for vehicles)
die	Auskunft	information
	aussteigen	to get off (train)
das	Boot	boat
die	Einfahrt	entrance (for vehicles)
der	Eingang	entrance (on foot)
	einsteigen	to get on (train)
die	Ermäßigung	reduction
der	Fahrradverleih	bike hire
der	Flughafen	airport
die	Gepäckaufbewahrung	left luggage
der	Imbiss	snack
der	Notausgang	emergency exit
der	Rentner	pensioner
die	Sehenswürdigkeiten (pl)	sights
	(sich) sonnen	to sunbathe
	umsteigen	to change (trains)
die	Verbindung	connection
der	Wartesaal	waiting room
der	Zuschlag	supplement (to pay)

4.2 H Unterwegs ➡ *pages 78–79*

der	Aufenthalt	stay
	ausgezeichnet	excellent
	(sich) entschließen	to decide
	erkunden	to explore
der	Führerschein	driving licence
	geschlossen	closed
der	Hauptbahnhof	main station
der	Leihwagen	hire car
	mieten	to rent
der	Reisebus	coach
die	Richtung	direction
	sammeln	to collect
die	Straßenbahn	tram
die	Umgebung	surrounding area
	unabhängig	independent
	vermeiden	to avoid
	wiederholen	to repeat
die	Wohltätigkeitsveranstaltung	charity event
die	Wüste	desert
der	Zweck	cause, goal

Topic 4.3 Past experiences, future plans

4.3 F Das werde ich machen ➡ *pages 80–81*

die	Ahnung	idea
	allein	alone
	Australien	Australia
	baden	to bathe
	besuchen	to visit
	erlauben	to allow
	getrennt	separate(ly)
die	Gondel	gondola
der	Kanal	canal
die	Klassenfahrt	school trip
	schrecklich	terrible
der	See	lake
die	See	sea
	seekrank	seasick

	sehenswert	worth seeing
	stören	to bother, to disturb
	tagsüber	during the day
	Venedig	Venice
	verbessern	to improve
der	Wohnwagen	caravan

4.3 H Berlin ist cool! ➡ *pages 82–83*

	Ägypten	Egypt
	aufregend	exciting
	berühmt	famous
	Bundestagsgebäude	German parliamentary buildings
	grillen	to have a barbecue
die	Hütte	mountain hut
	klettern	to climb
	kulturell	cultural
der	Kurs	course
	leider	unfortunately
die	Mauer	wall
der	Mensch	person
	segeln	to sail
die	Sitzung	meeting
der	Stadtteil	part of town
	surfen	to surf
	tauchen	to dive
das	Tier	animal
	(sich) verstecken	to hide
	(sich) verstehen (mit)	to get on with

Higher – Exam practice

 info

These pages give you the chance to try GCSE-style practice exam questions at grades B–A*, based on the AQA Context of Leisure.

 **Hinweis**

Foundation practice exam questions (grades D–C) are available at the end of this Context in the Foundation book.

Zell am See und Kaprun

Zell am See und Kaprun im Winter

Willkommen in Österreich. Ob Skianfänger oder Profi – 138 Kilometer Abfahrten und 57 Pisten machen jedem Wintersportler Spaß. Die leichten Pisten sind blau markiert und sind besonders gut für Anfänger. Wenn Sie schon ein besserer Skifahrer sind, dann wählen Sie eine von den 49 Kilometer langen roten Pisten oder die schwierigen Pisten der schwarzen Kategorie.

Sie sind noch nie Ski gefahren? Dann haben unsere Skilehrer die richtigen Tipps für Sie. Wir haben Englisch, Französisch, Italienisch, Polnisch und natürlich Deutsch sprechende Skilehrer. Wählen Sie zwischen einem halben Tag Unterricht von 10 bis 13 Uhr oder 13.30 bis 16.30 Uhr, oder den ganzen Tag. Wir bieten ihnen Einzelunterricht oder Unterricht in Gruppen bis maximal zehn Personen.

Sie wollen Snowboarden? Die drei Snow-Parks auf dem Kitzsteinhorn sind der richtige Ort dafür. Die sechs Meter hohe Superpipe ist nur eine der vielen Highlights im 30 000 Quadratmeter großen Mellow Park. Man kann hier immer üben, denn Schnee liegt hier auf dem Gletscher garantiert das ganze Jahr.

1a The local tourist office for Zell am See and Kaprun advertises activities. Read the advertisement and answer the questions.

1 Which country are Zell am See and Kaprun in?
2 What colour slope is recommended if you are a beginner skier?
3 What languages do the skiing instructors speak? (5)
4 What is the maximum number of people who can learn to ski in one group?
5 When do they have snow on the Kitzsteinhorn?

(**Total** = 9 marks)

1b Read the text again and decide whether the statements are true (**T**), false (**F**) or not in the text (**?**).

1 There are 49 kilometres of red slopes.
2 Difficult slopes are marked in black.
3 You have to book a whole day of skiing lessons.
4 Parents can learn how to ski with their children.
5 You can learn how to snow board.

(**Total** = 5 marks)

2 📖 Five teenagers talk about their pocket money. Read the statements on the right and decide whether their statements are positive (**P**), negative (**N**) or positive and negative (**P+N**).

1 Lina 4 Sabrina
2 Sebastian 5 Tarik
3 Ahmed

Total = 5 marks

3a 🎧 Five teenagers speak about the use of technology and media. Listen to Anja, Mathias, Daniela, Christian and Erika. Decide whether their statements are positive (**P**), negative (**N**) or positive and negative (**P+N**).

1 Anja 4 Christian
2 Mathias 5 Erika
3 Daniela

Total = 5 marks

3b 🎧 Listen again. Who says what? Write the correct name.

Who says that …
1 … they couldn't live without a mobile?
2 … friends talked behind their back?
3 … it helps them practise foreign languages?
4 … modern media and technology can be a waste of time?
5 … that you have to go with the times?

Total = 5 marks

4 🎧 Listen to the advertisement for Kaprun and Zell am See in summer. Choose the five words which apply to what you hear.

Families with children	Beach
Extreme sports	Altitude
International guests	Horse riding
Mountain village	Sunbathing

Total = 5 marks

Total for Reading and Listening = 34 marks

Lina
Ich bekomme 50 Euro pro Monat von meinen Eltern. Ich denke, das ist nicht genug, weil ich meine Hefte und Stifte davon kaufen muss. Ich finde meine Eltern wirklich nicht fair, weil mein Bruder viel mehr bekommt.

Sebastian
Von meinen Eltern bekomme ich jede Woche 10 Euro. Ich kriege auch noch Taschengeld von meinen Großeltern, aber das spare ich für meine Ferien. Ich habe also genug und freue mich schon auf meinen Urlaub.

Ahmed
Ich möchte gern Taschengeld, aber meine Eltern geben mir keines. Sie sagen ich muss für mein Geld arbeiten. Ich helfe also im Haushalt. Dafür bekomme ich nur 25 Euro im Monat. Das ist zwar nicht genug, aber es bereitet mich auf die Zukunft vor. Ich weiß, dass ich für mein Geld arbeiten muss, und das ist nützlich.

Sabrina
Ich bekomme 100 Euro im Monat. Meine Freunde und Freundinnen glauben, dass das zu viel ist. Ich muss aber davon alles selbst kaufen – meine Kleidung, Schulsachen, Eintritt ins Kino. Da bleibt am Ende des Monats nicht viel übrig. Was mir gefällt, ist, dass ich flexibel mit meinem Geld sein kann, aber es ist nicht so gut, wenn man schon als Teenager viel Verantwortung hat.

Tarik
Ich habe genug Taschengeld. Ich bekomme 80 Euro im Monat, und meine Eltern kaufen mir alles, was ich will. Besser kann man es nicht haben.

Higher – Speaking

Einkaufen ist toll!

You are in the home of your Austrian exchange partner. He or she wants to take you on a shopping trip in Vienna and wants to know what kind of things you like spending money on.

Your teacher will play the role of your exchange partner.
He or she could ask you the following:

1. How much pocket money do you get?
2. What do you like buying?
3. Where do you like to go shopping?
4. What have you bought recently?
5. What are the best and worst things you have ever bought?
6. What would you buy if you won a lot of money?
7. !

! Remember you will have to respond to something you have not yet prepared.

info

Important information:
This sample task is for practice purposes only and should not be used as an actual assessment task. Study it to find out how to plan your Controlled Assessment efficiently to gain maximum marks and / or work through it as a mock exam task before the actual Controlled Assessment.

---

1. **How much pocket money do you get?**
   - say how much pocket money you get, who from and how often
   - say whether you think it is enough and give a reason for your answer
   - mention whether you have to do some work for your pocket money
   - say whether you think it is a good idea to work for your pocket money

Strategie

Start your plan. Write a maximum of six words for each sub-division. Here are some suggested words for the first one: *Taschengeld, Eltern, ausreichen, helfen, ungerecht, ausgeben*. Remember that the maximum number of words allowed in your plan is 40.

Link your sentences together, for example by using *aber*, *jedoch*, *trotzdem*. Remember that *jedoch* and *trotzdem* are followed by a verb.

---

2. **What do you like buying?**
   - mention the kinds of things you like buying
   - give a reason for your answer
   - give examples of what your friends spend their money on
   - say what you think about this

Strategie

Suggested words for your plan: *kaufen, verschwenden, finden*. Add three more words to this list.

Use some advanced vocabulary and sentences to talk about your friends' shopping habits. You can list things they buy and give an example of what one friend has bought recently. By doing so you mix different tenses.

For example: *Mein bester Freund verschwendet meiner Meinung nach sein Geld. Er hat kürzlich ... gekauft, was ich viel zu teuer finde.*

---

3. **Where do you like to go shopping?**
   - say which town or city you normally shop in
   - say whether you prefer larger or smaller shops
   - give a reason for your choice
   - say whether you prefer internet shopping or real shops and give a reason

Strategie

Suggested words for your plan: *lieber, Kunden, persönlich*. Add three more words to this list.

Show that you can use the comparative. For example, for the last sub-division you can say where you prefer shopping but also use phrases such as *das ist besser als ... / nicht so teuer wie ...*

4 What have you bought recently?
- mention the kinds of things you have bought recently
- give a description of one item you have bought recently
- say how much money you spent on the item and why you bought it
- say whether it was worth the money and whether you are still happy with it

Strategie

Suggested words for your plan: *gekauft, kürzlich, sich lohnen*. Add two more words to this list.

Use an advanced structure such as *Als ich kürzlich in der Stadt war, habe ich … gekauft*. By doing so you show that you can use complex structures. Remember that the word **when** in the past tense is *als* in German.

Try to be imaginative when you describe the item: use detailed descriptions.

5 What are the best and worst things you have ever bought?
- mention the best thing you have ever bought
- give a number of reasons why it was such a good buy
- mention the worst thing you have ever bought
- give details of why it was such a bad buy

Strategie

Suggested words for your plan: *beste, schlechteste, Geldverschwendung*. Add three more words to this list.

This is a good opportunity for you to be creative. You could talk about how you thought that something was a real bargain but turned out to be a waste of money as it didn't work or was cheaper elsewhere. You may want to use the conditional tense here to say what you would do or buy in future instead.

6 What would you buy if you won a lot of money?
- say what you would buy with your money and how much money you would need
- say why you would spend money on these things
- say whether you would share your money with other people
- explain whether you feel that money makes people happy

Strategie

Suggested words for your plan: *Lottogewinn, sparen*. Add four more words to the list.

Use a variety of starter phrases to introduce your plans: *Wenn ich Geld gewinne, möchte ich …*; *Falls ich im Lotto gewinnen würde, würde ich …* . All of these phrases need a verb in the infinitive at the end of the sentence, e.g. *würde ich mein Traumhaus kaufen*.

This part of the Controlled Assessment allows you to be very creative and imaginative. Try to give detailed information in order to have access to the highest grades.

7 ! At this point you may be asked to …
- say whether you think you shop too much
- say what else you do with your pocket money, e.g. saving
- mention what you feel about shopping on the high street
- say what the ideal amount of pocket money is
- say whether you think it is good for teenagers to work for their pocket money.

Strategie

Think about what the surprise question could be. There are some suggestions in the sub-divisions. Then work out what your answer would be to each of those and any other questions you think might be asked.

You should have four words left to add to your list, so choose carefully, e.g. if you want to talk about high street shops, then you might want the word *Ladenketten*. Another useful word could be *Summe* for answering the fourth sub-division.

Pick words that you haven't already used in your preparation, as you're more likely to need help remembering these.

Your answer does not have to be long but it needs to contain a conjugated verb.

Remember to check the total number of words you have used. It should be 40 or fewer.

Hinweis

Foundation sample assessment tasks for this Context can be found in the Foundation book.

Higher – Writing

Meine Ferien

You are on holiday and are posting about it on your blog to keep everyone back home up to date. You could include:

1 location and weather
2 your journey there
3 food and accommodation
4 local sights
5 holiday activities
6 a comparison with past holidays
7 your future holiday plans.

1 Location and weather
  – say which country or city you are in at the moment and where it is located
  – say why you decided on this location
  – say what the weather has been like so far
  – say what type of holiday you generally prefer and why

Strategie

Start your plan. Remember that you are allowed a maximum of 40 words. Some suggested words for the first sub-division: *Hauptstadt, Norden, entschieden, Augenblick, geregnet, generell.*

Don't write too much basic information about the weather but focus on the other sub-divisions where you can be more creative.

You may want to use a phrase such as *Ich habe mich für … entschieden, weil … ;* or *Als ich meinen Urlaub geplant habe, wollte ich …*

This introduces complex language from the start.

2 Your journey there
  – say how you travelled to your destination
  – say how long the journey took
  – give an account of your journey to your destination
  – mention whether you will choose this mode of transport again and why

Strategie

Suggested words for your plan: *Transportmittel, Stau, preiswert.* Add no more than three words to this list.

The third sub-division allows you to list events by using time indicators such as *zuerst, dann, danach, zum Schluss.*

3 Food and accommodation
  – say what type of accommodation you are staying in and mention some of the facilities
  – say whether you would recommend it or not and give a reason for your decision
  – say what food you have tried already and give your opinion
  – mention what you are going to eat this evening and give a reason for your choice

Strategie

Suggested words for your plan: *empfehlen, versucht, probiert.* Add no more than three words to this list.

Think of various ways of expressing your opinion in the past tense, e.g. *Ich habe geglaubt, dass es gut schmecken würde. Ich habe gedacht, dass es schrecklich schmecken würde. Ich war der Meinung, dass das Essen ausgezeichnet war.* Remember to put the verb to the end of the clause after *dass.*

You can write down past participles in your plan such as the word *probiert* as they do not count as conjugated verbs.

4 Local sights

- mention some of the major local sights you have already seen
- give your opinion of them
- mention what one other member of your family thought about them
- mention one other sight you are going to see tomorrow and why

Strategie

Suggested words for your plan: *Sehenswürdigkeiten, sehenswert, Stadtrundfahrt.* Add no more than three words to this list.

You can use the structures *Am besten hat mir… gefallen* or *Am liebsten war mir…* to express which sights you liked the best.

This sub-division gives you another opportunity to use a variety of tenses, which will enable you to have access to the highest grades. See Exam technique W5.

5 Holiday activities

- say what you are currently doing
- give a detailed account of what you have already done on your holiday
- say whether you feel that it has been a good holiday so far and why
- give details about your plans for the rest of your holiday

Strategie

Suggested words for your plan: *gerade, schon, morgen.* Add no more than three words to this list.

Putting time indicators on your list of words allows you to think about the tenses you want to use, with *gerade* referring to the present tense, *schon* to an event in the past and *morgen* to the future.

Think about other family members on this trip. You may want to think about what things they might do in future that are not the same. This gives you the opportunity to show the examiner that you can talk about other people.

For example: *Ich werde an den Strand gehen, aber meine Eltern werden eine Galerie besuchen.*

6 A comparison with past holidays

- mention another holiday you have been on previously
- give an account of what you did on that holiday
- explain what you liked and didn't like about the previous holiday
- say which holiday you prefer and give a reason

Strategie

Suggested words for your plan: *besucht, gereist, Vergleich.* Add no more than three words to this list.

You may want to talk about a very different holiday you have been on recently: for example, a winter holiday if the main part of your Controlled Assessment is about a summer holiday. This allows you to use new language.

Use phrases such as *Ich denke, im Gegensatz zu … sind Ferien in … besser* or *Im Vergleich zu … sind Ferien in … nicht so schön.*

7 Your future holidays plans

- say where you will go on holiday and give reasons
- mention one or two activities you would like to do there
- say what type of holiday you would never want to go on and why
- say what would be your dream holiday and give reasons for your choice.

Strategie

Now count up how many words you have left, ideally about five or six. If you have fewer than this, you may want to go back and take some out of your lists for previous sub-divisions, as you can only have 40 words in total. Suggested words for your plan: *Zukunft, Kreuzfahrt.* Add four more words to this list.

This sub-division gives you the opportunity to use the future tense. Don't forget that there are a number of ways to express the future tense, e.g. *ich werde, ich will, ich möchte.*

Try to add other phrases which express the future tense, such as *ich habe vor, … zu …, ich habe mir vorgenommen … zu …, ich plane … zu … .*

 **Hinweis**

Foundation sample assessment tasks for this Context can be found in the Foundation book.

Exam technique – Speaking

S4 Help available

Your teacher is allowed to discuss each task in English with you, including the kind of language you may need and how to use your preparatory work. You can have access to a dictionary, your German books, Kerboodle and internet resources. This is the stage when you will prepare your plan using the Task Planning Form.

When you actually perform the task, you will only have access to your plan and your teacher's comments (i.e. the Task Planning Form).

S5 AQA administration

For the Speaking part of your exam, you have to do two different tasks (at two different times). One of the tasks will be recorded and sent to a moderator. Each task will last between 4 and 6 minutes. When your teacher thinks that you have been taught the language you need and feels that you are ready, you will be given the task to prepare. It could be a task designed by the AQA Examination Board or a task designed by German teachers in your school.

S6 Marking of the tasks

Your teacher will mark your work. A moderator (i.e. an examiner) will sample the work of your school and check that it has been marked correctly. A senior examiner will check the work of the moderator. This complicated but secure system ensures that candidates are given the correct mark.

The Speaking part of your exam counts for 30% of the German GCSE. Each task is marked out of 30 marks. As there are two Speaking tasks, the number of marks available for Speaking is 60.

For each task, the marks are divided in the following way, with the maximum number of marks available shown in each case: 10 marks for Communication, 10 marks for Range of language and Accuracy, 5 marks for Pronunciation and Intonation, 5 marks for Interaction and Fluency.

Grade booster

To reach grade B, you need to …

- Develop most of your answers well, using some complex sentences, e.g. bullet point 2: linking up your shopping preferences and your friends' shopping preferences with opinions and reasons. *Ich kaufe normalerweise gern in … ein, weil … . Meine Freundinnen glauben jedoch, dass das Einkaufen in … besser ist, weil …*

- Answer without hesitation, using a good range of vocabulary, e.g. bullet point 6. Give information about what you would give to different people and give a reason for it.

To reach grade A, you need to …

- Attempt a variety of verb tenses, e.g. bullet point 4 gives you the opportunity to answer in the present when you express your view on the purchase, the past when you say what you have bought and the future or conditional if you say whether or not you will buy the item again.

- Express ideas and points of view using complex sentences and a very good range of vocabulary, e.g. bullet point 5 gives you the opportunity to compare your best and your worst buy. *Es ist viel schlechter, weil es teurer, aber viel schneller kaputt war.*

To reach grade A*, you need to …

- Have a wide range of vocabulary and use a number of more complex structures, e.g. bullet point 3: show that you can talk about other people as well by saying what experiences other members of your family or friends have had with internet shopping. *Mein Freund hat CDs im Internet gekauft, aber sie sind nie angekommen.*

- Respond readily and show initiative on several occasions, e.g. bullet point 5. Initiative can be shown in different ways, e.g. by going beyond the normal phrases and content. You can, for example, mention that it is important to you where and how items have been produced. *Ich versuche Produkte zu kaufen, die ökologisch hergestellt sind.*

Exam technique – Writing

W4 Responding to the bullet points

In a Writing task, there are typically between six and eight bullet points. All bullet points are written in English. Although you have to write a response to the title of the task, it is recommended that you deal with every bullet point that is given below it so that you don't miss out any important information.

W5 Using different tenses

If you are aiming at grade A, you should also show that you know the conditional.

W6 How much to write

If you are aiming at grades C–A*, you should produce 400–600 words across the two tasks (i.e. 200–300 words per task). Although there is flexibility, aim to write approximately 40 words per bullet point.

You may produce a draft, but this is for your use only. Your teacher cannot comment on it and you cannot have access to any draft when you write the final version.

Grade booster

To reach grade B, you need to …

- Be able to explain ideas, using appropriate vocabulary and complex sentences, e.g. bullet point 2: don't just mention that the journey took a long time, but that there was a traffic jam and the reasons for it. *Es hat lange gedauert, weil es einen Stau gab. Ich glaube, es war weil zwei Autos einen Unfall hatten.*

- Write with some accuracy. There may be errors in your attempt at more complex sentences but verb and tense formations are usually correct, e.g. bullet point 5. You are asked to use the present, past and future tenses here. Take care with the accuracy of verb endings.

To reach grade A, you need to …

- Write 40 to 50 words per bullet point, conveying a lot of relevant information clearly, e.g. bullet point 5. You could give a lot of information and details here. However, try to limit yourself to 40–50 words and focus instead on quality of communication so that you don't neglect the other bullet points of the task.

- Be generally accurate in your attempts at complex sentences and verb tenses. You should, for example, make sure that you can confidently use *weil / da / obwohl* and that you don't forget to move the verb to the end. Likewise you should remember that the word order does not change after *denn*.

To reach grade A*, you need to …

- Use a wide variety of vocabulary and structures with accuracy, e.g. bullet point 4. Use vocabulary and give information that shows that you either have actually been to a particular place or that you have done research on it by describing some of the actual sights in detail. … *wurde im Jahr … von … erbaut.*

- Use more complex sentences and verb tenses successfully, e.g. bullet point 6: combine complex structures and verb tenses, e.g. *Den Urlaub, den ich bis jetzt am schlimmsten gefunden habe, ist der Urlaub in … , denn …*

5.1 F Wo ich wohne

Lernziele

Talking about house types and describing rooms

Using knowledge of cultural and social differences

Prepositions showing position

1 **V** Match the pictures to the types of housing.

1 Wohnblock   5 Bauernhaus
2 Mehrfamilienhaus   6 Doppelhaus
3 Reihenhaus   7 Mietwohnung
4 Einfamilienhaus

2a 🎧 Listen to these people talking about where they live and answer the questions using their names. Who says that they live …

1 somewhere with three bedrooms?
2 somewhere with a garden?
3 somewhere modern?
4 somewhere which is very big?
5 somewhere which is over a century old?

| Britta | Mehmet | Stefan | Rudi | Jana |

2b 🎧 Listen again and note down in English what type of house each person lives in.

Strategie 2a–2b

Using knowledge of cultural and social differences

It is important to remember that the way of life in other countries is not always the same as in Britain. This is particularly true of housing. Far more Germans, for example, choose to rent a flat (*eine Mietwohnung*), rather than buy one (*eine Eigentumswohnung*) or a house. Being aware of this is useful in various skill areas, e.g. when listening to someone from Germany describe their home, it is likely to be a flat (*Wohnung*) as part of a larger house (*Mehrfamilienhaus*) rather than a semi-detached house.

3a 📖🎧 Read Lisa's email on page 97. Are the statements about her room true (**T**), false (**F**) or not in the text (**?**)?

1 Lisa's room is small.
2 The curtains are pink.
3 She has a double bed and a wardrobe.
4 There is a computer in her room.
5 She has pictures of a band on the wall.
6 She would like to have a TV in her room.
7 She keeps her books on her bedside table.

3b 🖊 Read Lisa's email again and draw a plan of her room. Label everything that is in it and use colours where required.

◄ | ⌂ | | 🔍 Suche |

Startseite | Index | Hilfe | Kontakt | Textversion

Mein Schlafzimmer ist klein, aber sehr schön. Die Wände sind rosa und ich habe bunte Vorhänge. Es gibt natürlich ein Einzelbett und einen Kleiderschrank. Ich möchte einen Computer hier im Zimmer haben, aber das geht im Moment nicht. Ich habe Bilder von meiner Lieblingsgruppe an der Wand. Auf meinem Nachttisch steht eine Lampe. In der Ecke gibt es ein Radio aber keinen Fernseher.
Ich habe ein paar Bücher aber leider kein Bücherregal. Meine Oma hat mir neulich ein paar Kopfkissen gekauft. Sie sind auf meinem Bett.

Lisa

Lisa

4a 🄶 Which preposition would fit to describe the picture you see here?

Das Buch ist (**1**) dem Tisch.
Der Tisch ist (**2**) dem Bett.
Das Bett ist (**3**) dem Regal.
Das Regal ist (**4**) der Wand und (**5**) der Tür. (**6**) der Tür liegt der Hund!

4b 🄶 Can you use the other prepositions to make up more sentences about this room?

an	auf	hinter	in
neben	über	unter
vor	zwischen

5 🖊 Say what type of house you live in or would like to live in! Use your imagination and think where you might live if you were a celebrity. Describe it briefly and then give a description of what is in the bedroom. Use a dictionary to find additional vocabulary.

Prepositions showing position

Some prepositions can take either the accusative (to indicate movement) or dative (to show the position of something). When they take the dative, they are useful for describing where things are in a room. In the dative plural you also need to add an -*n* to the noun. You will learn more about these prepositions taking the accusative later in this topic.

neben **dem** Schrank (masc.)	next to the wardrobe
auf **dem** Tisch (masc.)	on the table ('on' as in 'on top of')
an **der** Wand (fem.)	on the wall ('on' as in 'against')
vor / hinter **der** Tür (fem.)	in front of / behind the door
unter **dem** Bett (neut.)	under the bed
zwischen **den** Zimmern (pl.)	between the rooms

Also revise how to use es *gibt*.   *See page 108* ➡

Grammatik   *Seite 176*

◯◯◯ **Hinweis**

5.1 Groundwork is available in the Foundation Book.

5.1 H Bei uns, bei euch

Wie sieht die ideale Wohnung aus?

Unsere Reporterin hat Folgendes für unsere Leser herausgefunden.

- Genug Zimmer! Die Kinder wollen ein eigenes Schlafzimmer mit Platz für einen Fernseher, einen Computer, ein Bücherregal usw. Die Farbe möchten sie natürlich selbst wählen.
- Eine moderne Küche mit einer Mikrowelle, einem Tiefkühlschrank und einer Spülmaschine.
- Ein ruhiges Wohnzimmer, wo man sich nach der Arbeit entspannen kann. Das Sofa ist vielleicht aus Leder und es gibt auch bequeme Sessel, einen Farbfernseher und noch viel mehr.
- Ein Balkon, wo man sich sonnen kann, und hoffentlich auch eine Grünanlage oder einen Spielplatz in der Nähe. Wenn man Glück hat vielleicht auch Gartenbenutzung (leider nicht möglich, wenn man in einem Wohnblock wohnt).
- Das Badezimmer soll eine Dusche haben und es ist besser, wenn die Toilette nicht im Badezimmer ist, besonders bei einer großen Familie. Im Moment sind Farben wie türkis, weiß und lila modisch.

Und das ideale Haus?

Natürlich hat es auch einen schönen Garten, eine Sonnenterrasse und vielleicht auch einen Wintergarten. Es gibt wahrscheinlich auch einen Dachboden und einen Keller.

1a 📖 🎧 Read the article and find the German words to match the English ones below.

Beispiel: 1 *Platz für einen Fernseher*

1 room for a TV
2 dishwasher
3 where you can sunbathe
4 a play area nearby
5 use of the garden
6 colours such as turquoise
7 an attic

1b 📖 🎧 Look at the article again and decide whether these statements are true (**T**), false (**F**) or not in the text (**?**):

Beispiel: 1 *F*

1 Die Kinder haben nichts dagegen, ein Schlafzimmer zu teilen.
2 Die richtige Farbe ist sehr wichtig für sie.
3 Viele Leute möchten aktiv sein, wenn sie abends nach Hause kommen.
4 Alle wollen einen Garten haben.
5 Eine separate Toilette ist nicht so wichtig für große Familien.
6 Das ideale Haus sollte viele Zimmer haben.

2 🎧 Listen to the young people talking about their homes. Do they like where they live (✓) or not (✗)? Give reasons.

Beispiel: a *Martin, ✓, small but comfortable*

a Martin
b Anna
c Olivia
d Michael
e Henrik
f Udo

ⓖrammatik *Seite 176*

Using prepositions taking the dative case

Some prepositions take the dative only when they are showing the position of something, but others are **always** followed by the dative. If you need a reminder about the dative case, see page xx.

aus	out of / made of
bei	at someone's house / with
mit	with / by (transport)
nach	after
seit	since / for (a length of time)
von	from / by / of
zu	to

gegenüber opposite (this preposition often comes after the noun)

You typically see shortened versions of *bei*, *von* and *zu*:

beim = bei dem, vom = von dem, zum = zu dem and *zur = zu der*.

Wie komme ich zur Stadtmitte?

Der Wald liegt nicht weit vom Dorf.

Also learn how to compare things.

See page 109 ➡

---

3 ⓖ Complete the sentences by using *dem*, *der* or *den*.

Beispiel: 1 *dem*

1 Das Sofa ist gegenüber _____ Fenster.
2 Ich wohne im Moment bei _____ Familie meiner Freundin.
3 Das Haus mit _____ großen Garten ist sehr schön.
4 Was machst du nach _____ Abendessen?
5 Der Kleiderschrank steht links von _____ Kommode.
6 Wir wohnen seit _____ Sommerferien in diesem Haus.

Strategie 4

Different ways of saying 'at someone's house'

The prepositions *bei*, *zu* and *in* can be useful in phrases to say where someone lives. Note the use of the dative case in these phrases.

bei mir / bei uns / bei ihr / bei ihm / bei ihnen

at my / our / her / his / their house

in unserem Haus – in our house

im Haus von meiner Freundin – in my (girl)friend's house

Although the word for house is *das Haus*, you add an -e in these two set expressions which never change:

zu Hause – at home
Ich bin zu Hause.

nach Hause – (to) home
Ich gehe nach Hause.

---

4 🗨 Work with a partner to describe what your house is like and compare it to his or hers. You don't have to tell the truth! Then swap roles.

Beschreib mir euer Haus.

| Ich finde | unser Haus
unsere Wohnung
mein Zimmer | in Ordnung /
schlecht / nicht
schlecht, | weil es / sie | (zu) groß
(zu) eng
gemütlich
geräumig
dunkel
hell
(zu) neu
(zu) alt
wunderschön
größer
ruhiger
älter
moderner
nicht so groß
nicht so gemütlich | ist. |

5.2 F Meine Gegend, deine Gegend

in der Nähe des Industriegebiets	im Seengebiet	in einem Vorort
auf dem Land	an der Küste	in einer Großstadt	in den Bergen

1 **V** The phrases above all relate to areas where you might live. Sort them into two groups and say what they mean in English. Which phrase will overlap both groups?

a rural environments (countryside)
b urban environments (town)

> **Nils**
> Die Landschaft um mein Dorf herum ist schön, aber die Jugendlichen hier wissen nicht, was sie mit sich anfangen sollen. Das Beste hier ist die Kneipe, aber ich bin noch zu jung, um dorthin zu gehen. Es gibt keine guten öffentlichen Verkehrsmittel, und das neue Hallenbad ist immer noch nicht fertig. Die Luft ist aber sehr sauber und man hat die schönste Aussicht auf den See. Der Wald in der Nähe ist auch wunderschön.

> **Martina**
> Ich wohne in einer Großstadt im Rheinland. Die Einkaufsmöglichkeiten sind sehr gut, und für sportliche Leute gibt es Tennisplätze, Schwimmbäder und vieles mehr. Erst abends geht es hier richtig los, was ich toll finde! Es gibt so viele Restaurants, Diskos und drei Kinos. Meine Freunde und ich gehen am liebsten am Samstagabend in die Stadt.

> **Axel**
> Ich wohne erst seit drei Monaten in dieser Industriestadt und es gibt Vorteile und Nachteile. Die Stadt ist nicht sehr schön und auch ziemlich schmutzig, aber man kann viel unternehmen. Man kann sehr billig mit dem Bus ins Stadtzentrum fahren. Das ist wichtig für mich, da ich im Stadtzentrum arbeite.

2 📖 🎧 Read what these people are saying about where they live, then read the statements below. For each statement, write **T** (true), **F** (false) or **?** (not in the text).

1 Nils lives in an unattractive place.
2 Nils isn't old enough to go to the pub.
3 There is a frequent bus service from Nils's village.
4 Martina likes going shopping for clothes.
5 Martina likes going out in the evenings.
6 Axel has been living in his town for three years.
7 Axel thinks the public transport is good.
8 Axel works in a factory.

Using grammar to work out meaning

Strategie 2

Man hat die schönste Aussicht auf den See.

What does the above sentence mean? *See* can mean 'sea' (*die See*) or 'lake' (*der See*). Which is it here?

Tip! If you have problems remembering the gender, think that *die* rhymes with 'sea'.

If you remember that the masculine version (*der*) means 'lake' and that the article *den* can never refer to a feminine noun, then it's clear that the house has a view of the lake.

3 **G** Complete the sentences with *in* + accusative or *in* + dative. Remember to decide whether there is movement or not!

Beispiel: **1** *in dem (im)*

1 Ich wohne _____ Haus.

2 Ich darf noch nicht _____ Kneipe gehen.

3 Willst du heute Abend _____ Kino kommen?

4 Das Sofa _____ Wohnzimmer ist sehr alt.

5 Mein Bruder geht lieber _____ Hallenbad schwimmen, aber ich gehe gern _____ Nordsee schwimmen.

6 Treffen wir uns _____ Restaurant?

7 Ich gehe gerne _____ Stadt, aber mein Freund geht lieber _____ Park.

8 Meine Schwester fährt mit dem Bus _____ Stadtzentrum.

Grammatik *Seite 177*

Using *in* with the dative or accusative

In the reading text, Axel says the following things about where he lives:

Man kann sehr billig mit dem Bus ins Stadtzentrum fahren.

Das ist wichtig für mich, da ich im Stadtzentrum arbeite.

Why does it say *ins* in the first sentence and *im* in the second, when both mean '*in*' in English?

In the first sentence, he uses *in* followed by the accusative case (*in das* = *ins*). This is because there is movement, following the preposition he is going into the town centre. In the second, he uses *in* followed by the dative (*in dem* = *im*). This is because there is no movement, he is describing where he works.

So, to say 'in to' use the ACCUSATIVE, to say 'in' without movement, use the DATIVE:

	masc.	fem.	neut.	pl.
accusative	*in den Dom*	*in die Schule*	*in das / ins Haus*	*in die Geschäfte*
dative	*in dem / im Dom*	*in der Schule*	*in dem / im Haus*	*in den Geschäften*

Also learn about superlative adjectives. *See page 108* ➡

4a 🎧 Listen to Christa, Theo, Mary and Heiko talking about what there is to do where they each live. Note down the letters of each thing available in their town. Take care – they will also mention things which aren't there!

Beispiel: *Christa a, g …*

4b 🎧 Now decide whether each person likes living in their town or village. Add a tick or a cross for each.

5 🗨 Work with a partner. Practise giving information about where you live. One partner asks questions and the other answers. Then swap roles. Talk about:

- location (*Wo …?*)
- the type and size of your town or village (*Was für eine Stadt ist … / Wie groß ist …?*)
- what there is to do (*Was gibt es …?*)
- opinions (*Wie findest du …?*)

Hinweis

5.1 Groundwork is available in the Foundation Book.

5.2 H Kommen Sie nach Baden-Württemberg!

Entdecken Sie Baden-Württemberg!

Baden-Württemberg liegt in Südwestdeutschland und ist das drittgrößte Bundesland mit 10,7 Millionen Einwohnern (fast so viele wie Belgien).

Man kann sich auf das Klima hier verlassen: im Sommer schön warm und meistens sonnig, und im Winter kälter mit Schnee, aber nicht zu viel!

Wer das Bundesland Baden-Württemberg besucht, muss unbedingt Städte wie Freiburg, Tübingen, Ulm und Ravensburg besuchen. Warum diese Städte? Sie sind nicht so groß wie zum Beispiel Stuttgart oder Heidelberg, aber sie bieten trotzdem viel für den Besucher.

Freiburg

Es gibt so viel zu sehen und zu tun. Die Landschaft ist abwechslungsreich: der Bodensee im Süden, die Berge im Schwarzwald, wo man schöne Wanderungen oder Radtouren machen kann, und es gibt auch viel für die Leute, die sich für Geschichte interessieren: In Tübingen kann man das alte Rathaus und das Schloss besuchen. Die Uni dort ist außerdem eine der ältesten in Deutschland.

Natürlich sind die Einkaufsmöglichkeiten auch sehr gut – Kaufhäuser gibt es viele. In Freiburg in der Fußgängerzone gibt es eine Menge Geschäfte und in der alten Marktstraße in Ravensburg kann man, wenn Markt ist, frisches Gemüse und Obst kaufen.

Industrie gibt es auch – zum Beispiel „Ravensburger AG", eine Firma, die Kinderspiele macht. Diese Spiele kann man überall in der Welt kaufen. Jeden Sommer kann man neue Spiele im „größten Spielzimmer der Welt" ausprobieren.

1 📖🎧 Read the article about Baden-Württemberg. Which of the sentences below are backed up by the article? Write down the letters of the four that are.

1 Baden-Württemberg is a region in the South East of Germany.
2 It is bigger than Belgium.
3 The weather here is unpredictable.
4 The town of Ravensburg is smaller than Stuttgart.
5 The region is renowned for its countryside as well as its history.
6 The university of Tübingen is the oldest university in Germany.
7 It is a good place to go shopping.
8 Children all over the world play with toys manufactured here.

> **Using knowledge from other topic areas**
>
> If you are careful to learn the vocabulary for each topic really thoroughly as you go along, you are more likely to encounter familiar words in new topics. Where might you have already come across language relating to different regions and countries?
>
> *Strategie 1*

2 🎧 Listen to these people responding to questions about their region, country or city. Match each person with the correct place from the box. There are more places than people, so be careful! Try also to note down one extra detail each time.

Beispiel: *Jessica – Southern Germany (weather warmer than in the north)*

| Jessica | Lana | Andreas | Johannes | Bernd | Christina | Anna |

| Southern Germany | East of England | Northern Scotland | South America | South West England |
| Austria | Munich | Northern Germany | France | South Africa | Switzerland | London |

3 🎧 Peter is talking about life in Switzerland. Listen carefully and answer the questions in English.

1   What do most people assume about Switzerland?
2   What example does he give to prove that this is not the case?
3   What is important for many inhabitants?
4   Why do tourists like Switzerland? Give two reasons.
5   What does Peter think of sport?
6   What is his overall opinion of Switzerland?

4 **G** Add the correct adjective endings to this brochure text advertising a German town.

Beispiel: **1** die schönst*e* Stadt

Besuchen Sie **1** die schönst_ Stadt Süddeutschlands!
2 Das wunderschön ＿＿ Schloss und **3** die mittelalterlich ＿＿
Pauluskirche mit **4** dem hoh ＿＿ Turm sind weltberühmt.
Sie können auch **5** die renoviert ＿＿ Altstadt besuchen.
Dort gibt es **6** den alt ＿＿ Brunnen und **7** das historisch ＿＿
Museum. Im Sommer gibt es **8** das regional ＿＿ Schützenfest
und unsere Stadt hat auch **9** die best ＿＿ Geschäfte in
10 der ganz ＿＿ Gegend.

5 🖋 Produce a brochure for German-speakers visiting your home region. Include details on:

- location
- climate
- activities for tourists

Remember to include opinions and justifications – you need to sound convincing! Use the phrases here to help you.

> **Using adjective endings** *Grammatik* · *Seite 177*
>
> If you use an adjective in front of the thing it describes, you will need to add an ending.
>
> *Das Rathaus ist alt.*
>
> BUT *Man kann das alte Rathaus besuchen.*
>
> *Die Marktstraße ist alt.*
>
> BUT … *in der alten Marktstraße*
>
> When using an adjective with the definite article ('the') to describe something, use the endings shown in the table on page 177.
>
> You also use the same endings with *dieser* and *jeder*. If you get stuck, remember that the endings are either -e or -en.
>
> Also practise using adjective endings with superlatives.
>
> *See page 108* ➡

Kommen Sie nach / in den / die / das Besuchen Sie	[meine Gegend] !		
[Meine Gegend]	bietet	viele Geschäfte / Sehenswürdigkeiten / eine abwechslungsreiche Landschaft / interessante Kultur	für den Besucher.
Hier können Sie sich		entspannen / wohlfühlen.	
Wer [meine Gegend] besucht, muss unbedingt		die schönen Dörfer besichtigen, das alte Rathaus sehen,	weil sie sehr malerisch sind. weil es weltberühmt ist.
Es gibt auch viel für Leute, die sich für		Geschichte / Musik / Kunst	interessieren.
Wir freuen uns auf Ihren Besuch! Hier werden Sie Spaß haben!			

5.3 F Ich helfe im Haushalt

Lernziele

Saying what you do to help around the house

Separable verbs (revision)

Listening for hints to meaning

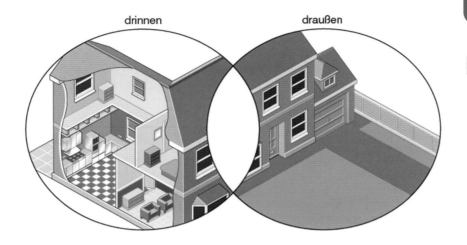

drinnen   draußen

Auto waschen

auf Kinder aufpassen

bügeln

abwaschen

Rasen mähen

aufräumen

abtrocknen

staubsaugen

kochen

Fahrrad reparieren

1 **ⓥ** These phrases are all activities that you might do to help around the house. Which would you be likely to do indoors (*drinnen*) and which outdoors (*draußen*)? Could any be both?

2 📖 🎧 Read the comments young people have left on a website about whether they help at home. Then answer the questions, giving the name of the correct person each time.

1 Who earns some money for helping out?
2 Who treats their mother on Mother's Day?
3 Who has been excused from helping as it is their birthday?
4 Who works with the whole family to clean the house for a special day?
5 Who only helps when he wants to receive presents?

Listening for hints to meaning

When you are listening to people speaking for the first time, listen out for their tone of voice. This may help you to understand what they are trying to express. Listen to Philipp's response to *Was machst du im Haushalt?* His tone gives away that he doesn't think much of the question!

Strategie 2

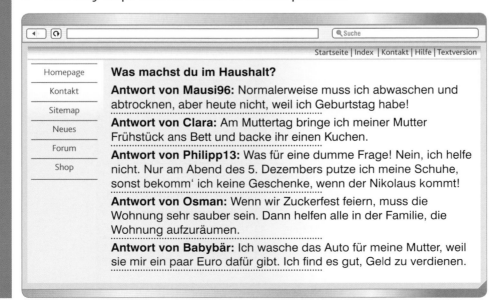

Startseite | Index | Kontakt | Hilfe | Textversion

Homepage
Kontakt
Sitemap
Neues
Forum
Shop

Was machst du im Haushalt?

Antwort von Mausi96: Normalerweise muss ich abwaschen und abtrocknen, aber heute nicht, weil ich Geburtstag habe!

Antwort von Clara: Am Muttertag bringe ich meiner Mutter Frühstück ans Bett und backe ihr einen Kuchen.

Antwort von Philipp13: Was für eine dumme Frage! Nein, ich helfe nicht. Nur am Abend des 5. Dezembers putze ich meine Schuhe, sonst bekomm' ich keine Geschenke, wenn der Nikolaus kommt!

Antwort von Osman: Wenn wir Zuckerfest feiern, muss die Wohnung sehr sauber sein. Dann helfen alle in der Familie, die Wohnung aufzuräumen.

Antwort von Babybär: Ich wasche das Auto für meine Mutter, weil sie mir ein paar Euro dafür gibt. Ich find es gut, Geld zu verdienen.

3 **G** Answer these questions in German, saying either 'yes' or 'no' as indicated. Keep to the same tense.

1 Räumst du dein Zimmer auf? Ja, ich …
2 Trocknest du ab? Nein, ich …
3 Ziehst du dich jetzt an? Ja, ich …
4 Rufst du deine Freundin an? Nein, ich …
5 Hast du gestern abgewaschen? Nein, ich …
6 Bist du früh aufgestanden? Ja, ich …

4a 🎧 Listen to what Tina and Jürgen say they do to help at home, then match each picture to the correct name.

Beispiel: **a** *Tina*

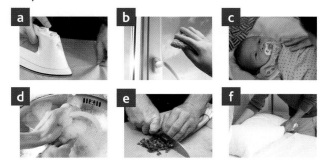

4b 🎧 Which activities do you hear mentioned which are not shown in the pictures?

5 ✏ Imagine you are adding your own comments to the website in activity 2 to say what you do to help at home. Include:

■ Several things you do to help and how often you do them
■ One thing you should do, but do not and why
■ Something you do differently on a special day

> ### Grammatik · Seite 182
>
> **Separable verbs (revision)**
>
> Separable verbs, e.g. *aufräumen* (to tidy up) consist of two parts: *auf* and *räumen*.
>
> Present tense: *Ich räume auf.* (I tidy up.) In a longer sentence, the separable prefix (*auf*) goes right to the end:
>
> *Ich **räume** jeden Tag **auf**.*
>
> In the perfect tense the past participle is *aufgeräumt*: *Ich habe mein Zimmer **aufgeräumt**.*
>
> Also learn about prepositions taking the accusative. *See page 108* ➡

Hinweis

5.3 Groundwork is available in the Foundation Book.

Ich passe auf Kinder auf, / Ich mache mein Bett, / Ich wasche ab, / Ich trockne ab, / Ich helfe im Garten, / Ich wasche das Auto, / Ich mähe den Rasen,		weil ich Taschengeld dafür bekomme. um meinen Eltern zu helfen. weil ich sehr hilfsbereit bin.
Ich sollte bügeln / mein Zimmer aufräumen / in der Küche helfen	aber ich mache das nicht,	weil es keinen Spaß macht. obwohl es Spaß macht. da ich keine Zeit dafür habe. weil ich ziemlich faul bin.
Wenn Weihnachten / Ostern / Muttertag / Ramadan ist,		stehe ich später auf. helfe ich mehr im Haushalt. essen wir etwas Besonderes mit der Familie zusammen. frühstücke ich früher und esse nichts bis zum Abend.

5.3 H Feier mit uns!

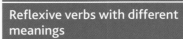

Traditionelle Feste

Karneval oder Fasching feiert man meistens im Rheinland und in Süddeutschland. Am Rosenmontag gibt es Straßenumzüge und viele Leute gehen verkleidet durch die Straßen, um Spaß zu haben. Die Faschingszeit endet am Aschermittwoch und die Fastenzeit beginnt, die 40 Tage bis Ostern dauert.

Zu Ostern malen die Kinder Eier an und hängen die bunten Eier an einem Zweig in der Wohnung auf. Natürlich isst man viel Schokolade, wie in England. Der Osterhase bringt Eier für kleine Kinder. Alle Kinder freuen sich auf Ostersonntag, weil die Eltern an diesem Tag die Eier im Garten oder in der Wohnung verstecken. Kurz vor Ostern machen viele Familien „Frühjahrsputz". Alle machen mit, um die Wohnung so gründlich wie möglich zu putzen.

Vor Weihnachten gibt es Weihnachtsmärkte, wo man zum Beispiel Lebkuchen kaufen kann. In der Nacht zum 6. Dezember kommt der Nikolaus und bringt den Kindern Geschenke. Die Kinder putzen ihre Schuhe und stellen sie vor die Tür. Weihnachten ist anders als in England: Die Kinder müssen nur bis zum 24. Dezember warten, bevor sie ihre Geschenke öffnen dürfen. Am Heiligabend liegen sie schon unter dem Weihnachtsbaum. Viele Leute gehen in die Kirche. Am 25. Dezember isst man Gans, Pute oder manchmal auch Fisch.

Silvester in Berlin

Silvester ist am 31. Dezember und in Deutschland feiert man das oft mit Feuerwerken. Man trinkt auch meistens Sekt.

1 📖 🎧 Copy the sentences and fill in the gaps with one of the words below.

Beispiel: 1 *Karneval*

1 Fasching ist ein anderes Wort für _____.

2 Während der Karnevalszeit _____ man sich sehr.

3 Kinder _____ die versteckten Ostereier.

4 Im Frühling macht man die Wohnung _____.

5 Der Nikolaustag findet _____ Weihnachten statt.

6 Am 24. Dezember _____ die Kinder Geschenke.

7 Man _____ viele Feuerwerke am 31. Dezember.

| suchen | Karneval | hört | bekommen |
| amüsiert | sauber | vor |

2 **G** Complete the following sentences using one of the reflexive verbs given below.

1 Ich _____ _____ auf Weihnachten, weil ich viele Geschenke bekomme.

2 Mein Bruder _____ _____, weil ich seinen Geburtstag vergessen habe.

3 _____ _____, sonst kommen wir zu spät zur Party!

4 Ich kann _____ nicht _____, was ich meiner Mutter zu Weihnachten schenken soll.

5 Als ich jünger war, bin ich immer zum Karneval gegangen, aber ich kann _____ nicht mehr daran _____.

6 Meine Schwester _____ _____, wenn sie im Haushalt helfen soll.

| sich ärgern | sich beeilen | sich entscheiden |
| sich erinnern | sich freuen | sich beschweren |

3 🎧 Listen to the young people (a–g) talking about special occasions. Copy and complete the table, using occasions from the list below. Note down extra details if you can!

Person	Occasion	Enjoy it (✓) or not (x)
a	National holiday	✓
b		
c		

Christmas Eve	Carnival	Easter	Birthday
Wedding	New Year	Name day
National holiday	Munich beer festival

4 💬 Prepare to answer some questions about a special occasion celebrated in your home. Practise asking and answering the questions with a partner.

- Wann findet dieses Fest statt?
- Beschreibe, wie man dieses Fest normalerweise feiert.
- Was isst und trinkt man?
- Wie gefällt dir dieses Fest, und warum?

Grammatik Seite 180

Reflexive verbs with different meanings

Some verbs are always used reflexively, even though the reflexive element may not always be obvious in the meaning.

Reflexive verbs use a subject pronoun and a reflexive pronoun:

Ich erinnere mich. – I remember (I remind myself).

Usually the reflexive pronoun is accusative. The accusative reflexive pronouns are as follows:

*ich erinnere **mich***

*du erinnerst **dich***

*er / sie / es erinnert **sich***

*wir erinnern **uns***

*ihr erinnert **euch***

*sie erinnern **sich***

*Sie erinnern **sich***

For dative reflexive pronouns and their use, see page 180 in the grammar reference section.

Also look at using adjective endings after the indefinite article. See page 109 ➡

Completing gap-fill tasks

Strategie 2

When using words to fill gaps, in addition to understanding the gist, it helps if you can make use of your knowledge of grammar:

1 *Ich _____ mit dem Bus nach München.*

2 *Er hat keine _____, das Oktoberfest zu besuchen.*

gefahren   gute   Zeit

fahre   das

For (**1**), it is clear you need a verb. As the gap is straight after *ich* it cannot be a past participle, so the answer is *fahre*.

keine is the clue in (**2**). It shows that you need either a feminine or plural noun in the gap, so the answer here is *Zeit*.

G # Home and local area

1 Choose the correct indefinite article in each of these sentences. Watch out for gender and whether the noun is singular or plural.

1 Im Wohnzimmer gibt es ein / einen / eine / keine **Fernsehapparat**.

2 In meinem Zimmer gibt es ein / einen / eine / keine **Bett**.

3 Es gibt ein / einen / eine / keine **Vorhänge** in diesem Zimmer.

4 In der Küche gibt es ein / einen / eine / keine **Kühlschrank**.

5 Draußen im Garten gibt es ein / einen / eine / keine **Tisch** aber ein / einen / eine / keine **Stühle**.

6 In unserem Haus gibt es ein / einen / eine / keine **Badezimmer** oben und ein / einen / eine / keine **Dusche** unten.

2 Choose superlatives from below to complete the sentences to correspond to the English meanings.

1 *My room is the biggest.* Mein Zimmer ist …

2 *Her bed is the smallest.* Ihr Bett ist …

3 *In our family I am the oldest.* In unserer Familie bin ich …

4 *Karl is the youngest.* Karl ist …

5 *Our town is the most beautiful.* Unsere Stadt ist …

6 *This school is the newest.* Diese Schule ist …

der älteste	am kleinsten	am neuesten
der jüngste	die schönste	am größten

3 Copy the sentences and fill in the gaps with a preposition taking the accusative which makes sense.

1 Ich bügele Kleider _____ die ganze Familie.

2 Manchmal koche ich _____ die Hilfe meiner Mutter.

3 Mein Onkel wohnt _____ die Ecke. Ich wasche das Auto _____ ihn.

4 Ich helfe meinem Vater. Ich stelle die Leiter _____ die Wand.

Grammatik Seite 175

In diesem Zimmer gibt es … (revision)

Remember that you use the accusative case after *es gibt*:

(masc.) *Es gibt einen Herd.*
(fem.) *Es gibt eine Toilette.*
(neut.) *Es gibt ein Regal.*

In the plural there is no article unless you are using *keine*:

Es gibt Stühle.
Es gibt keine Stühle.

You should also note that when you are describing where things are, you use the dative case after *in*. Remember to use the correct form of the definite article:

*In **der** Küche gibt es einen Herd.*

(masc.) *auf dem Tisch*
(fem.) *in der Ecke*
(neut.) *in dem (im) Zimmer*

Note: in the masculine and neuter dative *in + dem* becomes *im*.

Grammatik Seite 178

Superlative adjectives

To say something is the biggest, smallest, best etc., you need to use superlative adjectives.

In German you add *-st* to the adjective:

*klein – klein**st**-*

*Mein Bruder ist der **jüngste** in der Familie.*

*Mein Zimmer ist das **kleinste**.*

*Ist deine Schule die **neueste** in der Stadt?*

You also find the superlative in this form:

*klein – **am** klein**sten***

*Mein Schlafzimmer ist **am kleinsten**.*

Mein Schlafzimmer ist das kleinste Zimmer im Haus.

If the adjective ends in *-t* or a vowel, then add *-est*:

neu – neuest (am neuesten)

Some superlatives are irregular:

gut – beste (am besten)

hoch – höchste (am höchsten)

nah – nächste (am nächsten)

viel – meiste (am meisten)

Grammatik Seite 176

Prepositions always taking the accusative

Prepositions are small words, such as *in* and *für*, usually placed before nouns. Few prepositions are always followed by the accusative, but you do need to know the main ones:

bis	until, as far as	*gegen*	against
durch	through	*ohne*	without
für	for	*um*	around

4 With a partner practise comparing your home / home area using … *als* and *nicht so … wie*. Use the adjectives below as prompts but try to think of your own too!

Beispiel: Unser Garten ist kleiner als euer Garten.
Unser Garten ist nicht so groß wie euer Garten.

bunt   gemütlich   groß   klein

ruhig   schmutzig   schön

Grammatik · Seite 178

Comparing things

If you want to make comparisons in German, you can use comparative adjectives. Usually you need to add -*er* to the end of the adjective you are using (as also often happens in English):

klein – kleiner – Unser neues Haus ist kleiner.

small – smaller – Our new house is smaller.

Some comparatives add an umlaut: Many short adjectives add an umlaut if they can.

alt – älter   jung – jünger

Others are irregular:

gut – besser   viel – mehr
hoch – höher   gern – lieber

To compare something with something else use the word *als*:

*Unser neues Haus ist **kleiner als** das alte Haus.*

You can also compare things by saying that something is 'not as … as ' – *nicht so … wie*:

*Das alte Haus ist **nicht so groß wie** unser neues Haus.*

You should also be aware of phrases such as 'the bigger, the better':

***je** größer, **desto** besser*

---

5 Using comparative and superlative adjectives make sentences comparing the following items. Work with a partner, deciding how the items should compare, then write up your answers.

Beispiel: *Das Schlafzimmer ist größer als das Badezimmer, aber das Wohnzimmer ist das größte Zimmer.*

1   das Zimmer: das Schlafzimmer – das Badezimmer – das Wohnzimmer (groß)
2   die Stadt: Bonn – Berlin – Wien (schön)
3   das Haus: das Doppelhaus – das Reihenhaus – das Einfamilienhaus (klein)
4   das Gebäude: die Kirche – der Dom – das Schloss (alt)
5   der Fluss: die Themse – die Donau – der Rhein (lang)
6   die Straße: die Poststraße – die Hauptstraße – die Bergstraße (breit)

Grammatik · Seite 178

Superlative adjectives in front of the noun

When you use a superlative in front of a noun, remember it is an adjective like any other so you need normal adjective endings.

*Mein Schlafzimmer ist das klein**ste** Zimmer im Haus.*

*Wir haben den größ**ten** Fernseher gekauft.*

For help with adjective endings, see page 177.

---

6 Read what Ralf tells you about his family and his friend, Karl, and pick out the indefinite adjective endings, stating what gender and case they are.

Beispiel: *einem kleinen Dorf – neuter, dative*

Meine Familie wohnt in einem kleinen Dorf. Es liegt nicht weit von einem schönen Wald entfernt. In der Nähe gibt es auch einen kleinen Bauernhof – dort wohnt mein bester Freund Karl. Ich habe eine kleine Schwester. Mein älterer Bruder studiert in Berlin. Berlin ist die Hauptstadt Deutschlands und liegt im Norden.

Letztes Jahr habe ich mit meinen Eltern einen kurzen Urlaub im Schwarzwald verbracht. Wir haben in einem bequemen Hotel in der Nähe von schönen Wäldern gewohnt. Die Landschaft war sehr hübsch, aber ich möchte lieber in einer großen Stadt wie München leben.

Grammatik · Seite 178

Adjective endings after the indefinite article

After *ein*, possessive adjectives (*mein, dein* etc.) and the negative article *kein*, you need to use a different set of adjective endings from those used after *der / die / das*.

	masc.	fem.	neut.	pl.
nom.	-er	-e	-es	-en
acc.	-en	-e	-es	-en
dat.	-en	-en	-en	-en

*Ich habe ein rot**es** Sofa.* – accusative, neuter, singular

*Wir wohnen in einer klein**en** Stadt.* – dative, feminine, singular

Home and local area

Topic 5.1 Types of homes and what is in them

5.1 F Wo ich wohne ➡ pages 96–97

	altmodisch	old-fashioned
das	Bauernhaus	farmhouse
	bequem	comfortable
das	Doppelhaus	semi-detached house
die	Eigentumswohnung	flat (owned rather than rented)
das	Einfamilienhaus	detached house
	hässlich	ugly
der	Kleiderschrank	wardrobe
die	Kommode	chest of drawers
das	Kopfkissen	pillow
das	Mehrfamilienhaus	house for several families
die	Mietwohnung	rented flat
	möbliert	furnished
der	Nachttisch	bedside table
das	Regal	shelf
das	Reihenhaus	terraced house
der	Spiegel	mirror
die	Tür	door
der	Vorhang	curtain
der	Wohnblock	block of flats

5.1 H Bei uns, bei euch ➡ pages 98–99

der	Abstellraum	storeroom
der	Dachboden	attic
die	Dusche	shower
die	Gartenbenutzung	use of a garden
	gemütlich	cosy
	geräumig	roomy
die	Grünanlage	green space/area
	hervorragend	excellent
der	Keller	cellar
	mies	grotty

	modisch	fashionable
der	Spielplatz	playground
die	Spülmaschine	dishwasher
	teilen	to share
der	Tiefkühlschrank	freezer
die	Toilette	toilet
	türkis	turquoise
	umziehen	to move house
	wählen	to choose
der	Wintergarten	conservatory

Topic 5.2 Where you live and what the area is like

5.2 F Meine Gegend, deine Gegend
➡ pages 100–101

die	Aussicht	view
der	Berg	mountain
der	Dom	cathedral
die	Fußgängerzone	pedestrian zone
das	Hallenbad	indoor swimming pool
das	Industriegebiet	industrial area
die	Kneipe	pub
die	Küste	coast
das	Land	country
die	Luft	air
der	Marktplatz	market square
die	Möglichkeit	possibility
der	Nachteil	disadvantage
	öffentliche Verkehrsmittel (pl.)	public transport
	schmutzig	dirty
der	See	lake
die	See	sea
der	Verkehr	traffic
das	Verkehrsamt	tourist information
der	Vorteil	advantage

5.2 H Kommen Sie nach Baden-Württemberg!
➡ *pages 102–103*

	abwechslungsreich	varied
die	Altstadt	old part of town
	ausprobieren	to try out
	außerdem	besides
der	Besucher	visitor
	bieten	to offer
der	Brunnen	fountain, well
der	Einwohner	inhabitant
die	Firma	company
das	Klima	climate
	malerisch	picturesque
die	Menge	a lot, plenty
	mittelalterlich	medieval
das	Rathaus	town hall
das	Schloss	castle
die	Sehenswürdigkeiten (pl)	sights
der	Turm	tower
der	*Vorort*	suburb
die	Wanderung	walk, hike
	weltberühmt	world famous

Topic 5.3 Life at home day to day and on special occasions

5.3 F Ich helfe im Haushalt ➡ *pages 104–105*

	abtrocknen	to dry up
	abwaschen	to wash up
	anrufen	to telephone
	aufpassen (auf)	to look after
	aufräumen	to tidy up
	backen	to bake
	bügeln	to iron
	feiern	to celebrate
das	Geschenk	present
der	Haushalt	household
	hilfsbereit	helpful
	kochen	to cook
die	Leiter	ladder

	mähen	to mow
der	Muttertag	Mother's Day
der	Rasen	lawn
	sauber	clean
	staubsaugen	to vacuum
	verdienen	to earn
das	Zuckerfest	Islamic festival of breaking the fast

5.3 H Feier mit uns! ➡ *pages 106–107*

	erlauben	to allow
	(sich) erinnern	to remember
der	Fasching	traditional German celebration ending on Ash Wednesday
das	Feuerwerk	firework
	(sich) freuen (auf etwas)	to look forward to something
die	Gans	goose
	gründlich	thoroughly
der	Heiligabend	Christmas Eve
die	Hochzeit	wedding
	malen	to paint
das	*Oktoberfest*	Munich beer festival
die	Pute	turkey (meat)
der	Rosenmontag	Monday before Ash Wednesday
der	*Sekt*	sparkling wine
der	Sprudel	sparkling water
der	Truthahn	turkey (bird)
der	Umzug	parade
	verkleidet	disguised
	verstecken	to hide
der	*Zweig*	branch

6.1 F Rettet die Umwelt!

1 Ⓥ Match the problem to the photo.

Beispiel: 1 *c*

a	Spraydosen
b	Müll
c	Aussterben von Tieren
d	Waldsterben
e	Luftverschmutzung

2 📖🎧 The headlines are all about environmental issues in the world today. Read them and then say which one relates to each of the problems listed below.

1 pollution
2 nuclear power
3 acid rain
4 skin cancer
5 the hole in the ozone layer

a **Kaufen Sie nicht so viele Spraydosen! – Das Ozonloch soll nicht größer werden!**

b *Noch mehr Luftverschmutzung im Industriegebiet.*

c **Atomkraft in Japan – jetzt zu gefährlich?**

d **Ärzte warnen vor Hautkrebs – lieg im Urlaub nicht nur in der Sonne!**

e Saurer Regen auch in Asien? Jeden Tag sterben Bäume!

3a 🎧 Listen to these young people talking about environmental problems. Which words in the boxes show what each one is concerned about? There are two words / phrases for each person.

1 Bruno
2 Jasmin
3 Otto
4 Thomas
5 Carolin

acid rain	river
ultra violet rays	pesticides
ozone layer	farmers
water pollution	nuclear power station
	sea	trees

3b 🎧 Listen again and then choose the correct word to complete each sentence.

1 Bruno ärgert sich über die a Tiere / b Bauern.
2 Jedes Jahr wird das Ozonloch a kleiner / b größer.
3 Ottos Brieffreund wohnt in a England / b Irland.
4 Thomas wohnt in der Nähe a des Meers / b der Berge.
5 Es gibt viele a Flüsse / b Bäume da, wo Carolin wohnt.

4 🅖 Fill in the gaps using the correct imperative form of the verb given in brackets.

Beispiel: 1 *Fahren Sie*

1 (Fahren) nicht so schnell, Frau Becker!
2 Verena, (bringen) die Flaschen zum Container!
3 Martin und Anna, (machen) die Lichter aus!
4 (Kaufen) frisches Obst, meine Damen und Herren!
5 (Sparen) mehr Wasser, Vati!
6 (Wegwerfen) nicht so viel Müll, Herr Biber!

5 ✏️ Produce a poster on an environmental issue that interests you. The poster should include the problem and some slogans using the imperative. You can choose to address the reader as *du*, *ihr* or *Sie*, but stick to the same form for the whole poster.

Rette / Rettet / Retten Sie	die Umwelt!
Spar / Spart / Sparen Sie	Wasser!
Trenn / Trennt / Trennen Sie	Müll!
Mach / Macht / Machen Sie	mit!

Hinweis
6.1 Groundwork is available in the Foundation Book.

Grammatik *Seite 186*

Using the imperative

The imperative is used to give a command or when telling someone what to do. There are three forms of the imperative, depending on which word for 'you' is being used.

Talking to an adult or a group of people you don't know very well, you use the *Sie* form of the verb, but with *Sie* following the verb:

Machen Sie das Licht aus!

Talking to someone you know or someone your age, you use the *du* form of the verb without the pronoun and -*st* ending:

Mach das Licht aus!

Note: if the *du* form usually has *ä* in, it drops the Umlaut in the imperative, e.g. *du fährst > Fahr!*

Talking to a group of people you know you use the *ihr* form of the verb without the pronoun:

Macht das Licht aus!

Remember that the prefix of a separable verb still goes to the end of the sentence:

Dreh die Heizung herunter!

Also revise articles.   *See page 120* ➡

Strategie 5

Checking your work carefully

With any written work, make sure you check carefully for errors. Use this check list as a starting point:

1 Is my spelling correct? (Check in a dictionary or other word list.)
2 Have I used capital letters for nouns?
3 Is the word order correct? (Identify the verb in every clause and decide whether it's in the right place.)
4 Have I included any English words by mistake?
5 If I have used a separable verb, have I remembered to include both parts?
6 Have I used the correct form of different tenses and the imperative?

6.1 H Unsere Welt, unsere Umwelt

■ Thema Umwelt

Stefan

„Für mich ist das Thema sehr wichtig, weil ich mein Bestes tun will, um die Umwelt zu retten. Ich interessiere mich sehr für Tiere und hier in Deutschland sind einige Tiere vom Aussterben bedroht, z. B. Fische und Vögel. Die Menschen sind schuld daran, weil wir zu viel Lärm machen und die Vögel können sich nicht mehr in der Nähe von Straßen zwitschern hören. Es gibt auch weniger Wohnraum wie Wälder, Buschland und Wasser für viele Tierarten. Ich möchte mehr Naturschutzgebiete sehen, um die Tiere zu retten. Auch sollten wir alle umweltfreundliche Produkte kaufen und Energie sparen."

Gisela

„Ich finde die Luftverschmutzung am schlimmsten. Ich wohne auf dem Land, aber ich sehe jeden Tag, wie wir die Luft verschmutzen: Autos mit Kohlenmonoxid und anderen Abgasen, und FCKWs aus Spraydosen, verpesten die Luft. Es gibt nicht genug alternative Energiequellen wie Wind und Sonne und wir produzieren zu viel Müll. Öl, Gas und Kohlendioxid fördern den Treibhauseffekt und ich habe Angst, dass es bald zu spät sein wird – die Umweltverschmutzung ist wahrscheinlich schon zu weit fortgeschritten."

1a 📖🎧 Read Stefan's and Gisela's views on environmental issues and pick out the German for these words and phrases.

1 to save the environment
2 threatened with extinction
3 people are to blame
4 nature reserves
5 to save energy
6 alternative energy sources
7 carbon dioxide
8 greenhouse effect
9 too far advanced

1b 📖🎧 Answer the questions in English.

1 How important does Stefan feel environmental issues are?
2 Which problem does he then go on to talk about?
3 In his view, how are humans to blame?
4 How would he try to solve the problem?
5 Why might it be surprising that Gisela talks about air pollution?
6 Name two things that she feels contribute most to the problem.
7 Why does she mention oil and gas?
8 What is her main fear?

Grammatik Seite 184

The future tense with *werden* (revision)

To use the future tense you need to use the present tense of *werden* plus an infinitive.

ich werde + infinitive (*kaufen, recyceln, sparen* …)

du wirst

er / sie / es wird

wir werden

ihr werdet

sie werden

Sie werden

Remember that the infinitive needs to go at the end of the sentence or clause:

Ich werde in Zukunft Energie sparen.

Wir werden viel mehr recyceln.

Also learn about prepositions taking the genitive on page 120.

2a 🎧 Listen to an interview about energy sources and how Germany is changing to renewable energies after the Fukushima nuclear disaster. Which of these statements match what you have heard? Write a, b or c

1 Germany's reaction to the Fukushima disaster in 2011 was that
   a they immediately shut down their own nuclear power plants.
   b they made sure their own nuclear power plants were safe.
   c they decided to get rid of all nuclear power plants in future.
2 Fossil fuels
   a are not as bad for the environment as people think.
   b have traditionally been an important energy source.
   c will become more important by 2020.
3 35% of electricity
   a needs to be produced through energy sources such as wind and sun in future.
   b is now being produced through energy sources such as wind and sun.
   c has traditionally been produced through burning fossil fuels.

2b 🎧 Listen again and match up these beginnings and endings of sentences.

1 Die Katastrophe von Fukushima   a sind fossile Brennstoffe.
2 Kohle, Gas und Öl   b werden die deutschen Atomkraftwerke schließen.
3 In Deutschland versucht man,   c hat der Umwelt geschadet.
4 Bis zum Jahr 2022   d neue Energiequellen zu finden.

3 Ⓖ Rewrite these sentences in the future tense using *werden*.

1 Ich wohne auf dem Land.
2 Meine Familie ist sehr umweltfreundlich.
3 Wir benutzen weniger Brennstoffe.
4 Es gibt neue Energiequellen.
5 Man produziert nicht so viel Atomkraft.
6 Deutschland wird grüner.

4 🗩 What do you consider to be the biggest environmental problems facing the world today? Prepare a short presentation mentioning at least three issues, including energy. Use these questions as a guide:

■ Was sind deiner Meinung nach die schlimmsten Umweltprobleme für unsere Welt heute?

■ Welche Energiequellen werden wir in Zukunft benutzen und warum?

Be prepared to answer some questions following on from what you have said.

Structuring your speaking				Strategie 4

Structuring your speaking

Divide what you are going to say into different points by using expressions like these:

erstens	firstly	*einerseits*	on the one hand
zweitens	secondly	*andererseits*	on the other hand
drittens	thirdly	*im Großen und ganzen*	on the whole
zum Schluss	finally		

Remember to invert the verb if you start your sentence with these:

Erstens werde ich über die Luftverschmutzung sprechen.

6.2 F Umweltfreundlich oder umweltfeindlich?

Lernziele

Discussing environmental problems and solutions

Using separable verbs after a modal verb

Making what you say and write more expressive

1 **V** Look at the vocabulary items on the right and decide whether they are good or bad for the environment, then put them under the correct heading.

Umweltfreundlich	Umweltfeindlich

Flugzeug   Abgase

Fahrrad   zu Fuß gehen

Energiesparlampen   Auto

Solarenergie   FCKWs

wegwerfen   recyceln

Sind wir umweltfreundlich oder umweltfeindlich?

Die Schüler und Schülerinnen des Schiller-Gymnasiums haben neulich eine Umfrage gemacht und hier sind die Ergebnisse.

86%   trennen den Müll.

75%   würden mit dem Zug fahren, wenn es billiger wäre.

70%   schalten Geräte nur ein, wenn man sie braucht.

62%   haben zum Beispiel eine Dose auf der Straße weggeworfen.

55%   glauben, dass Abgase nicht so umweltfeindlich wie saurer Regen sind.

40%   wollen mehr machen, haben aber nicht genug Zeit.

33%   benutzen umweltfreundliches Papier.

21%   haben in letzter Zeit Energiesparlampen gekauft.

14%   sind der Meinung, dass Spraydosen schlechter als Plastiktüten für die Umwelt sind.

Weniger als 10% sparen Wasser.

2 📖🎧 Look at the results of the survey on the environment, and write down the correct percentage for each of the statements.

Beispiel: 1 *Less than 10%*

   1 Save water.
   2 Think that plastic bags harm the environment less than aerosols.
   3 Have recently bought energy-saving light bulbs.
   4 Use recycled paper.
   5 Think that acid rain is more of a problem than exhaust fumes.
   6 Admit to having dropped litter rather than using a bin.
   7 Always switch off electrical appliances.
   8 Sort their rubbish.
   9 Would use public transport if it was not so expensive.
   10 Are prevented from doing more because they are too busy.

3 **G** These sentences all include a modal verb and a separable verb. Rewrite them using the modal verbs in brackets as in the example.

Beispiel: 1 *Wir können die Zeitung wegwerfen.*

1 Wir werfen die Zeitung weg. (können)
2 Er macht das Licht aus. (sollen)
3 Ich werfe mein altes Fahrrad weg. (müssen)
4 Mein Vater schaltet den Computer aus. (dürfen)
5 Schaltest du den Fernseher aus? (können)
6 Schalte ich das Licht an? (dürfen)

4 🎧 Listen to these people talking about the environment. For each person, find a corresponding picture. Try to add any extra details.

Beispiel: *Johannes, e + better for the environment*

 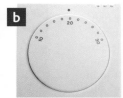 

5 🗨️🖊️ Produce your own survey on how environmentally friendly your class is. You can use the reading survey as a basis for the questions you ask or make up your own. Once you have completed the survey, you can present your results.

Bist du umweltfreundlich?		
Ja, ich bin	sehr / ziemlich / wirklich	umweltfreundlich.
Nein, ich bin	gar nicht / kaum / überhaupt nicht	umweltfreundlich.
Trennst du den Müll? / Fährst du mit öffentlichen Verkehrsmitteln? / Sammelst du Altpapier?		
Ja, ich trenne / fahre / sammle	immer / oft / normalerweise	den Müll / mit dem Zug / Altpapier.
Nein, ich trenne	nie / niemals / selten	den Müll.

Grammatik · Seite 182

Using separable verbs after a modal verb

Separable verbs come in two parts:

*wegwerfen: Ich **werfe** den Abfall **weg**.* – I throw the rubbish away.

*ausschalten: Ich **schalte** den Fernseher **aus**.* – I turn the TV off.

When you use separable verbs after a modal verb, e.g. to say what you can, must or are supposed to do, the two parts come back together in the infinitive, e.g.

*Du kannst den Abfall **wegwerfen**.* – You can throw the rubbish away.

*Man soll den Fernseher **ausschalten**.* – You are supposed to turn the TV off.

Remember, after a modal verb the 2nd verb needs to go to the end of the sentence.

Also learn how to use time phrases.

See page 120 ➡️

Strategie 5

Making what you say and write more expressive

There are several ways in which you can do this:

Using qualifiers:

Ich bin total umweltfreundlich. (See page 178)

Varying the adjectives you use:

Das finde ich interessant / lustig / amüsant.

Using comparatives or superlatives:

Recyceln ist mir am wichtigsten. (See page 178)

Varying opinion phrases.

Hinweis

6.2 Groundwork is available in the Foundation Book.

6.2 H Global denken, lokal handeln

UMWELTAKTION: Wie eine Stadt umweltfreundlicher geworden ist!

Sauberstadt hat beschlossen, umweltfreundlicher zu werden. Warum? „Weil die Einwohner das so wollen", sagt der Bürgermeister Herr Brinkmann.

Vor ein paar Jahren gab es viele Probleme hier: Abfall auf den Straßen, Staus auf der Umgehungsstraße, keine Radwege und nicht genug Recyclingcontainer. Viele Leute wollten nicht in die Stadtmitte fahren, weil es nicht genug Parkplätze gab. Die Geschäfte waren oft fast leer und Arbeitslosigkeit war auch ein Problem.

Die meisten Einwohner waren überhaupt nicht umweltbewusst: Sie trennten ihren Müll nicht, kauften viele Produkte in Verpackungen, Einwegflaschen und benutzten immer Plastiktüten. Die Luft in der Stadt wurde durch die Industrie verpestet und es gab keine Fische im Fluss am Stadtrand, da er total verschmutzt war. In den Schulen interessierte sich fast niemand für die Umwelt, und man sah nur wenig Abfalleimer.

Und jetzt? Was hat sich geändert?

Die Stadtmitte wird zu einer Fußgängerzone und die Einwohner sind total dafür. Bei schönem Wetter kann man draußen vor dem Café sitzen. Dieses Jahr wird ein „Park und Ride" gebaut und Kinder und ältere Leute werden zum halben Preis fahren können. Die Geschäfte werden bald mehr Kunden haben, die Straßen werden sicherer für alte Leute und Kinder, und es wird auch ruhiger. In den Schulen sieht man keine Plastikbecher mehr, man macht die Fenster zu und dreht die Heizung herunter, um Energie zu sparen. Eine Bürgerinitiative hat dafür gesorgt, dass es wieder Fische im Fluss gibt.

Vorher

Nachher

1a 📖 🎧 Find the German for the following words or phrases in the text.

Beispiel: 1 *beschlossen*

1 decided
2 the residents want it that way
3 a few years ago
4 there weren't enough car parks
5 not at all
6 they separated

7 non-refundable bottles
8 completely in favour
9 safer for children
10 you don't see any plastic cups
11 a community action group

1b 📖 🎧 Which three sentences are correct?

1 The town council decided to improve the town.
2 There used to be no recycling facilities.
3 The residents always used to use plastic bags.
4 There used to be a pedestrian zone in the town centre.

5 The cafés have seating outside.
6 The streets are becoming safer for old people.
7 Unemployment is no longer such a problem.
8 The shops are now full of customers.

2 🎬 These people are being interviewed for the local news about the environment in their area. Watch and listen carefully, then answer the questions in English.

Beispiel: 1 *He thinks everyone should do something.*

1   What is Jens' attitude towards the environment?
2   What does his family do?
3   What has been done in his village?
4   What is Barbara's opinion of her fellow students' attitude towards the environment?
5   Name two things the 'Greenteams' do in Thomas' town.
6   Why is Thomas in favour of these teams?
7   What would a lot of people in Anke's area like?
8   What is her mother's view and why?

3 **G** Decide whether these sentences need *zu* to make them correct and write out the correct version if they do. Make sure you include a comma before each clause containing *zu*.

Beispiel: 1 *Yes. Er hat versucht, Energie zu sparen.*

1   Er hat versucht Energie sparen.
2   Ich will mit dem Bus fahren.
3   Mein Bruder vergisst immer das Licht ausmachen.
4   Meine Stadt könnte „Park und Ride" Parkplätze einführen.
5   Wir fangen an umweltfreundlicher sein.
6   Ich hoffe in der Zukunft nach Amerika fahren.
7   Die Einwohner möchten mehr Radwege.

4 ✏️ Write a paragraph about the positive and negative aspects of where you live from an environmental point of view. Consider these questions in your response:

■ Welche Probleme gibt es in deiner Stadt / in deinem Dorf / bei dir zu Hause?
■ Was hat man schon für die Umwelt getan?
■ Hat sich etwas geändert?
■ Was könnte man noch machen?

Strategie 2

Decoding compound nouns

Recognising how compound nouns are formed is a very useful technique. The formation of German words is often like a series of building blocks.

Einwegflaschen > *ein* (one) > *Weg* (way) > *Flaschen* (bottles)

Umwelt > *um* (around) > *Welt* (world)

schmutzig > dirty
Umweltverschmutzung > 'dirtying of the world around us' i.e. environmental pollution

Can you work out the logic and meaning of these words?

Mehrwegflaschen *Autoabgase*

Grammatik   Seite 185

Verbs with *zu*

Some verbs require you to use *zu* + the infinitive of the second verb that follows.

The main ones you are likely to need are *versuchen, beschließen, hoffen, beginnen, anfangen, vergessen* and *helfen*.

The sentence can be divided into 2 parts:

Part 1, where you use one of the above verbs followed by a comma;

Part 2, where you need *zu* and the infinitive, which comes at the end.

Sauberstadt hat beschlossen, umweltfreundlicher zu werden.

With a separable verb the *zu* goes in the middle of the infinitive, after the prefix.

Meine Stadt hat neulich begonnen, billigere Busfahrkarten anzubieten.

Remember *zu* is not needed with modal verbs, e.g. *Ich möchte umweltfreundlicher werden.*

Also learn about using separable verbs in the future.   *See page 121* ➡

Hier / in meiner Stadt / Bei mir Zu Hause	gibt es	zu viel Lärm / nicht genug Busse / Luftverschmutzung.	
Auf der anderen Seite	ist es schön,	weil viele Menschen	ihren Müll trennen / Flaschen recyceln / Stofftaschen benutzen.
Neulich	hat man	eine Fußgängerzone / einen autofreien Tag / Umweltaktivitäten für Kinder	eingerichtet. eingeführt. organisiert.
In der Zukunft	könnte man	eine Fußgängerzone / einen autofreien Tag / Umweltaktivitäten für Kinder	einrichten. einführen. organisieren.

(G) Environment

1 Choose the correct form of the definite or indefinite article for these German nouns. The gender is given in brackets.

1. the hole in the ozone layer _____ Ozonloch (n)
2. a forest _____ Wald (m)
3. the people _____ Menschen (pl)
4. a town _____ Stadt (f)
5. the animal _____ Tier (n)
6. the air _____ Luft (f)

> **Articles (revision)**
>
> **Remember:**
>
> All German nouns have a gender and are either masculine, feminine or neuter
>
> ■ You need to know which gender a noun is in order to use the words for 'the' and 'a' correctly.
>
> ■ 'The' is called the definite article and 'a' is called the indefinite article.
>
> ■ The nominative case is used when you name a noun, e.g. *der Fluss* (the river), *ein Fluss* (a river) and when this is the subject of the sentence: *Der Fluss ist lang*.

2 Choose the correct time phrase to complete these sentences. The English is given in brackets.

1. _____ kaufen wir Umweltschutzpapier. (*usually*)
2. Die Luftverschmutzung wird _____ schlimmer. (*every year*)
3. Ich benutze _____ öffentliche Verkehrsmittel. (*all the time*)
4. _____ ist das Problem so groß wie nie zuvor. (*now*)
5. Das Wetter _____ ist besser als gestern. (*today*)
6. _____ gibt es so viele Umweltprobleme. (*nowadays*)

> **More time phrases (revision)**
>
> You have already come across some examples of adverbial phrases of time. Here are some more you might find useful:
>
> | | |
> |---|---|
> | *jedes Jahr* | every year |
> | *jetzt* | now |
> | *gewöhnlich* | usually |
> | *die ganze Zeit* | all the time |
> | *heute* | today |
> | *heutzutage* | nowadays |
>
> These can all be used with the present tense. Remember that if the time phrase comes first in the sentence, you have to invert the verb and subject, e.g.
>
> *Heutzutage sind Abgase ein Problem.*

3a Complete the sentences below, adding the correct genitive preposition.

Beispiel: 1 *Trotz*

1. _____ des starken Verkehrs ist die Luft im Stadtzentrum nicht so schmutzig.
2. _____ der hohen Preise fahren wir nie mit dem Zug.
3. Wenn ich mit dem Rad zur Schule fahre, komme ich _____ fünfzehn Minuten an.
4. _____ der Stadt ist die Natur wunderschön.

> **Using prepositions with the genitive**
>
> The genitive case is normally used to show possession:
>
> *das Haus meiner Mutter* – my mother's house.
>
> Some prepositions are followed by the genitive:
>
> | | |
> |---|---|
> | *(an)statt* | instead of |
> | *außerhalb* | outside of, excluding |
> | *innerhalb* | inside of, within |
> | *trotz* | in spite of |
> | *während* | during |
> | *wegen* | because of |

Grammatik

Grammatik Seite 179

Grammatik Seite 176

3b Complete the following texts by adding the correct forms of the definite article in the genitive case. See page 176 for the endings of the definite article.

Beispiel: 1 *der*

Ich wohne außerhalb **1**_____ Stadt und bin auch umweltfreundlich. Deswegen fahre ich mit dem Bus zur Arbeit. Während **2**_____ Reise lese ich. Wegen **3**_____ hohen Fahrtkosten geht mein Bruder lieber zu Fuß zur Schule. Das dauert aber länger.

Trotz **4**_____ kalten Wetters während **5**_____ Winters verbrauche ich nicht viel Energie, weil ich warme Kleidung trage, anstatt die Heizung einzuschalten. Innerhalb **6**_____ letzten Jahre habe ich dadurch viel Geld gespart.

4 You and your family have good intentions about caring for the environment but have yet to put your plans into action! Change the following text from the present tense to the future tense with *werden*.

Ich bin umweltfreundlicher als meine Freundin. Ich recycle alles. Meine Familie kauft keine Einwegflaschen und bringt Flaschen zum Container. Mein Bruder fährt mit dem Rad zur Schule und mein Vater geht zu Fuß in die Stadtmitte. Meine Schwester schaltet den Fernseher am Abend aus. Im Winter schalten wir die Heizung nicht immer ein. Wir werfen weniger weg.

5 Use the verb tables on pages 190–193 and the list of infinitives to help you fill in the correct form of the present or imperfect tense of the verbs in the following sentences. Then translate each one into English.

Beispiel: 1 *isst*
He always has dinner at 7.30.

1 Er _____ immer um halb acht zu Abend.
2 _____ Sepp morgen bei seiner Freundin?
3 Letzten Sommer_____ sie jeden Tag ein gutes Buch.
4 _____ Torsten gestern nach Hamburg?
5 Das Buch _____ dieses Hotel aber leider nicht.
6 Letzten Juli _____ es kaum genug Regen.
7 Richard _____ immer den Zug, wenn es möglich ist.
8 Louisa _____ vor zwei Wochen sechzehn.

rennen	nehmen	sein	lesen
essen	fahren	werden	empfehlen

Grammatik

Using prepositions with the genitive

Articles in the genitive case are as follows:

	masc.	fem.	neut.	pl.
def.	*des*	*der*	*des*	*der*
indef.	*eines*	*einer*	*eines*	–

For singular masculine and neuter nouns you also add an -*s* to the end of the noun or -*es* for one-syllable nouns like *Mann*:

Wegen des Wetters fahre ich nicht in die Berge.

Seite 176

Using separable verbs in the future

When forming the future tense with *werden*, remember that separable verbs need to appear in their infinitive form at the end of the sentence or clause, e.g.

Present tense
*Ich **werfe** keine Verpackungen **weg**.*

Future tense
*Ich **werde** keine Verpackungen **wegwerfen**.*

Seite 182

Understanding verb tables 1

The verb tables on pages 190–193 are very useful if you want to look up different tenses of irregular verbs. The first column contains the infinitive, e.g. *beginnen*, which is the equivalent of 'to begin' in English.

The second column contains the *er / sie / es* form, known as the 3rd person singular, of the present tense, e.g. *beginnt*. You need to either put *er, sie, es, man* or the name of someone or something before it.

e.g. *er beginnt* means 'he begins' or 'he is beginning'.

The third column contains the 3rd person singular of the imperfect tense.

You often get a clue as to whether you need the present tense or a past tense by looking at the time phrases in each question, e.g. if a sentence contained the phrase *letzten Monat* (last month) it would need a past tense verb.

Seite 190

Environment

Topic 6.1 Current problems facing the planet

6.1 F Rettet die Umwelt! ➡ *pages 112–113*

	ärgern	to annoy, to bother
das	Atomkraftwerk	nuclear power station
der	Bauer	farmer
der	Biomüll	organic waste
das	Düngemittel	fertiliser
die	Flasche	bottle
	gefährlich	dangerous
der	Hautkrebs	skin cancer
die	Heizung	heating
	herunterdrehen	to turn down
die	Luft	air
der	Müll	rubbish
das	Ozonloch	hole in the ozone layer
die	Ozonschicht	ozone layer
	retten	to save
	saurer Regen	acid rain
	schaden	to damage, to harm
der	Strahl	ray
	trennen	to separate
	verwenden	to use

6.1 H Unsere Welt, unsere Umwelt
➡ *pages 114–115*

	Abgase (pl)	gas emissions
	aussterben	to die out, to become extinct
	bedrohen	to threaten
der	Brennstoff	fuel
die	Energiewende	energy revolution
	FCKWs	CFCs
	fortgeschritten	advanced
die	Kohle	coal
das	Kohlenmonoxid	carbon monoxide
der	Lärm	noise

das	Naturschutzgebiet	conservation area
das	Öl	oil
die	Quelle	source
	schädlich	harmful
	schuld an etwas sein	to be to blame for something
der	Treibhauseffekt	greenhouse effect
das	Unglück	disaster
	verpesten	to pollute
	verschwinden	to disappear
	zwitschern	to twitter

Topic 6.2 Local issues and actions

6.2 F Umweltfreundlich oder umweltfeindlich? ➡ *pages 116–117*

	ausmachen	to turn off
	ausschalten	to turn off
	benutzen	to use
die	Dose	can
	einschalten	to turn on
die	Energiesparlampe	energy-saving lightbulb
das	Ergebnis	result
	faul	lazy
das	Gerät	equipment
	hassen	to hate
das	Licht	light
	neulich	recently
	sammeln	to collect, to gather
die	Solarenergie	solar power
	stecken	to put
die	Tüte	bag
die	Umfrage	survey
	umweltfeindlich	environmentally unfriendly
	umweltfreundlich	environmentally friendly
	wegwerfen	to throw away

6.2 H Global denken, lokal handeln

➡ *pages 118–119*

der	Abfalleimer	waste bin
die	Arbeitslosigkeit	unemployment
der	Becher	cup
	beschließen	to decide
die	Bürgerinitiative	community action group
	dafür	in favour of, for it
	dagegen	opposed to it, against it
	einführen	to introduce
	enttäuschend	disappointing
	leer	empty
	leider	unfortunately
	pflanzen	to plant
der	Radweg	cycle path
	reinigen	to clean
	sorgen für	to ensure
der	Stau	traffic jam
die	Stofftasche	textile bag
	umweltbewusst	environmentally aware
die	Verantwortung	responsibility
	verschwenden	to waste

Learning frequently used words

The words in the two 'frequently used words' lists are some of the most common words in the German language. They come up in every single GCSE Topic and you will find that it is a really good investment of your time to learn them all by heart.

Frequently used words 1

als	as, when (in the past), than
also	so, therefore
an	at, on
auch	also
auf	on, in, at
aus	out, out of, from
bei	by, with, at the house of
bis	until
da	there, because
damit	with it, so that
dann	then
dass	that
denn	because
doch	however, still
durch	through, by means of
eigentlich	actually
entweder … oder	either … or
für	for
ganz	quite, whole

Frequently used words 2

immer	always
jedoch	however
jetzt	now
kaum	hardly
mehr	more
am meisten	most of all
mit	with
nach	after, to(wards)
neu	new
noch	still, yet, another
nur	only
oben	above
schon	already
sonst	otherwise
über	over
um	around
viel	a lot of, many
von	from, of
wieder	again
zu	to, at, too

Higher – Exam practice

info

These pages give you the chance to try GCSE-style practice exam questions at grades B-A* based on the AQA Context of Home and environment.

Hinweis

Foundation practice exam questions (grades D-C) are available at the end of this Context in the Foundation book.

■ Umwelt in Gefahr

Wir haben mit vier Experten gesprochen. Hier sind ihre Meinungen über unsere Umwelt heute.

Zoologin, Frau Meyer

Heutzutage gibt es zwischen zehn und hundert Millionen verschiedene Arten auf der Erde. Früher gab es viel mehr – etwa 99% aller Arten sind schon ausgestorben. Was ist passiert? Vielleicht eine Katastrophe wie eine Supernova? Viele Leute sind der Meinung, dass saurer Regen, ultraviolette Strahlen, Biomüll, Schwefeldioxid, FCKWs und Insektizide dafür verantwortlich sind: aber wer produziert z.B. Insektizide und Biomüll? Wir Menschen!

Wissenschaftler, Herr Dirks

Das Klima hat sich in den letzten Jahren verändert und hat den Treibhauseffekt verursacht – die Temperatur ist seit Beginn der Industrialisierung um 1 Grad gestiegen und seit 1980 hat sich dieser Prozess noch beschleunigt. Man kann in den nächsten fünfzig Jahren mit einem weiteren Anstieg der Temperatur rechnen. Es regnet öfter und der Meeresspiegel steigt jedes Jahr.

Bäuerin, Frau Haag

Bald wird man in Ländern wie Deutschland, Dänemark und Schottland exotische Früchte und Gemüse pflanzen können. Einerseits ist das ein Vorteil, andererseits ein Nachteil, weil andere Pflanzen wegen der Hitze nicht mehr wachsen werden.

Umweltschützer, Herr Marschner

Saurer Regen macht die Wälder krank, wegen Kohlendioxid aus Auspuffgasen wird die Erde wärmer und unser Trinkwasser wird durch Umweltverschmutzung gefährdet. Wir fahren überall mit dem Auto hin, fliegen ins Ausland, kaufen immer mehr elektrische Produkte und werfen zu viel weg, statt unseren Müll zu trennen oder zu recyceln.

Aus Alt mach Neu! Kauf Taschenrechner mit Solarzellen! Verwende nur Flaschen, die man recyceln kann! Die Heizung nicht voll aufdrehen – trag lieber einen warmen Pulli!

1a Read the article, then read the following sentences. For each sentence write **T** (true), **F** (false) or **?** (not in the text).

1 The first expert is a zoologist.
2 A natural catastrophe killed lots of animal species.
3 Climate change is a recent occurrence.
4 It will get even warmer in the next half century.
5 Drinking water is not in danger.
6 The environmentalist believes we are now doing enough recycling.

Total = 6 marks

1b 📖 Read the article again and answer the following questions in English.

1 Apart from insecticides, what are three of the other main causes of the problem raised by the zoologist? (3)

2 Other than the rise in temperature, what are two other effects of the changing climate? (2)

3 How does the farmer feel about being able to grow exotic fruits in Northern Europe? (2)

4 What exactly does the environmentalist think is the main cause of the earth warming up?

5 What is the environmentalist's overall advice? Give one specific example he mentions. (2)

6 What impression do the experts give overall of the environment today?

Total = 11 marks

2 📖 Read the following text about the environment and then select the correct word from the list below.

Die Umwelt ist für (1)_____ sehr wichtig. Ich versuche, keine Spraydosen zu (2)_____. Ich mache mich Sorgen um die (3)_____ in unserer Stadt. Das ganze Stadtzentrum (4)_____ und man bekommt (5)_____ frische Luft. Am liebsten (6)_____ ich auf dem Land (7)_____.

benutzen   Energiesparlampen   hätte   keine
Luftverschmutzung   mich   stinkt   wohnen   würde

Total = 7 marks

3 🎧 Listen to the radio item on saving the environment and answer the following questions in English.

1 What are the benefits of solar energy, according to the speaker? (2)

2 What is of the greatest importance to him? Give one reason why. (2)

3 Why does he think his ideas might not be popular?

4 Give three suggested alternatives to using cars. (3)

5 Who does the speaker say can join in with saving the environment?

Total = 9 marks

Total for Reading and Listening = 33 marks

Strategie 1b

Linking statements with the text

When you have an exam task where you have to answer a number of questions about the text, you will find that they go in roughly the same order as the text, rather than jumping about. In order to answer 1b, therefore, you do not need to read the text six times.

The first thing you will find is information on how the problem is caused for question 1. This is in the first mini text by the zoologist. However, as you are working at Higher level, don't expect it to be completely straightforward. The text mentions insecticides twice, but these are both towards the end of the paragraph. You'll have to go further back to find the other causes.

You can then move on to the second mini text to find the information to answer question 2.

Strategie 3

Preparing well for Higher Listening questions

There are many types of Higher Listening task, but they all have one thing in common: a high concentration of complex vocabulary. Use the preparation time you have before all the recordings start and again in between questions as wisely as you can.

Have a look at task 3. It might be difficult to anticipate what the answer to question 3 might be, as it is very open-ended. However, it would be easy to think of key vocab in German for alternatives to cars in question 4. You could make a list of words like *Bus*, *Rad*, *Zug* and *Fuss* and then see which ones come up.

Higher – Speaking

Umweltsumfrage

You have agreed to take part in a survey about environmental issues at your exchange school in Germany. Your teacher will play the role of the person carrying out the survey. He or she could ask you the following:

1 What do you do at home to look after the environment?

2 What are the advantages and disadvantages of using public transport?

3 What environmental problems are there in your local area?

4 What have you done so far to improve your environment?

5 What are the worst environmental problems worldwide?

6 What could be done in the future to improve the environment?

7 !

! Remember you will have to respond to something that you have not yet prepared.

> **info**
>
> **Important information:**
> This sample task is for practice purposes only and should not be used as an actual assessment task. Study it to find out how to plan your Controlled Assessment efficiently to gain maximum marks and / or work through it as a mock exam task before the actual Controlled Assessment.

1 What do you do at home to look after the environment?
- say what you do at home to protect the environment and say how long you've been doing this
- say what the impact of your actions is
- say what your family doesn't do at home for the environment
- explain why this is not important to you / them

> **Strategie**
>
> Now start your plan. Write a maximum of six words for each bullet point. Here are some suggested words for the first bullet point: *recyceln, trennen, Müll, abschalten, Dusche, Energiesparlampen.*
> Remember that verbs need to go on your notes in the infinitive, but when you say them, the *ich, er / sie* and *wir* forms will all have different endings.
> *Ich trenne, er / sie trennt, wir trennen.*
> You could also say whether you agree with your family's choices for sub-division 4.

2 What are the advantages and disadvantages of using public transport?
- explain the advantages of using public transport
- explain the disadvantages of using public transport
- give your opinion on whether you like using public transport or not
- briefly describe the last time you used public transport and say what it was like

> **Strategie**
>
> Suggested words for your plan: *öffentliche Verkehrsmittel, Vorteil, Nachteil, teuer, warten.*
> To make comparisons, you can either use comparative adjectives such as *praktischer als, schneller als*, or for variety use the format *nicht so [zuverlässig] wie.*

3 What environmental problems are there in your area?
- describe the area you live in
- mention one or two good or bad points in terms of the environment
- mention an issue that was an environmental problem in the past and say whether it is still an issue
- compare your area with another area which is nearby

> **Strategie**
>
> Suggested words for your plan: *Umwelt, schaden, Hauptprobleme, Verschmutzung.* Add two more words to this list.
> When you start talking about the problems in the past, you will need to use the imperfect tense: *In der Vergangenheit gab es zu viele Staus in der Stadt. Wir hatten keine frische Luft.*

4 What have you done so far to improve the environment?

- say what people have been doing already and for how long
- give ideas of what individuals, groups and the local council could do to further improve the area
- say whether you think that these ideas would be successful
- say which idea you prefer and why

> **Strategie**
>
> Suggested words for your plan: *verbessern, Lösung, reinigen, seit.* Add two more words to this list.
>
> You could use *man könnte* to say what could be done or *das wäre* to say what would be a good idea. Make sure your word order is correct!
>
> *Die Leute in London könnten weniger Müll auf die Straße werfen.*

5 What are the worst environmental problems worldwide?

- say what the most important worldwide environmental problems are
- say how they affect the environment and in which areas of the world
- explain why you are particularly interested in these issues
- give a practical solution to the problems and explain why you think it would work

> **Strategie**
>
> The vocabulary you require here is very specific, so make sure you focus on the key words you really need to help you. Suggested words for your plan: *Ausland, weltweit.* Add four more words to this list.
>
> You could start off by saying *Das schlimmste Problem* or *Das Hauptproblem ist …*
>
> You could use *man könnte* to say what could be done. Make sure your word order is correct!

6 What could be done in the future?

- say whether you think the environment is improving or declining
- explain why you think this is the case
- say what you plan to do personally
- explain why you feel it's important to take this action

> **Strategie**
>
> Suggested words for your plan: *verschlechtern, wegen* (you will need to use the genitive with this preposition). Add four more words to this list.
>
> There are a few different ways of talking about the future. Whichever one you use, start with a time phrase like *in der Zukunft.* Then move onto a verb such as *könnte ich, hat man vor …, würden wir, hoffe ich* or *sollte man.* If you mix and match these, be careful to get the right verb ending.
>
> Using *um … zu …* to explain why something is a solution will improve your mark.
>
> For top marks, use the conditional: *Wenn ich Zeit hätte, würde ich …*

7 **!** At this point you may be asked to …

- describe how important the environment is to teenagers generally
- say what you think the environment will be like in 20 years' time
- say whether you think that the environment is a local or global problem
- say who you think is responsible for looking after the environment and who should be!

> **Strategie**
>
> Think about what the surprise question could be. There are some suggestions in the sub-divisions. Then work out what your answer would be to each of those and any other questions you think might be asked.
>
> You should have four words left to add to your list, so choose carefully. You might choose: *verantwortlich, zukünftige.*
>
> Pick words that you haven't already used in your preparation, as you're more likely to need help remembering these.
>
> Your answer does not have to be long but it needs to contain a conjugated verb.
>
> Remember to check the total number of words you have used. It should be 40 or fewer.

> **Hinweis**
>
> Foundation sample assessment tasks for this Context can be found in the Foundation book.

Higher – Writing

 **Hinweis**

Foundation sample assessment tasks for this Context can be found in the Foundation book.

Mein Wohnort

Your Austrian friend has asked you to write an article about your home and local area for his or her school magazine. The piece is entitled *Mein Wohnort*. You could include:

1 where the town / village is situated and what the weather is like

2 a description of your house

3 a description of the town

4 what there is for tourists and young people

5 something you and your friends recently did there

6 the advantages and disadvantages of living there

7 whether you want to live there in the future

info

Important information:
This sample task is for practice purposes only and should not be used as an actual assessment task. Study it to find out how to plan your Controlled Assessment efficiently to gain maximum marks and / or work through it as a mock exam task before the actual Controlled Assessment.

1 Where the town / village is situated and what the weather is like

- briefly describe your town / village, giving its location, size and saying what type of place it is
- give some information about what the town was like in the past
- if it is a small place, say how far it is from the nearest larger town and compare it to that town
- say what the weather is like in the different seasons

Strategie

Now start your plan. Write five or six words for each bullet point, remembering that verbs will need to have the correct ending when you write them in your assessment but, like *liegen* below, they can only be in your list in the infinitive. Suggested words for your plan for this bullet point: *Südwestengland, historisch, Hauptstadt, Klima, früher, größer.*

To write about the town's history in the second sub-division you could use the time phrases *in der Vergangenheit* or *vor zwanzig Jahren* and the verbs *es gab, wir hatten* or *die Stadt war …*

Show that you can use adjectives and their endings competently and correctly. *Manchester ist eine große Industriestadt, die in Nordwestengland liegt.*

2 A description of your house or flat

- say where you live in relation to the town centre
- briefly describe the house – size, number of rooms, garden
- describe your own room
- give your opinion of both your house / flat and own bedroom, saying what you would change

Strategie

Suggested words for your plan: *Vorort, Stadtmitte, Land, Zimmer, Wohnung, Reihenhaus.*

Remember that the items that follow *es gibt* and *wir haben* will take the accusative case. Using adjectives to describe your house / room will make your language more developed, and so more likely to score top marks. *Ich habe einen sehr alten Tisch in meinem Zimmer.*

When giving opinions, always try to justify them. *Ich finde, dass unser Haus nur mittelmäßig ist, weil es nicht geräumig genug ist. Ich würde gern in einem größeren Haus wohnen.*

3 A description of the town

- say what the main buildings in the town are and where they are in relation to each other
- say when some of the buildings were built or founded
- say what public transport is like
- say how you prefer to travel and why

Strategie

Suggested words for your plan: *öffnen, Bahnhof, gründen, gegenüber von.* Add one more word to this list.

Remember to use the correct case (dative or accusative) after prepositions. *Das Sportzentrum liegt neben dem Bahnhof.* Use the passive to say when things were built or founded. *Das Rathaus wurde im Jahr 1840 erbaut.*

Vary the way you give your preferences: *Ich ziehe es vor, mit dem Zug zu fahren …. / Ich fahre lieber mit dem Zug …*

4 What there is for tourists and young people

- say what there is for tourists and give your opinion of one of the attractions
- say what there is for young people
- say which of these facilities you use and why
- say what attractions you would like in your town

Suggested words for your plan: *sich entspannen, ausgezeichnet.* Add three more words to this list.

You could use *man kann, man sollte* or *man muss* to say what there is to do, e.g. *Man kann die alte Kirche besuchen.* Remember that after a modal verb, the infinitive goes to the end of the sentence.

When saying which facilities you use and why, you could compare yourself to a friend using *während* (whereas).

Link sentences using less common conjunctions such as *damit*, *obwohl* and *so dass*, but make sure your word order is correct. You can find information on how each one behaves on page 187.

Strategie

5 Something you and your friends recently did there

- give a brief description of the activity you and your friends did, including the location, the cost and who went
- say what one of your friends did whilst they were there
- give your opinion of the activity and give reasons
- say what you and your friends plan to do next weekend

Suggested words for your plan: *vorhaben, nächsten Samstag.* Add three more words to this list.

Use the Grammatik section to help you show that you can use different tenses accurately. Look up the perfect (page 182) the imperfect (page 183), the pluperfect (page 184), the future (page 184) and the conditional (page 184). See if you can put a couple of examples of each one in your answer.

Make sure you use the correct verb endings when you use the *ich, er / sie* and *wir* forms of the verb, as they are all different!

Strategie

6 The advantages and disadvantages of living there

- give advantages and disadvantages of your town, and reasons to back these up
- give your overall opinion of where you live, including different reasons
- compare your town to another town nearby
- say if you prefer your town to the other one and why (not)

Suggested words for your plan: *Landschaft, Aussicht.* Add four more words to this list.

You could use less common adjectives and qualifiers here to add depth to your opinions, e.g. *Ich glaube, dass die Eisdiele ziemlich enttäuschend ist* or *Meiner Meinung nach ist das Einkaufszentrum total überteuert.*

At Higher level you need to be able to give complex opinions, so try to think of unique reasons (but not too off-the-wall!) when you give your overall opinion of where you live: *Newton ist kleiner als meine Stadt, bietet aber bessere Wassersportmöglichkeiten.*

Strategie

7 Whether you want to live there in the future

- say what improvements or facilities you would like your town to have in the future
- say where you would like to live in the future and give reasons
- compare where you live now with your future choice
- say why you would (not) like to live in the mountains, in the countryside or on the coast (choose one) and say why (not)

If you start a sentence with a time phrase, remember that the main verb is then the second idea, e.g. *In der Zukunft werde ich in London wohnen.*

Don't forget that you don't have to use *ich werde* to imply the future. You could use *ich habe vor, ich will, ich möchte, ich könnte, ich sollte, ich hoffe … zu …* or *ich würde gern.* All these constructions will send your second verb to the end of the sentence or clause.

Now count up how many words you have left, ideally about 5 or 6. If you have fewer than this, you may want to go back and take some out of your list for previous bullet points, as you can only have 40 words in total. Useful words to add here could be: *Verbesserungen, später.*

Strategie

Exam technique – Speaking

S7 Ideas for practising

Treat each bullet point as a mini-task. Practise your answer to one bullet point at a time. Look at one word on your plan and say aloud all the things that the word is reminding you to say. Repeat the process for each word on your plan. Next, try to account for two words, then for three words, etc. Time your answer for one whole bullet point. Repeat the process for each bullet point. Record yourself if possible.

You can also practise with a partner. Together, work out the questions that your teacher might ask you in the exam and practise your answers to these questions in turn.

S8 Info about Interaction and Fluency

Fluency is your ability to speak without hesitation. Try and speak with fluency but not too fast. If you are likely to be nervous when performing the task, practise it and practise it again. Time your whole response. Make a point of slowing down if you feel that you are speaking too fast. Practise with your plan in front of you so that you know what you are going to say next and therefore do not hesitate in the exam itself.

Interaction is about your ability to contribute to the conversation. To gain good marks, you will need to show initiative (see S10).

S9 Info about Communication, Range of language, and Accuracy

The marks that you get for Communication are for getting the message over to the teacher who is examining you. The marks for Range of language are awarded if you have a good variety of vocabulary and grammatical structures in your responses. The marks that you get for Accuracy will be linked to how well you know and use the rules of German grammar and pronunciation. These three are closely linked because if you get the grammar wrong, it can change the meaning of your message. If this happens, you will lose both Communication / Range of Language and Accuracy marks.

Exam technique – Writing

W7 Marking of the tasks

AQA examiners will mark your work. A senior examiner will check the work of the Examiner. This is to ensure that candidates are given the correct mark for their work.

The pair of Writing tasks count for 30% of the whole GCSE German exam, so each of the Writing tasks is worth 15%. Your work will be marked in terms of Content, Range of language, and Accuracy. Each task will be marked out of 30. 15 of these marks are for Content, 10 are for Range of language and 5 are for Accuracy.

W8 Info about Range of language

If you are aiming at grade A, you must use a wide variety of vocabulary and structures. You must also include more complex sentences and use different verb tenses (see W5).

W9 Info about 'Content'

You will be awarded marks under the heading 'Content' for

- the amount of relevant information you give
- expressing and explaining ideas and points of view
- developing the points you make
- producing a well-structured piece of work.

Refer to W6 for the number of words you should aim to write.

Grade booster

To reach grade B, you need to ...

- Have a good variety of vocabulary and structures, e.g. in bullet point 6, use a variety of ways to give a balanced argument e.g. *auf der einen Seite ... auf der anderen Seite / ein Vorteil ist ..., aber ein Nachteil ist / einerseits ... andererseits.*

- Convey a lot of information clearly, e.g. in bullet point 5, give many details about your last trip out in your area, e.g. what you did, who with, when, why, the cost, your opinion, etc.

To reach grade A, you need to ...

- Develop the majority of the points you make, whilst being accurate, particularly with regards to verb and tense formations, e.g. in bullet point 4, say what there is for young people to do. You can then develop your answer by saying why you rate the facilities you use. Give clear reasons to get the best marks.

- Express and explain ideas and points of view with clarity, e.g. in bullet point 6, give your overall opinion of where you live after summing up the advantages and disadvantages of the area. Focus on accuracy and use phrases like *zum Schluss* to make it clear that this is part of your conclusion.

To reach grade A*, you need to ...

- Give a fully relevant and detailed response to the task which is largely accurate, e.g. in bullet point 7, write at least 50 words to cover all the ideas included in this bullet point.

- Handle complex sentences with confidence, making very few errors in the process, e.g. in bullet point 5, include different tenses in your answer to say what the weather was like (imperfect), what activity you chose (perfect), what you think of that particular activity now (present), what you had done the previous weekend (pluperfect), your plans for your next outing (future) and what you'd like to do if you had the time or money (conditional).

7.1 F
Ich möchte meine Schule beschreiben

Lernziele

Describing your school

Saying where you do things

Giving impressive answers to questions

1 ⓥ Using the vocabulary list on page 146, unscramble the anagrams. Then translate the words into English.

Beispiel: 1 *Stunde (hour, lesson)*

Hinweis

7.1 Groundwork is available in the Foundation Book.

1 Sunted
2 härFec
3 suchteelsmaG
4 diFbear
5 muGsmainy
6 fetH
7 rentatIn
8 lAau

◀ ⏺ [   ] 🔍 Suche

Startseite | Index | Hilfe | Kontakt | Textversion

Hermann-Friedrich-Gesamtschule

Schule

Fachbereiche

Fotos

Personal

Schulordnung

Hallo, mein Name ist Stefan Reuter. Ich bin in der Klasse 9b und darf unsere Schule vorstellen. Sie ist eine ganz neue Gesamtschule, die 2002 eröffnet wurde. Sie liegt in der Nähe von Hannover.

In der Schule haben wir viele Klassenzimmer, wo allerlei Fächer unterrichtet werden, zum Beispiel Mathe, Erdkunde, Geschichte und Deutsch. Naturwissenschaften machen wir in den neuen Labors und für Fremdsprachen wie Englisch und Französisch gibt es ein modernes Sprachlabor. Jedes Klassenzimmer hat die neueste Technik und ich finde es gut, dass man immer das Internet benutzen kann.

Mein Lieblingsfach ist Sport. Dafür gibt es sowohl einen großen Sportplatz hinter der Schule als auch eine Turnhalle und ein Hallenbad.

In unserer Schule beginnt die erste Stunde normalerweise um halb acht. Jede Stunde dauert 45 Minuten. Wir haben sieben Stunden pro Tag und zwei große Pausen und dürfen schon um 1.35 Uhr nach Hause gehen, weil die Schule dann aus ist.

Am Mittwoch sieht es anders aus. Da haben wir auch nachmittags Schule. Nach der siebten Stunde gehen wir zuerst einmal in die Schulkantine, wo wir zu Mittag essen können. Ich finde das Essen dort lecker und billig, aber zu Hause ist es besser! Am Nachmittag macht dann jeder eine AG. Ich bin Mitglied in der Theatergruppe, aber man kann auch Sport treiben, eine dritte Fremdsprache lernen oder einfach Hausaufgaben machen, bevor man nach Hause geht. Toll, nicht wahr?

2a 📖 🎧 Read about Stefan's school. Then copy these sentences and fill in the gaps with one of the words opposite.

Beispiel: 1 *Die Hermann-Friedrich-Schule ist eine Gesamtschule.*

1 Die Hermann-Friedrich-Schule ist eine _____.
2 Die Schule ist ganz _____.
3 In den _____ machen wir Biologie, Chemie und Physik.
4 Die Schule hat ein _____, wo man schwimmen kann.
5 Um _____ Uhr dreißig beginnt die erste Stunde.
6 Das _____ in der Schule schmeckt gut.
7 Stefan findet es _____, dass er am Mittwoch Ganztagsschule hat.

acht   Freibad

alt   Gesamtschule

Klassenzimmer

langweilig   prima

Hallenbad   modern   Labors

sieben   Essen

2b 📖 🎧 Read about the school again and look at these statements. Write **T** (true), **F** (false) or **?** (not in the text).

Beispiel: 1 *F*

1 The school is situated in the centre of Hanover.
2 Students are able to use a language laboratory.
3 Spanish is taught in addition to English and French.
4 The classrooms have up-to-date equipment.
5 Every student has a tablet computer.

6 First lesson is at 8.30 a.m.
7 They finish early in the afternoon except on Fridays.
8 He thinks the food at school is as good as at home.
9 Everyone has to do an activity or homework on Wednesday afternoon.
10 They are allowed to listen to music if they are doing homework at school.

3 Ⓖ Join these phrases using *wo*.

Beispiel: 1 *Es gibt einen Sportplatz, wo wir Hockey spielen.*

1 Es gibt einen Sportplatz. Wir spielen Hockey.
2 Ich gehe in die Schulkantine. Ich esse zu Mittag.
3 Die Schule hat viele Labors. Wir machen Experimente.
4 Es gibt auch ein Sprachlabor. Ich kann Englisch sprechen.
5 Neben meinem Klassenzimmer ist die Bibliothek. Ich mache meine Hausaufgaben.
6 In der Schule gibt es eine Turnhalle. Man kann Gymnastik machen.

4 🎧 Listen to Axel and Christina talking about their schools and choose the correct answers.

Beispiel: 1 *c*

1 Axel goes to a school in …   a Southern Germany   b Eastern Germany   c Northern Germany.
2 His school is a …   a boarding school   b comprehensive school   c grammar school.
3 He particularly likes the …   a language laboratory   b canteen   c sports hall.
4 After school yesterday, he was involved with the …   a theatre group   b orchestra   c film club.
5 Christina …   a hates her school   b quite likes her school   c likes her school a lot.
6 She says the classrooms are …   a modern   b not big enough   c dirty.
7 She thinks school meals are often …   a unhealthy   b cheap   c tasty.
8 School finishes at …   a 1 p.m.   b 2 p.m.   c 3 p.m.

5 🗪 Taking it in turns, interview a partner about your school.

Ⓖrammatik   Seite 187

Saying where you do things

If you use the word *wo* to join two clauses, the <u>verb</u> in the clause after *wo* goes to the <u>end</u>. Remember to put a comma after the first clause.

Meine Schule hat ein Sprachlabor, wo ich Französisch lerne.

Notice that when there is a modal verb in the clause as well as the infinitive, the modal verb must go to the very end.

*Es gibt ein großes Hallenbad, wo man schwimmen **kann**.*

Also learn how to use prepositions with the words 'it' or 'that'.   *See page 144* ➡

Strategie 5

Giving impressive answers to questions

When answering questions remember ADORE:

Answer the question in full sentences, add
Details,
Opinions and
Reasons, to produce
Excellent work!

• Was für eine Schule besuchst du?
• Wie alt ist die Schule?
• Wann beginnt die Schule und wann ist sie aus?
• Was gibt es in deiner Schule?
• Wie findest du die Schule?
• Warum?

7.1 H Meine Schule ist anders

Lernziele

Comparing schools in different countries

Using the imperfect tense of modal verbs

Revising vocabulary

Paula

Für mich war der Austausch ganz interessant. Wir besuchten ein Gymnasium, dessen Stundenplan überhaupt nicht wie bei uns in England war. Wir mussten sehr früh aufstehen, weil die erste Stunde schon um 7:55 Uhr begonnen hat! Die Stunden dauerten auch nur 45 Minuten. Das habe ich gut gefunden, da man sich nicht so lange konzentrieren musste. Nach der dritten Stunde hatten wir eine große Pause, und wir konnten uns dann unterhalten oder auf dem Schulhof spielen. Das beste daran war, dass wir zu Mittag nach Hause gehen durften, denn die letzte Stunde endete um Viertel nach eins.

Tom

Die Schule meines Austauschpartners war völlig anders als in England. Ganz toll war natürlich, dass ich jeden Morgen meine Jeans und ein T-Shirt anziehen durfte, denn in Deutschland braucht man keine Schuluniform zu tragen. Die Pausen waren ziemlich kurz, nur 10 Minuten meistens, aber in den Pausen durften wir in den Klassenzimmern essen und trinken. Und wir waren den ganzen Tag im gleichen Klassenzimmer. Das hat mir gut gefallen, weil die Lehrer immer zu uns kommen mussten. Nur an einem Tag sind wir nachmittags in der Schule geblieben. Das war Mittwoch, glaube ich, und die deutschen Schüler mussten alle eine AG machen. Mein Austauschpartner war in der Schulmannschaft für Handball und durfte an dem Nachmittag trainieren.

Revising vocabulary

Strategie 1a

If you are having difficulty revising vocabulary try to:

1 Find pairs of words which mean the same, e.g. *beginnen / anfangen*.

2 Find pairs of words which mean the opposite, e.g. *kurz / lang*.

3 Challenge yourself to make a list of 10 words from the same category, e.g. 10 places in school.

Remember, vocabulary revision is best done little and often. Set yourself a realistic target each week or even each day and increase your word power! Also, to help you remember what you have learnt, it is a good idea to review this vocabulary a week later. If you do this regularly, you will soon build up the number of words you know.

1a 📖 🎧 Read Paula and Tom's descriptions, picking out the key words relating to the topic of school life.

- Which words are familiar?
- Which are new but easy to work out?
- Which did you need to look up?

Make a list of new words to revise and use again in future!

1b 📖 🎧 Read the descriptions again and answer the following questions in English:

1   Why did Paula have to get up so early?
2   Why did she think the shorter lessons were good?
3   What was Paula able to do in the main break?
4   What did Paula find best about the school day in Germany?
5   What is the first positive thing Tom mentions about school life in Germany?
6   What was Tom allowed to do at break time?
7   Why was Tom pleased about being in one classroom for all lessons?
8   What did the German pupils do on Wednesday afternoons?

2 Ⓖ Rewrite these sentences in the imperfect tense.

Beispiel: 1 *Ich musste um 8 Uhr aufstehen.*
1   Ich muss um 8 Uhr aufstehen.
2   Im Klassenzimmer darf ich nicht essen.
3   In der Pause kann ich mich mit meinen Freunden treffen.
4   In Deutschland müssen die Schüler eine AG machen.
5   Wir können zu Mittag in der Schulkantine essen.
6   In Deutschland darf man tragen, was man will.

3 🎧 These pupils are talking about their school day. Find the correct four statements.

1   Hans's school day begins early at half past 8.
2   Paul likes not having to wear a uniform at school.
3   Martina buys a sandwich from the caretaker at break.
4   Bettina goes to a comprehensive school.
5   She has every afternoon free.
6   Michael does drama every Thursday afternoon.

4 ✏ Imagine you have just been to an Austrian school on an exchange visit. Write a short report saying what was different. Use Paula and Tom's texts to help you.

> **Using the imperfect tense of modal verbs**   *Grammatik*
>
> | | |
> |---|---|
> | *ich musste* | 'I had to' |
> | *ich konnte* | 'I was able to' |
> | *ich durfte* | 'I was allowed to' |
> | *ich wollte* | 'I wanted to' |
> | *ich sollte* | 'I was supposed to' |
> | *ich mochte* | 'I liked to' |
>
> Notice that the imperfect tense never has an Umlaut.
>
> Look for other forms of these verbs (e.g. *wir mussten*) in Paula and Tom's texts.
>
> Remember that the second verb still needs to go to the end of the clause:
>
> *Wir mussten sehr früh aufstehen.* – We had to get up very early.
>
> Also learn the pluperfect tense.
> *See page 145* ➡

In Österreich / In der Schule meines Austauschpartners / meiner Austauschpartnerin	musste ich / man konnte ich / man durfte ich / man	früh aufstehen. keine Uniform tragen. im Klassenzimmer … am Nachmittag …
Die Unterrichtsstunden in Österreich	dauerten	fünfzig Minuten / anderthalb Stunden …
	waren	lustig / langweilig / amüsant / einfach / schwierig.
Ich finde das Schulwesen in	Österreich / England	besser, weil …

7.2 F Hast du Stress in der Schule?

Lernziele

Talking about school stress

Subordinate clauses

Looking for verbs in the 'wrong' place

1 **V** With the help of a dictionary and the vocabulary on page 146, place these words which refer to school stress in the correct category: Discipline – Assessment – Feelings.

Beispiel: **Discipline Assessment Feelings**
                              Prüfung

Prüfung nervös Abitur
streng nachsitzen Note
peinlich Klassenarbeit
Abschluss Angst sitzen bleiben

Hilfe!

1

Ich bin nicht so gut in der Schule wie meine Schulfreunde und bekomme immer schlechte Noten. Letzte Woche hatte ich mich sehr gut vorbereitet, aber ich bekam trotzdem nur eine Drei. Ich habe Angst, dass ich vielleicht nächstes Jahr sitzen bleibe. Ich werde nervös, wenn ich eine Klassenarbeit oder eine Prüfung habe. Was soll ich machen?

Klaus

2

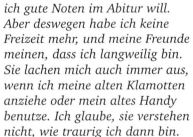

Ich möchte auf die Uni gehen und brauche dafür einen guten Abschluss. Ich muss viel arbeiten, wenn ich gute Noten im Abitur will. Aber deswegen habe ich keine Freizeit mehr, und meine Freunde meinen, dass ich langweilig bin. Sie lachen mich auch immer aus, wenn ich meine alten Klamotten anziehe oder mein altes Handy benutze. Ich glaube, sie verstehen nicht, wie traurig ich dann bin.

Gabi

3

Es ist alles zu viel für mich. Ich treibe viel Sport, spiele ein Instrument im Schulorchester und muss dann auch nach der Schule Zeit für Hausaufgaben usw. finden. Kein Wunder, dass ich manchmal vergesse, sie zu machen und deshalb nachsitzen muss. Das ist mir immer peinlich.

Wilhelm

2a 📖 🎧 Read the problem page letters. Which of the teenagers …

1 … wants to get good marks in order to go to university?
2 … gets nervous about exams?
3 … sometimes has to stay behind after school?
4 … is worried about having to repeat a year?
5 … has lots of hobbies?
6 … uses an old mobile phone?

Looking for verbs in the 'wrong' place

When working out what a sentence means, it can be off-putting if the verb isn't where you expect it. So if you see a verb at the end of a clause or sentence, think what is making it go there. This should help you to understand the rest of the sentence. For example, in Klaus's letter in the third sentence, the verb *bleibe* is at the end because of the subordinating conjunction *dass*.

Strategie 2a

2b 📖 🎧 Now read the responses and match each to the correct letter (1–3).

a

Du solltest deine Zeit besser organisieren. Du könntest alles in einen Terminkalender eintragen.

b

Du solltest dir keine Sorgen machen. Du könntest die Situation mit deinen Lehrern besprechen. Sie werden dich bestimmt verstehen und dir helfen.

c

Freizeit und Freunde sind immer wichtig. Du solltest versuchen, mehr Spaß zu haben und mehr Zeit mit deinen Freunden zu verbringen. Vielleicht könntest du das Wochenende dafür frei lassen. Du solltest ihnen auch sagen, dass du traurig wirst, wenn sie dich immer auslachen. Gute Freunde werden dann damit aufhören.

3a Ⓖ Join the phrases below using the conjunctions indicated.

Beispiel: 1 *Ich gehe ins Bett, nachdem ich meine Hausaufgaben gemacht habe.*

1 Ich gehe ins Bett. Ich habe meine Hausaufgaben gemacht. (nachdem)
2 Ich mag meine Schule. Ich habe viele Freunde hier. (weil)
3 Ich finde Englisch in Ordnung. Der Lehrer ist streng. (obwohl)
4 Ich muss fleißig arbeiten. Ich will gute Noten bekommen. (wenn)
5 Ich finde es doof. Ich muss jeden Abend Hausaufgaben machen. (dass)

3b Ⓖ Once your teacher has checked your answers, rewrite the sentences from activity 3a, starting each with the subordinating conjunction.

Beispiel: 1 *Nachdem ich meine Hausaufgaben gemacht habe, gehe ich ins Bett.*

4a 🎧 Clara is spending the school year in England. What problems does she have? Listen to the first part of the recording and complete the sentences.

1 Clara is studying at a _____ school.
2 She finds the _____ too long.
3 She has little time for her _____.

4b 🎧 Now listen carefully to the next part and complete the sentences.

1 Clara does not understand her fellow pupils when _____.
2 She find the teachers hard to understand because they _____.
3 She cannot always do her work because _____.

5 🖊 Using the letters on page 136 to help you, write to an agony aunt explaining that you have the following problems:

■ homework   ■ exams
■ teachers   ■ no free time

> **Subordinate clauses** *Grammatik* *Seite 187*
>
> A subordinating conjunction sends the verb to the end of its clause:
>
> *Ich mache meine Hausaufgaben, **nachdem** ich zu Abend gegessen **habe**.*
>
> Remember that if you start a sentence with a subordinating conjunction, you will have 'verb - comma - verb' in the middle of your sentence:
>
> ***Nachdem** ich zu Abend gegessen **habe**, **mache** ich meine Hausaufgaben.*
>
> Also learn about ways of denoting possession.
>
> *See page 144* ➡

 **Hinweis**

7.2 Groundwork is available in the Foundation Book.

7.2 H   Wir haben zu viel Druck

Antonia: Es tut mir leid, Herr Meier, aber ich verstehe mich nicht so gut mit dem neuen Fremdsprachenassistenten. Wenn wir Gruppenarbeit machen, stellt er mir gar keine Fragen. Das nervt mich, weil ich meine Sprachkenntnisse verbessern möchte.

Lehrer: Ich verstehe schon, Antonia. Ich werde mit ihm darüber reden.

•••••••••••••••••••••••••••••

Ben: Fräulein Müller, ich bin so eifersüchtig. Am Montag haben wir eine Klassenarbeit geschrieben und ich habe eine Drei bekommen. Dafür habe ich mich stundenlang vorbereitet, aber mein Freund Christof hat fast nichts gemacht und er hat eine Eins bekommen. Das finde ich so ungerecht!

Lehrerin: Es kann sein, dass Christof neue Sachen schneller versteht. Du solltest aber mit dem Wiederholen nicht aufhören. Wenn du vielleicht etwas nicht verstanden hast, kannst du mit mir reden.

Claudia: Meine Freundinnen sind so gemein. Sie gehen mir auf die Nerven. Weil ich mich nicht schminke oder keine kurzen Röcke trage wie sie, lachen sie mich aus. Ich will keine Außenseiterin werden, aber ich habe wirklich keine Lust, mich so anzuziehen.

Mutter: Mach dir keine Sorgen, Claudia! Es wäre viel besser, wenn du andere Freundinnen kennen lernen könntest. Diese Mädchen sind keine echten Freundinnen. Außerdem bist du auch ohne Schminke sehr schön.

•••••••••••••••••••••••••••••

Markus: Nächste Woche habe ich meine Abschlussprüfung, aber ich weiß nicht, ob ich dafür genug gearbeitet habe. Ich will gute Noten bekommen, aber in der Schule ist der Leistungsdruck wirklich schrecklich. Das kann ich einfach nicht leiden.

Vater: Du solltest jeden Abend versuchen, ein paar Stunden mit Wiederholen zu verbringen. Es ist dabei sehr wichtig, dass du dich entspannst und nicht zu spät ins Bett gehst.

1a 📖🎧 Read the dialogues and find the German phrases for the following:

Beispiel: 1 *Dafür habe ich mich stundenlang vorbereitet.*

1 I prepared for hours.
2 I don't want to become an outsider.
3 Don't worry.
4 The pressure to achieve at school is really terrible.
5 That annoys me.
6 I think that's so unfair.
7 I simply can't stand it.

1b 📖🎧 Read the dialogues again and look at these statements. Write **T** (true), **F** (false), or **?** (not in the text).

Beispiel: 1 *T*

1 Antonia feels that she isn't making enough progress in her language lesson.
2 She gets on well with her class mates.
3 Ben thinks his friend does more revision than him.
4 His teacher offers to help him.
5 Claudia is being bullied.
6 Her mother thinks Claudia should leave her mobile phone at home.
7 Markus thinks he is prepared for the exam.
8 His father suggests that he should spend longer on revision.

2 **G** Complete these sentences with the correct German form for either 'could' or 'should'.

1 Vor deiner nächsten Prüfung _____ ich dir beim Wiederholen helfen. (können)

2 Meine jüngere Schwester _____ sich mehr um ihre Hausaufgaben kümmern. (sollen)

3 Wenn ich meine Zeit besser organisieren _____, würde ich ab und zu ins Kino gehen. (können)

4 Wenn du die Schule nicht verlassen willst, _____ du nächstes Jahr weiterlernen. (können)

5 Ich _____ fleißig sein und hart arbeiten, aber ich habe keine Lust dazu. (sollen)

6 Was _____ wir machen, um bessere Noten zu bekommen? (sollen)

3 🎧 Listen to Caroline, Florian, Annika and Patrick talking about their problems at school. Read these possible solutions and match them with the names.

1 Morgen werden die Leute über etwas anderes lachen. Vergiss es!

2 Du solltest dich ein bisschen entspannen, wenn du nicht in der Schule bist.

3 Vielleicht könntest du versuchen, selbstbewusster zu werden. Sprich zum Beispiel mit jemandem über Hobbys.

4 Freizeit ist wichtig. Du solltest versuchen, Zeit mit Freunden zu verbringen.

4 💬 What problems do you have at school? Work out how to tell your partner about your problems. When you are both ready, take it in turns to get things off your chest! Your partner should try to offer some advice.

In der Schule habe ich Schwierigkeiten mit		meinen Mitschülern. / Mitschülerinnen.
Den Leistungsdruck finde ich	furchtbar / unglaublich / unerträglich.	
Ich bin	bestimmt / gar	nicht selbstbewusst.
Ich finde	Französisch / Mathe / Prüfungen	nutzlos / total blöd / eine Zeitverschwendung …
	meine die meisten	Lehrer	unangenehm / unhöflich / schlecht gelaunt …
Ich habe viel Angst vor	meinen Lehrern / Mitschülern, denn sie sind immer …	
Meine Freunde lachen mich aus, weil	ich nicht die „richtigen" Klamotten trage. ich immer versuche, fleißig zu arbeiten.	
Du könntest Du solltest	fleißiger sein / mit … sprechen . Hilfe von deinem Bruder bekommen. deiner Lehrerin	
Du könntest / solltest versuchen,	dich mehr zu entspannen. andere Freunde / Freundinnen kennen zu lernen.	

Grammatik Seite 185

Saying what you could or ought to do

You have already seen one form of the imperfect subjunctive: *ich möchte …* to say that you 'would like' something (see page 73). To talk about things you 'could' or 'should' do, you need to use the imperfect subjunctive of the modal verbs *können* and *sollen*.

sollen – *ich sollte, du solltest,* etc. ('ought to')

e.g. *Ich sollte meine Hausaufgaben machen.*

können – *ich könnte, du könntest,* etc. ('could')

e.g. *Du könntest andere Freundinnen kennen lernen.*

Also learn four more subordinating conjunctions.

See page 145 ➡

Strategie 4

Starting sentences in different ways

It is important that you vary your language. For example, when talking about yourself here, avoid starting lots of sentences with *ich*. Instead you could start with an adverbial phrase of time, e.g. *manchmal*, *oft*, or you could use an adverbial phrase of place, e.g. *in der Schule*. Alternatively, you could start with a subordinate clause, e.g. *Wenn ich in der Schule bin, …* (Don't forget inversion after all of these.) Varying your language like this will show that you are able to use a range of structures, which is important in an assessment test.

7.3 F Nach meinen Prüfungen

1 ⓥ Place the following phrases into categories. Which refer to continuing your education and which don't?

1 die Schule verlassen
2 eine Lehre machen
3 auf die Uni gehen
4 in einer Fabrik arbeiten
5 eine Weltreise machen
6 in die Oberstufe gehen
7 mit der Schule weitermachen
8 einen Job finden

Meine Zukunft

Lena   Felix   Martina

Felix
Im Juni mache ich das Abitur. Wenn ich gute Noten bekomme, will ich auf die Uni gehen. Ich muss im Durchschnitt mindestens eine Drei haben. Ich werde wahrscheinlich Informatik studieren, weil ich mich für Computer interessiere. Danach werde ich bestimmt einen gut bezahlten Job bekommen.

Lena
Ich werde eine Lehre machen. Mein Vater ist Mechaniker und ich werde mit ihm arbeiten. Ich glaube, das wird sehr interessant sein. Es ist harte Arbeit, das weiß ich, aber das macht mir gar nichts aus. In der Zukunft will ich mein eigenes Geschäft gründen und er kann dann für mich arbeiten. Das wäre toll!

Martina
Ich bin mir überhaupt nicht sicher, was ich beruflich machen werde. Es gibt so viele Möglichkeiten. Ich bin nicht intelligent genug, um auf die Uni zu gehen, aber ich will auch nicht sofort einen Job haben. Ich will doch zuerst ein bisschen leben. Ich werde also nächstes Jahr eine Weltreise machen, bevor ich anfange zu arbeiten. Nachher werde ich keine Zeit mehr dafür haben.

2 📖🎧 Read these statements and find the correct three.

1 Felix has to get good grades.
2 He is hoping to work abroad.
3 Lena doesn't mind working hard.
4 She would like to work in a shop one day.
5 Until she can decide on a career, Martina wants to carry on studying.
6 She would like to see the world.

3 ⓖ Write the correct form of *werden* and add the infinitive in German of the word in brackets.

Beispiel: 1 *Ich werde nächstes Jahr Mathe und Physik studieren.*

1 Ich _____ nächstes Jahr Mathe und Physik _____. (*study*)
2 Meine Freundin _____ eine Lehre als Klempnerin _____. (*do*)
3 Nach den Prüfungen _____ wir uns Teilzeitjobs _____. (*look for*)
4 Im September _____ ich _____. (*continue studying*)
5 Mein Freund _____ hoffentlich in einer Fabrik _____. (*work*)
6 _____ Andreas einen Job _____? (*find*)
7 _____ du eine Weltreise _____? (*do*)
8 In der Zukunft _____ ich vielleicht auf die Uni _____. (*go*)

4a 🎧 Listen to these four young people describing their plans for the future. Match them with the following statements.

Beispiel: 1 *Speaker b*

1   … would like to be a professional football player.
2   … wants to study medicine or law at university.
3   … wants to be an electrician.
4   … says s/he works hard.
5   … says s/he hasn't decided yet what to do.
6   … wants to get good qualifications first.
7   … spends a lot each month.
8   … wants to work in a school or sports centre.

4b 🎧 Listen again then answer the following questions in English.

1   Where would Speaker **a** like to work?
2   What would Speaker **b** ideally like to do?
3   What does he hope to study?
4   What does Speaker **c** want to do straightaway?
5   What would make her happy?
6   Why is Speaker **d** uncertain about her plans?
7   What will she need to do to achieve her goal?

5 🗨 With a partner, take it in turns to interview each other about what you want to do after the exams. Explain why.

Was wirst du nach den Prüfungen machen?		
Nach den Prüfungen	werde ich will ich möchte ich	die Schule verlassen. eine Lehre machen. weiter zur Schule gehen. in einer Fabrik / in einem Büro arbeiten. zuerst Urlaub machen.
Ich habe die Nase voll von	Prüfungen / der Schule / Lehrern.	
Ich interessiere mich für	Naturwissenschaften / Informatik / Medienwissenschaft.	
Ich kann	die Schule / die Lehrer / den Direktor / die Schulordnung	… nicht leiden.

Grammatik • Seite 184

Talking about the future

Remember that when talking about what is going to happen you usually use the appropriate part of *werden* followed by an infinitive (see page 77).

Ich werde in Deutschland arbeiten.

You could also use the present tense and a future time reference like we sometimes do in English. *Nächstes Jahr arbeite ich in Deutschland.*

Also learn about using linking words.   *See page 144* ➡

Strategie 4a

Matching people to information

Read the questions carefully and decide what information you are looking for. Listen for a word or phrase which might show the answer is coming. For example, in questions 1 and 3, you should be listening for the names of jobs.

Strategie 5

Knowing which tenses to use

Look for clues in the question to help you with the tense of your answer. You should reuse the tense of the question in your answer:

*Was **machst** du nach den Prüfungen?*
*Ich **mache** eine Lehre.*
*Was **willst** du später machen?*
*Ich **will** auf die Uni gehen.*
*Was **wirst** du nächstes Jahr machen?*
*Ich **werde** die Schule verlassen.*

⚙ Hinweis

7.3 Groundwork is available in the Foundation Book.

7.3 H   Wie würdest du deine Schule verbessern?

◼ Als Direktor(in) meiner Traumschule würde ich ...

Thomas

Die neue Schule muss modern sein. Ich würde die neueste Technologie einführen. Die Schüler würden in jedem Klassenzimmer Computer benutzen, um ihre Aufgaben zu schreiben. Wir würden Experimente in den nagelneuen Labors machen und in allen Fächern Kameras, Handys und Video benutzen.

Martha

Ich würde Versammlungen organisieren, und die erste Stunde würde erst um halb zehn anfangen. Die Stunden müssten kürzer sein. Nach jeder Stunde müssten wir eine Pause haben. Wir würden anderthalb Stunden für das Mittagessen brauchen. Dann würden wir nicht nur essen sondern auch auf dem Sportplatz spielen oder Zeit für den Chor und das Schulorchester haben. Das Essen in der Kantine müsste auch billig und gesund sein. Keine fettigen Pommes mehr!

Jens

Ich würde eine Schuluniform tragen. Ich würde Prüfungen, Klassenarbeiten usw. verbieten. Kein Stress mehr! Sitzenbleiben ist auch unfair. Wir würden alle unsere Hausaufgaben in der Bibliothek oder in der Klasse machen und die Lehrer würden uns dabei helfen. Außerdem hätten wir mehr Zeit für Projekte, Sport und Drama.

1a 📖 🎧 Read what these people say about their ideal school. Find the German expressions for the following:

1 after every lesson
2 Apart from that we would have more time.
3 in all subjects
4 Repeating a school year is unfair too.

5 I'd introduce the latest technology.
6 one and a half hours
7 The teachers would help us with it.
8 Lessons would have to be shorter.

1b 📖 🎧 Read again what they say and match the names with the following statements.

Beispiel: 1 Martha

1 Food in the canteen would have to be cheap.
2 I would like to do my homework at school.
3 It is important that the school is up-to-date.
4 I would like school to start later than now.

5 I would get rid of exams.
6 There would be a break after each lesson.
7 Computers would be available in every classroom.

2 **ⓖ** What would these people say? Make up sentences to describe their thoughts using the conditional mood. The language structure box below will help you.

Beispiel: **a** *Ich würde einen neuen Tennisplatz bauen.*

a *einen neuen Tennisplatz*

d *einen Laptop*

b 9:30

c *keine Uniform*

e *viele Labors, viele Experimente*

3 🎧 Listen to Michaela asking her fellow pupils what they would like to see in their new school. Then answer the following questions in English.

1   Name **two** things Markus would like to have in school.
2   Name **two** things Matthias says about the building.
3   Name **two** ways he would improve the canteen.
4   Why do you have to get to the present canteen early?
5   When would Jutta's school be open?
6   What would the teachers do for the last part of the day?
7   Name **six** ways Maria would improve the sports facilities in school.

4 🖋 Have a competition where, working in a group, each of you writes a description of your ideal school. Decide who has the best one in your group, then it should be read out to the rest of the class. Include the following questions:

Ich würde	viele Labors / neue Sportplätze bauen.
Man würde	Prüfungen verbieten / abschaffen.
Die Schüle würde	Laptops kaufen.
Wir würden	interessantere Fächer einführen.
	keine Hausaufgaben machen.
	um 11 Uhr anfangen.

Meine (ideale) Schule	hätte	einen Laptop / gesundes Essen / viele Labors.
Jeder Schüler		
Jede Schülerin		

In der idealen Schule gäbe es	ein schönes Hallenbad / ein neues Theater.

Eine lange Pause / ein neuer Tennisplatz	... wäre eine gute Idee.

Die Lehrer / Lehrerinnen wären alle	hilfsbereit / begabt / gut gelaunt.

ⓖrammatik   Seite 184

Making conditional statements

To say what someone 'would do' in German you use the imperfect subjunctive of *werden* (*ich würde, du würdest* etc.) followed by an infinitive. This is called the conditional mood.

Die Schule würde um halb zehn anfangen. – School would begin at half past nine.

To say what someone 'could do / would be able to do', use the imperfect subjunctive form of *können* (*ich könnte, du könntest* etc.) followed by an infinitive.

Wir könnten nach Hause gehen. – We could go home.

To say what 'would have to happen', use the imperfect subjunctive form of *müssen* (*ich müsste, du müsstest* etc.) followed by an infinitive.

Die Stunden müssten kürzer sein. – Lessons would have to be shorter.

Also learn how to say 'would have' (*hätte*), 'would be' (*wäre*) and 'there would be', (*es gäbe*)

See page 145 ➡

• Wie wäre deine ideale Schule?
• Was würde man in deiner Schule machen?
• Welche Sportmöglichkeiten gäbe es?
• Wie wären die Lehrer und Lehrerinnen?

Avoiding the passive

The passive is used in English in sentences such as 'Exams would be banned'. It exists in German, but can be avoided by using *man*. So this sentence in German would be *Man würde Prüfungen verbieten* (lit. 'One would ban exams').

Strategie 4

School, college and future plans

1 Replace the underlined phrases with *dafür*, *darin* etc. as appropriate.

Beispiel: **1** *Darin gibt es viele Bücher.*

1 <u>In unserer Bibliothek</u> gibt es viele Bücher.
2 Hier ist die Aula. <u>Neben der Aula</u> liegt die Schulkantine.
3 <u>Nach der Pause</u> sind wir ins Klassenzimmer gegangen.
4 Meine Hefte sind <u>in meiner Schultasche</u>.
5 <u>Für Hobbys</u> habe ich im Augenblick keine Zeit. Ich habe zu viele Hausaufgaben.
6 Mein Kuli liegt <u>auf dem Tisch</u>.
7 Es gibt ein neues Gebäude <u>für Fremdsprachen</u>.
8 Heute bin ich nicht <u>mit dem Schulbus</u> gefahren, weil ich mit dem Rad kommen wollte.

> ### Using prepositions with 'it' / 'that' / 'them'
> If you want to use a preposition with the word 'it', 'that' or 'them' (when referring to things), add *da* in front of the preposition, e.g. *dafür* ('for it / that / them'), *daneben* ('next to it / that / them').
> If the preposition begins with a vowel, you add *dar*, e.g. *darin* ('in it / that / them'), *darauf* ('on it / that / them').
>
> *Grammatik*

2 Read the passage below. Make a list of the things described and who they belong to. How many different ways of showing possession can you find?

In Deutschland war das Klassenzimmer meines Austauschpartners prima. Ich habe ein Foto davon gemacht. Das Arbeitsheft meines Partners liegt auf dem Tisch. Die Jacke auf dem Stuhl gehört mir. Neben dem Fenster sieht man den Lehrer. Seine Butterbrote liegen neben dem Computer.

> ### Ways of denoting possession
> There is more than one way of showing possession in German. You could use the genitive case:
> *Hier ist **das Lineal meines Freundes**.*   See page 176 ➡
> *von* + the dative:
> *Hier ist **das Lineal von meinem Freund**.* See page 176 ➡
> add an *-s*, like in English (note that there is no apostrophe used in German and that this form of the possessive can only be used with names):
> *Hier ist **Peters Lineal**.*
> use possessive adjectives:
> *Hier ist **sein Lineal**.*   See page 175 ➡
>
> *Grammatik*

3 Copy out the sentences, starting the second one with a suitable linking word from the grammar box. Aim to vary your answers.

Beispiel: **1** *Ich will gute Noten bekommen. Dann / Danach will ich auf die Uni gehen.*

1 Ich will gute Noten bekommen. Ich will auf die Uni gehen.
2 Englisch finde ich sehr interessant. Ich will weiter zur Schule gehen.
3 Ich möchte in der Zukunft in Frankreich arbeiten. Ich muss gute Noten in Französisch bekommen.
4 In fünf Jahren will ich eine gute Stelle haben. Ich möchte eine Weltreise machen.
5 Eines Tages will mein Bruder Elektriker werden. Er muss zuerst eine Lehre machen.
6 Ich hasse die Lehrer hier. Ich will die Schule sofort verlassen.
7 Ich wollte in die Oberstufe gehen. Meine Noten sind nicht gut genug.

> ### Using linking words
> You can make your writing and speaking 'flow' (sound more natural) by using linking words such as *daher* ('therefore'), *deswegen* / *deshalb* ('therefore', 'that's why …'), *dann* ('then'), *danach* ('afterwards'), *vorher* ('beforehand'), *jedoch* ('however'), *also* ('so', 'therefore').
> Don't forget to put the verb next after these words. For more on this, see page 151.
>
> *Grammatik*   Seite 187

4 Translate the following sentences into German.

1 I was supposed to go to the computer room after I had been in the sports hall.
2 My friend (m) was ill because he had eaten in the canteen.
3 The teacher (f) was angry as we had not done our homework.
4 After she had eaten a sandwich, she went into the classroom.
5 We were allowed to chat to each other after we had read the book.

> ### The pluperfect tense
>
> The pluperfect tense refers to something that **had happened** before something else happened, e.g.
>
> *Ich bin in die Schule gegangen, nachdem ich gefrühstückt hatte.* – I went to school after I **had** eaten my breakfast.
>
> For the pluperfect the auxiliary is the appropriate form of the imperfect of *sein* or *haben*, e.g.
>
> *Ich **hatte** meine Arbeit gemacht.* – I **had** done my work.
>
> *Ich **war** in die Kantine gegangen.* – I **had** gone to the canteen.
>
> The past participle remains the same. For the imperfect forms of *sein* and *haben*, see page 183.
>
> *Grammatik — Seite 184*

5a Join the phrases below using the conjunctions indicated.

1 Ich war sehr fleißig. Ich war gestern Abend zu Hause. (als)
2 Meine Freundin spielt Klarinette im Schulorchester. Die Schule ist aus. (sobald)
3 Niemand durfte sprechen. Wir hatten Prüfung. (während)
4 Ich muss diese Verben lernen. Ich gehe ins Bett. (bevor)
5 Michael und ich machen unsere Hausaufgaben. Wir sind zu Hause angekommen. (sobald)
6 Wir durften auf den Schulhof gehen. Die Prüfung war zu Ende. (als)

> ### Four more subordinating conjunctions
>
> Try to include a wide variety of these when writing and speaking. For instance, avoid always using *weil*. For a change, use *da* instead. It will make your work more interesting and could gain you a higher mark too. Here are four more useful subordinating conjunctions which, like *weil*, send the verb to the end:
>
> *als* – when (referring to one occasion in the past)
>
> *bevor* – before   *sobald* – as soon as
>
> *während* – while
>
> For more on this, see page 151.
>
> *Grammatik — Seite 188*

5b Once your teacher has checked your answers, rewrite the sentences from the previous activity, starting each with the subordinating conjunction.

6 Use the conditional forms of the verbs *sein* and *haben* and / or the phrase *es gäbe* … to describe an ideal school as indicated by the pictures. The phrases in the box may also help you.

Beispiel: Meine ideale Schule wäre auf dem Land. Mein Klassenzimmer hätte die neueste Technologie.

eine moderne Sporthalle	ein modernes Labor
ein großes Zimmer, wo …	einen Sportplatz
eine kleine Schule	die neueste Technologie
ich könnte	nicht streng

> ### The conditional forms of *haben*, *sein* and *geben*
>
> The conditional (imperfect subjunctive) forms of *haben* and *sein* are the German equivalents of the English 'would have' and 'would be':
>
> | | |
> |---|---|
> | *ich hätte* | *ich wäre* |
> | *du hättest* | *du wärst* |
> | *er / sie / es hätte* | *er / sie / es wäre* |
> | *wir hätten* | *wir wären* |
> | *ihr hättet* | *ihr wärt* |
> | *sie hätten* | *sie wären* |
> | *Sie hätten* | *Sie wären* |
>
> To say 'there would be' you need to use the imperfect subjunctive form of *es gibt: es gäbe*.
>
> *Grammatik — Seite 185*

School, college and future plans

Topic 7.1 Comparing schools

7.1 F Ich möchte meine Schule beschreiben
➡ *pages 132–133*

die	AG	extra-curricular group activity chosen by students
	anders	different(ly)
der	Augenblick	moment
die	Aula	school hall
	dauern	to last
das	Fach	subject
das	Freibad	open-air swimming pool
die	Fremdsprache	foreign language
	(sich) freuen	to be pleased
die	Ganztagsschule	school that lasts all day
die	Gesamtschule	comprehensive school
die	Grundschule	primary school
das	Gymnasium	grammar school
das	Heft	exercise book
das	Internat	boarding school
das	Mitglied	member
das	Orchester	orchestra
	sowohl ... als auch	both ... and
die	Stunde	hour, lesson
	unterrichten	to teach

7.1 H Meine Schule ist anders ➡ *pages 134–135*

	anfangen	to start
	(etwas) anziehen	to put on (clothes)
der	Austausch	exchange
	beginnen	to begin
	brauchen	to need
	eben	just
	enden	to end, to finish
	früh	early
	gleich	same

der	Hausmeister	caretaker
die	Klassenarbeit	class test
	(sich) konzentrieren	to concentrate
die	Mannschaft	team
	plaudern	to chat
die	Schuluniform	school uniform
das	Schulwesen	school system
der	Schüler / die Schülerin	pupil, student
der	Stundenplan	timetable
	(sich) unterhalten	to talk to / with
	völlig	completely

Topic 7.2 Addressing school pressures and problems

7.2 F Hast du Stress in der Schule?
➡ *pages 136–137*

das	Abitur	exams taken at 18 (A-level equivalent)
der	Abschluss	final examination
	Angst haben	to be afraid
die	Aufgabe	task, job
	auslachen	to laugh at
	besprechen	to discuss
	gehören (+ dat)	to belong to
die	Klamotten (pl)	clothes
	kompliziert	complicated
	meinen	to think
	nachsitzen	to have detention
	nervös	nervous
	in Ordnung	fine, okay
	peinlich	painful, embarrassing
	schwer	difficult, hard
	sitzen bleiben	to repeat a school year
	trotzdem	nevertheless
	verbringen	to spend (time)
	versuchen	to try, to attempt
	(sich) vorbereiten	to prepare

7.2 H Wir haben zu viel Druck ➡ *pages 138–139*

der	*Außenseiter*	outsider
	deprimiert	depressed
	eifersüchtig	jealous
eine	*Frage stellen*	to ask a question
der	*Fremdsprachenassistent*	foreign language assistant
	hoffen	to hope
	jemand	someone
	(sich um etw.) kümmern	to worry (about)
der	*Leistungsdruck*	pressure to achieve
die	*Lust*	desire, pleasure
	(sich) schminken	to put on make-up
	selbstbewusst	self-confident
die	*Sprachkenntnisse (pl)*	knowledge of the language
	verbessern	to improve
	vergessen	to forget
	verlassen	to leave
	verstehen	to understand
	weiterstudieren	to do further study
	wiederholen	to revise

Topic 7.3 Present school, future school, ideal school

7.3 F Nach meinen Prüfungen ➡ *pages 140–141*

	ankommen auf etw.	to depend on sth.
	ausmachen	to matter
	ein bisschen	a little
	beruflich	career-wise, in terms of a job
der	*Elektriker / die Elektrikerin*	electrician
	entweder ... oder	either ... or
die	*Fabrik*	factory
	gründen	to found, to set up
der	*Klempner / die Klempnerin*	plumber
die	*Möglichkeit*	possibility
	noch nicht	not yet

die	*Oberstufe*	sixth form
die	*Qualifikation*	qualification
die	*Schulordnung*	school rules
	sicher	sure, safe
	sofort	straightaway
die	*Stelle*	job, position
	Teilzeit-	part-time
die	*Uni(versität)*	university
	unmöglich	impossible

7.3 H Wie würdest du deine Schule verbessern? ➡ *pages 142–143*

	anbieten	to offer
	anderthalb	one and a half
	außerdem	besides, apart from that
die	*Auswahl*	choice, selection
	bauen	to build
der	*Chor*	choir
	einführen	to introduce
	erstens	firstly
das	*Gebäude*	building
	mindestens	at least
	nicht nur ... sondern auch	not only ... but also
	notwendig	necessary
das	*Pflichtfach*	compulsory subject
	sonst	else, otherwise
die	*Speise*	dish, food
	übrig bleiben	to be left over
der	*Unterricht*	lessons, classes
die	*Versammlung*	assembly
	vorschlagen	to suggest
das	*Wahlfach*	optional subject

8.1 F Hast du einen Job?

Lernziele

Discussing part-time jobs

Not always using the indefinite article

Planning a piece of writing

1 ⓥ Match up the jobs with the workplaces.

Park   Straße   Lehrer   Krankenpfleger   Polizist

Schule   Gärtner   Verkäuferin   Krankenhaus

Geschäft   Restaurant   Köchin

◼ Mein Nebenjob

Karin

Ich habe viele Nebenjobs. Jeden Morgen muss ich früh aufstehen, um Zeitungen auszutragen, und abends gehe ich oft babysitten. Manchmal arbeite ich auch in einem Café, wo ich die Teller abwasche. Ab und zu bin ich auch Kellnerin im Café, aber nur wenn jemand krank ist. Ich habe fast so gut wie keine Freizeit, aber ich kann eine Menge Geld verdienen.

Georg

Ich arbeite samstags in einer Bäckerei. Ich möchte nämlich Bäcker werden, wenn ich mit der Schule fertig bin. Ich bekomme nicht viel Geld dafür, aber ich lerne viel. Der Nachteil an der Arbeit ist, dass es durch die Backöfen sehr heiß werden kann.

Monika

Am Wochenende helfe ich meinem Vater. Er ist Gärtner. Wir arbeiten natürlich im Freien und ich muss Rasen mähen usw. Er gibt mir nur €10 pro Tag und ich spare es für meinen Urlaub. Es macht Spaß, wenn die Sonne scheint, aber es ist auch anstrengend.

2 📖🎧 Read the texts about part-time jobs. Who does what? Match the pictures to the people.

Beispiel: a *Karin*

a   b   c   d   e   f

3 Ⓖ Decide which of the following sentences need an article. For those sentences which need one, fill in the gaps with the correct form of the article.

Beispiel: 1 *Er ist Mechaniker und arbeitet in einer Werkstatt.*

1 Er ist _____ Mechaniker und arbeitet in einer Werkstatt.

2 Sie ist _____ Tierärztin und arbeitet gern mit Tieren.

3 In der Stadtmitte gibt es _____ Bibliothek.

4 Sie ist _____ Klempnerin.

5 In unserer Stadt gibt es nur _____ Schule.

6 Er ist _____ LKW-Fahrer.

8 Samstags helfe ich meiner Tante. Sie ist _____ Bäckerin.

> **Ⓖrammatik** Seite 174
>
> ## Not always using the indefinite article.
>
> In German the indefinite article is not used if you want to express what someone's job is.
>
> *Er ist Koch.* – He is a chef.
>
> *Sie ist Kelllnerin.* – She is a waitress.
>
> You do use the indefinite article if you are talking about a job without identifying a particular person, e.g.
>
> *Wir suchen eine Kellnerin.* – We are looking for a waitress.
>
> Also learn about using alternative time phrases. *See page 160* ➡

4 🎧 Listen to Lennard and Christina talking about their part-time jobs. Choose the correct answers.

Beispiel: 1 *c*

1 Lennard babysits … **a** on Saturdays **b** twice a week **c** three times a week.

2 Yesterday he earned … **a** 3 euros an hour **b** 8 euros an hour **c** nothing.

3 He … **a** enjoys babysitting **b** doesn't like his cousin **c** has to babysit for a neighbour.

4 He thinks helping at weekends is … **a** a waste of time **b** good experience **c** a way to earn extra money.

5 On Saturday, Christina worked in a … **a** butcher's **b** baker's **c** hairdresser's.

6 She thinks the job is … **a** enjoyable **b** okay **c** boring.

7 Usually, she … **a** shampoos customers' hair **b** works on the till **c** tidies up.

8 In the future, she would like to … **a** be a police officer **b** have her own business **c** be a shop assistant.

5 ✏ Write a blog about your part-time job (real or imaginary). Mention what you do, how long you worked this week, how much you earned and what you thought about it. Mention any other details you can.

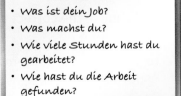

- *Was ist dein Job?*
- *Was machst du?*
- *Wie viele Stunden hast du gearbeitet?*
- *Wie hast du die Arbeit gefunden?*

> ## Planning a piece of writing
> **Strategie 5**
>
> ■ Make sure you know what you have to include in your work.
>
> ■ Write one paragraph per bullet point.
>
> ■ Make a checklist of the structures you want to use, e.g. tenses, subordinate clauses.
>
> ■ Remember ADORE. Look back at page 133.

> ⊖⊖⊖ **Hinweis**
>
> 8.1 Groundwork is available in the Foundation Book.

8.1 H Wie war dein Arbeitspraktikum?

Lernziele

Talking about work experience

Coordinating and subordinating conjunctions (revision)

Don't wait to be asked

Lehrer: Sonja, wo hast du dein Arbeitspraktikum verbracht?

Sonja: Ich habe mein Praktikum in einem Büro verbracht. Das war bei einer großen Firma am Stadtrand, die Rasenmäher herstellt.

Lehrer: Wann war das eigentlich?

Sonja: Das war letzten Oktober.

Lehrer: Und wie lange warst du da?

Sonja: Leider, nur eine Woche. Es war schade, dass ich nicht länger bleiben konnte.

Lehrer: Was hast du dort gemacht?

Sonja: Ich habe das Telefon beantwortet und manchmal Briefe getippt, obwohl ich manchmal Fehler gemacht habe. Gewöhnlich waren die Kunden am Telefon ganz höflich, aber das war nicht immer so.

Lehrer: Wie hast du dein Arbeitspraktikum gefunden?

Sonja: Die Arbeit war eigentlich nicht so interessant, zum Beispiel war es schade, dass ich ich keine Gelegenheit dazu hatte, meine Sprachkenntnisse zu benutzen. Trotzdem hat mir das Praktikum Spaß gemacht, weil meine Kollegen sehr lustig waren. Auch war die Chefin sehr sympathisch.

Lehrer: Und wie war die Arbeitszeit?

Sonja: Das Praktikum war besser als die Schule, aber am Ende des Tages war ich total müde. Bis siebzehn Uhr zu arbeiten war anstrengend. Gott sei Dank habe ich keine Schichtarbeit machen müssen.

Lehrer: Was möchtest du in Zukunft machen?

Sonja: Es hat mich sehr gefreut, diese Erfahrung zu machen, besonders weil die Kollegen so nett waren, aber ich will mein Leben nicht in einem Büro verbringen. Es ist mein Traum, in Zukunft mit Tieren zu arbeiten. Ich möchte Tierärztin werden.

1a 📖 🎧 Read the interview between Sonja and her teacher and find the German words / phrases for the following:

1 spent
2 manufactures
3 answered
4 customers
5 colleagues
6 working hours
7 shift work
8 experience

1b 📖 🎧 Read the interview again and choose the correct answers.

Beispiel: 1 *a*

1 Sonja did work experience at a factory making … **a** lawn-mowers **b** dish-washers **c** cookers.
2 She thought a week there was … **a** too long **b** about right **c** too short.
3 Sometimes she … **a** found writing letters easy **b** made mistakes **c** sent fax messages.
4 Customers on the phone were … **a** always polite **b** sometimes unclear **c** sometimes rude.
5 She used her languages … **a** never **b** occasionally **c** daily.
6 She … **a** disliked the boss **b** got on well with her colleagues **c** wasn't really accepted.
7 She was glad that she … **a** finished at seven **b** could work overtime **c** worked normal hours.
8 In the future she hopes to … **a** work abroad **b** work as a vet **c** gain more office experience.

2 **G** Link the pairs of sentences with the conjunction given in brackets.

Beispiel: 1 *Mein Arbeitspraktikum war ermüdend, aber es hat viel Spaß gemacht.*

1 Mein Arbeitspraktikum war ermüdend. Es hat viel Spaß gemacht. (aber)
2 Ich habe mich gefreut. Die Woche war zu Ende. (als)
3 Mein Vater musste mich täglich zur Fabrik fahren. Es gab keine guten Busverbindungen. (denn)
4 Ich habe im Büro gearbeitet. Ich habe viele nette Leute kennengelernt. (und)
5 Wir waren alle überrascht. Die Woche war so schnell vorbei. (dass)
6 Ich hatte die Nase voll. Ich hatte nur einen Tag in der Fabrik verbracht. (nachdem)
7 Meine Kollegen haben mir geholfen. Ich durfte den Computer allein benutzen. (bevor)

3 🎧 Listen to Florian and Brigitte talking about their work experience. Answer the questions in English.

1 What did Florian say about sorting the post?
2 What did he do next?
3 Which **three** things did he do in the afternoon?
4 How did he get home?
5 When exactly did Brigitte help the children with reading?
6 What did she say she did at lunchtime?
7 How did she feel about what she had to do in the afternoon?

4 🗨 Taking it in turns, interview a partner about work experience (real or imaginary), using the questions on the clipboard.

- Wo hast du gearbeitet?
- Wann war das?
- Wie lange warst du da?
- Was hast du gemacht?
- Wie hast du dein Arbeitspraktikum gefunden und warum war das so?
- Was möchtest du in Zukunft machen?

Grammatik *Seite 187*

Coordinating and subordinating conjunctions (revision)

Remember that after coordinating conjunctions *und* (and), *aber* (but), *denn* (because) the word order is unaffected:

*Meine Kollegen waren sehr nett, **aber** die Arbeit war langweilig.*

After subordinating conjunctions *weil* (because), *da* (since, as), *wenn* (when, if, whenever), *als* (when), *obwohl* (although), *dass* (that), *bis* (until), *ob* (whether), *bevor* (before), *nachdem* (after), *seitdem* (since), *sobald* (as soon as), *während* (while) the verb must go to the end of the clause or sentence:

*Mein Praktikum hat mir keinen Spaß gemacht, **da** ich nur Tee und Kaffee gekocht **habe**.*

Also revise how to use the perfect tense. *See page 161* ➡

Strategie 4

Don't wait to be asked

If you are asked a question and can give extra information after you have answered it, always do so. You don't have to wait for the teacher to ask you another question. For example, you are asked here about what you did on work experience, so if you did a few things, talk about all of them, not just one. The more information you can provide the better, as this is showing your ability to **narrate events**. In addition, because you are keeping the conversation going with a flow of information, you are showing **initiative**. These are both qualities which will enhance your performance in a Speaking assessment!

8.2 F Zukunftspläne

Lernziele

Discussing career plans

Using the future tense (revision)

Varying your language

1 **V** Using the vocabulary list on page 162, place these words which refer to jobs in the correct category: mainly outdoors – mainly indoors – both.

Beispiel: **mainly outdoors mainly indoors both**
Postbote

Postbote Apothekerin Bauarbeiter Bauer Beamte Fahrer

Feuerwehrmann Hausfrau Ingenieur Kassiererin Kauffrau

Maler Pfarrer Schauspielerin Reiseleiter Tischlerin

Jessica: Wenn meine Noten gut genug sind, hoffe ich, auf die Uni zu gehen. Ich will Erdkunde studieren, weil ich die Umwelt so faszinierend finde. Später möchte ich als Lehrerin arbeiten, denn junge Leute müssen verstehen, wie wichtig ihre Umwelt ist.

Lars: Nach meinem Studium will ich mein eigenes Geschäft gründen. In meiner Freizeit habe ich schon eine Webseite – einen Online-Markt, wo ich ein paar alte Sachen, zum Beispiel Kleidung, CDs, Spielzeuge usw. kaufe und verkaufe. Damit habe ich schon etwas Erfolg, also will ich ein richtiges Unternehmen haben.

Isabell: Nach der Uni hoffe ich natürlich, einen gut bezahlten Job zu finden, aber zuerst werde ich ein Jahr aussetzen. Danach möchte ich als Apothekerin arbeiten. Obwohl ich keine Ärztin werden will, interessiere ich mich für Medizin.

2a 📖📖 🎧 Three sixth formers have written about their career plans for the school magazine. Look at these statements. Write **T** (true), **F** (false), or **?** (not in the text).

Beispiel: 1 *T*

1 Jessica wants to continue studying.
2 She thinks history is fascinating.
3 She wants to go on a cruise.
4 She would like everyone to appreciate the environment.
5 Lars wants to go to university.
6 He sells things on the internet.
7 Isabell wants a job as soon as possible.

2b 📖📖 🎧 Read the plans again and match the names to the statements.

Beispiel: 1 *Lars*

1 I want to have a proper business.
2 I intend having a gap-year.
3 I am keen on geography.
4 I don't want to be a doctor.
5 The internet is important to me.
6 Getting good results is important for my career.
7 I hope to earn a lot of money.
8 I want to work in education.

3 🅖 Rewrite the following sentences using *werden* + infinitive:

Beispiel: 1 *Im November werde ich eine Lehre machen.*

1 Im November mache ich eine Lehre.
2 Nächstes Jahr geht meine ältere Schwester auf die Uni.
3 Was machst du in zehn Jahren?
4 Hoffentlich bekommen wir gute Noten.
5 Meine Freunde und ich machen im September mit der Schule weiter.
6 Welche Fächer wählt ihr in der Oberstufe?
7 Ich mache zuerst eine Weltreise.

4 🎧 Listen to Timo being interviewed by his teacher about his career plans. Choose the correct answers.

Beispiel: 1 *c*

1 After university, Timo wants to …
  a get an apprenticeship   b have a holiday   c work abroad.
2 Timo says he is interested in …
  a cooking   b languages   c sightseeing.
3 At school, he is studying …
  a two   b three   c four languages.
4 He wants to learn Spanish because of the …
  a weather   b people   c food.
5 His favourite subject is …
  a ICT   b French   c history.
6 He wants his first job to be as a …
  a hairdresser   b tour guide   c computer programmer.

5 🗨 Taking it in turns, interview a partner about their future career plans and why they want to pursue those plans.

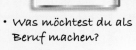

- Was möchtest du als Beruf machen?
- Warum?
- Wirst du vielleicht im Ausland arbeiten?
- Warum (nicht)?

Using the future tense (revision)

Grammatik · Seite 184

Remember that to form the future tense, you use the present tense of *werden* + infinitive (at the end of the sentence or clause).

	+ infinitive
ich werde	*gründen*
du wirst	*finden*
er / sie / es wird	*brauchen*
wir werden	*gehen*
ihr werdet	*bekommen*
sie / Sie werden	*studieren*

Wenn ich mit der Schule fertig bin, werde ich einen Job suchen. – After I am finished with school, I will look for a job.

In fünf Jahren werde ich ein erfolgreiches Unternehmen haben. – In five years' time I'll have a successful business.

Remember that there are different ways of talking about the future. *See page 160* ➡

Varying your language

Strategie 5

Try to vary the way you express your future plans. As well as the suggestions in the grammar box, you could also use *ich möchte* or *ich will* plus an infinitive to say what you want to do. Remember that *ich will* means 'I want', **not** 'I will'.

Ich möchte einmal	Lehrer(in) / Kaufmann / Kauffrau / Polizist(in)	werden.
Ich will / werde als		arbeiten.
Diese Arbeit interessiert mich sehr.		
Ich finde diesen Beruf	interessant / faszinierend.	
Ich werde	in England / Deutschland / in den USA	arbeiten, weil das Gehalt dort besser ist.
Ich will nicht im Ausland arbeiten,	da	meine Familie in … lebt. ich hier zufrieden bin.

⊝⊝⊝ **Hinweis**

8.2 Groundwork is available in the Foundation Book.

8.2 H Ich möchte mich um diese Stelle bewerben

Lernziele

Applying for a job

Saying 'when' (revision)

Inferring information when reading

1a 📖 🎧 Read Andrea's job application letter and identify the words which will fit into these categories:

job	workplace	personal quality
Köchin, …	Restaurant, …	freundlich, …

1b 📖 🎧 Read the letter again and answer the following questions in English.

Beispiel: **1** *By baking cakes*

1 How did Andrea help at home?

2 Name **two** things she enjoyed doing.

3 Which **three** things did she have to do on work experience?

4 Why does she like her Saturday job?

5 Why do you think she preferred her work experience?

6 When did she not get on with her colleagues?

7 What made her choose this career?

8 How can we tell she is a tolerant person?

9 How do we know she is ambitious?

10 What does she reassure the people she is writing to about?

2 🄶 Complete the sentences by using the correct word for 'when'.

Beispiel: **1** *Wann*

1 _____ können Sie anfangen?

2 _____ ich 15 war, habe ich in einem Restaurant gearbeitet.

3 _____ ich arbeite, bin ich immer fleißig.

4 _____ ich die Schule verlasse, werde ich einen Job suchen.

5 Ich habe oft Tee gekocht, _____ ich im Büro gearbeitet habe.

6 _____ hast du dort gearbeitet?

Sehr geehrte Damen und Herren,

ich möchte mich um die Stelle als Köchin in Ihrem Restaurant bewerben. Ich interessiere mich seit langem für das Kochen. Als ich jünger war, habe ich Kuchen gebacken, und ich war immer froh zuzuschauen oder mitzuhelfen, wenn meine Mutter Mahlzeiten zubereitet hat.

Letzten April habe ich ein Arbeitspraktikum in einem Hotelrestaurant gemacht, wo ich allerlei Aufgaben übernehmen musste, zum Beispiel Gemüse schneiden, die Küche aufräumen, Töpfe und Teller abwaschen usw. Auch habe ich Erfahrung als Kellnerin, weil ich samstags in einem Café arbeite. Ich bin eine freundliche Person und es gefällt mir dort, da ich die Gelegenheit habe, mit Kunden zu reden.

Ich muss jedoch sagen, dass mir die Arbeit in der Hotelküche mehr Spaß gemacht hat, obwohl es ein paar Nachteile gab. Weil alles möglichst schnell gehen musste, war die Arbeit anstrengend. Außerdem war es gewöhnlich sehr warm in der Küche. Meine Kollegen und ich sind meistens sehr gut miteinander ausgekommen, aber wenn ich ab und zu einen Fehler gemacht habe, dann war es anders – dann haben sie mich angeschrien. Am Ende jedes Tages war ich völlig erschöpft. Trotzdem hat es mir viel Spaß gemacht, denn ich habe dort viel gelernt – ich war so begeistert. Deswegen habe ich mich entschieden, dass Kochen mein Traumberuf ist.

Obwohl ich weiß, dass ich noch viel zu lernen habe, kann ich ehrlich sagen, dass ich fleißig und zuverlässig bin. Ich bin immer pünktlich und arbeite gern in einem Team. Eines Tages möchte ich die erfolgreiche Besitzerin eines eigenen Restaurants sein, aber ich will zuerst in Ihrem berühmten Restaurant arbeiten.

Wenn ich die Gelegenheit hätte, bei Ihnen zu arbeiten, dann bin ich sicher, dass Sie mit mir zufrieden wären. Ich wäre sehr dankbar, wenn Sie mir sagen könnten, wann die Vorstellungsgespräche stattfinden, weil ich im August im Urlaub bin. Ich freue mich auf Ihre Antwort.

Mit freundlichen Grüßen

Ihre

Andrea Schneider

3a 🎥 🎧 Listen to / watch Fräulein Kassel's interview and choose the correct answers.

1 The interviewers hope Fräulein Kassel …   a isn't nervous   b didn't have to wait long   c had a good journey.

2 Her current job is …   a not well paid   b boring   c tiring.

3 She …   a likes computers   b wants to avoid computers   c designs computers.

4 She has experience working with …   a animals   b children   c computers.

5 According to her, she …   a is reliable   b likes a joke   c is honest.

6 Before she can start, she will have to …   a supply a reference   b cancel a holiday   c hand in her notice.

7 If she gets the job, she will have to work …   a overtime   b shifts   c at weekends.

8 She asks about …   a flexi-time   b holidays   c her salary.

3b 🎥 🎧 Listen to / watch the interview again and answer the following questions in English.

Beispiel: 1 *More responsibility*

1 What does she say she would like to have in the new job?

2 What kind of experience does she have? Name **two** things.

3 Give **three** reasons why she thinks she should get the job.

4 Apart from being a team player, name **five** other personal qualities she mentions.

4 ✏️ Write an application for a job in Switzerland during the summer holidays. (You can decide which job you would like.) Use the letter on page 154 as a model.

Mention the following points:

- your qualities
- work experience
- what kind of work you want
- when you could start

Strategie 1b

Inferring information when reading

An important skill is being able to infer information, i.e. understand a point of information without it being said explicitly. For example, for question 9, Andrea doesn't actually say she is ambitious, but it can be understood that she is because she mentions she would like her own restaurant one day.

Grammatik   Seite 187

Saying 'when' (revision)

Wenn can mean 'when', 'if' or 'whenever' and is used to refer to the present, future or a habitual action in the past.

Wenn ich mit den Kunden gesprochen habe, waren sie meistens höflich.

Als means 'when' and refers to a particular event in the past.

Als mein Arbeitspraktikum zu Ende war, war ich ganz traurig.

Wann introduces a 'when' question, in any tense.

Wann haben Sie im Hotel gearbeitet?

Also learn how to use *seit*.

See page 161 ➡

Ich bin der Meinung,	dass ich	viele gute Eigenschaften / einen guten Sinn für Humor habe.	
Ich glaube,	ich bin	freundlich / ehrlich / pünktlich / fleißig / selbstbewusst.	
Meine Freunde meinen,	dass ich	ehrlich / treu / zuverlässig bin.	
Ich habe	in einer Fabrik / mit Kindern	gearbeitet.	
	aufgeräumt / Autos geputzt / Telefonanrufe geantwortet.		
	mein Arbeitspraktikum bei … verbracht.		
Ich war	eine Woche / zehn Tage dort.		
Meiner Meinung nach war das	sehr nützlich für meine künftige Karriere reine Zeitverschwendung.		
Das Praktikum hat mir (nicht) gefallen,	weil mir der Chef (nicht) vertraut hat. weil ich zu viel / sehr wenig zu tun hatte. da es mich (nicht) herausgefordert hat.		
Wenn möglich möchte ich	mich um die Stelle als Gärtner(in) / Koch / Köchin … bewerben.		
Ich könnte	Anfang August / Ende Juni	anfangen.	

8.3 F Am Arbeitsplatz

1 **V** Using the vocabulary list on page 163, unscramble these words and translate them into English.

Beispiel: 1 *Bewerbung (application)*

1 webgruben
2 prokeine
3 checkins
4 unage
5 lemia
6 prescheenb
7 getrulane
8 chirchtan

2a 📖 🎧 Read these messages for Mr Schmidt and match them to the following statements.

Beispiel: a *2*

a Mr Schmidt has to write something about his life and career.
b A colleague is ill.
c Someone has rung up.
d Mr Schmidt is looking for a new job.
e He has received some documents.
f He will be getting an email.

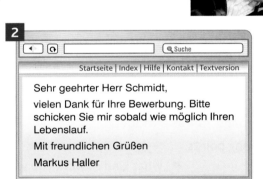

1

Fräulein Meier hat angerufen. Sie wollte etwas mit Ihnen besprechen, aber sie wird Ihnen jetzt eine E-Mail schicken. Sie müssen sie nicht zurückrufen.

2

Startseite | Index | Hilfe | Kontakt | Textversion

Sehr geehrter Herr Schmidt,

vielen Dank für Ihre Bewerbung. Bitte schicken Sie mir sobald wie möglich Ihren Lebenslauf.

Mit freundlichen Grüßen

Markus Haller

3

Hans,

Renate ist vorbeigekommen. Du solltest diese Unterlagen zuerst lesen, unterschreiben und dann kopieren, damit sie sie heute Nachmittag zurückhaben kann.

Gisela

4

Frau Kohl musste nach Hause gehen. Sie hat Magenschmerzen und Durchfall. Sie wird morgen mit Ihnen telefonieren.

2b 📖 🎧 Write these messages in German. Refer to the messages above to help you.

1 Mr Braun had to go home. He has a headache and sore throat. He will phone you on Monday.
2 Mrs Heinke has rung. You must ring back tomorrow.
3 Mr Bäcker called by. He wanted to discuss something with you.

3 **G** Complete the sentences by filling the gap with an appropriate dative pronoun (for the last two, translate the English given in brackets).

Beispiel: 1 *ihm*

1 Johann ist im Büro. Du sollst mit _____ telefonieren.
2 Serena kommt morgen. Du sollst _____ sagen, wo das Hotel liegt.
3 Ich habe kein Geld. Kannst du _____ 20 € geben?
4 Ich gehe mit _____ dorthin. (*them*)
5 Frau Gens hat _____ eine E-Mail geschickt. (*you – familiar plural*)

4a 🎧 Listen to the voicemails. Choose the four correct statements.

a You should ring Dirk on 453868.
b Frau Ballack will ring you tomorrow at 10.45.
c Frank is going to the dentist's tomorrow.
d The caller has received Andrea's email.
e You are going to meet at the town hall next week.
f Herr Müller has to use tram no. 7.
g Stefanie wants to meet up the day after tomorrow.

4b 🎧 Listen again. Fill in the missing details.

a You need to ring back on telephone number _____.
b Frau Ballack will meet Herr Bauer at _____ in _____.
c Frank is going to _____.
d The _____ looks good. Andrea should now _____.
e Next week's meeting will be at the _____.
f To get to the office Herr Müller should take the _____. The office is _____.
g Stefanie would like to see Julia _____. Julia needs to contact her by _____.

5 🖋 Write a business e-mail about your forthcoming visit to a company, giving details of exactly when and where you are meeting.

Sehr geehrter Herr _ / Sehr geehrte Frau _			
Ich komme gern	morgen am _	zu einem Vorstellungsgespräch zu einem Seminar	bei Ihnen. in Ihrem Büro. im Hotel Regent.
Ich will	um _ Uhr gegen Mittag	eintreffen.	
Mit freundlichen Grüßen [Name]			

Grammatik   **Seite 180**

Using dative pronouns

After some prepositions and some verbs the dative case is used:

*Ich gehe mit **ihm**.* – I'm going with him.

*Schicke **mir** eine Postkarte.* – Send me a postcard.

ich → mir	wir → uns
du → dir	ihr → euch
er / es → ihm	sie (pl) → ihnen
sie → ihr	Sie → Ihnen

Also revise interrogatives.

See page 160 ➡

Strategie 4a–4b

Listening for *nicht* and *kein*

Don't forget the effect of *nicht* or *kein*. Listen carefully to what you hear.

Jotting down notes

Sometimes when listening, there isn't enough time to write down the answer properly before you hear the next piece of relevant information. Therefore,

■ get used to jotting down key points briefly and quickly.

■ use your own shorthand version (in German or English) if it helps, so you can come back to them later.

■ When noting numbers, if the number has two digits, get used to writing them down as they are said in German, i.e. write the second digit first, e.g. *dreiundzwanzig* (23).

■ Fill in your correct answer in the proper place on the paper during a pause.

■ Do make sure that you cross out any notes so they are not confused with your actual answer and assessed by mistake!

🖙 **Hinweis**

8.3 Groundwork is available in the Foundation Book.

8.3 H Wie findest du deinen Job?

Lernziele

Talking about the good and bad points of jobs

Conditional sentences (revision)

Knowing interrogative pronouns

Jasmin

Ich bin LKW-Fahrerin. Es gibt nicht viele Frauen in meinem Beruf und man fragt mich immer, „Warum hast du diesen Job gewählt?". Ich mag einfach fahren! Ich musste natürlich meinen LKW-Führerschein machen, bevor ich den Job machen konnte. Das war für mich ganz schwierig, aber ich habe es geschafft und jetzt habe ich meinen Traumjob. Ich muss jeden Tag sehr früh aufstehen, denn der Arbeitstag beginnt schon um 6 Uhr! Dann bin ich den ganzen Tag unterwegs und ich bin froh, dass ich alleine arbeite.

Horst

Ich bin Friseur. Nach der Schulzeit habe ich zuerst eine Lehre gemacht. Dann habe ich drei Jahre lang für einen Freund gearbeitet, aber das fand ich langweilig und frustrierend. Deswegen habe ich mein eigenes Geschäft gekauft und ich kann jetzt viel mehr Geld verdienen. Mein Arbeitstag beginnt um halb neun und endet um 5 Uhr. Ich arbeite auch am Samstag, aber Montag habe ich frei. Ich finde meine Arbeit interessant, weil ich mit meinen Kunden sprechen kann, während ich arbeite.

Kai

Ich arbeite in einem Büro. Ich habe vier Jahre lang auf der Uni studiert und seitdem arbeite ich. Mein Arbeitstag ist fast immer langweilig. Ein Tag ist wie der andere. Ich fahre mit dem Auto zum Büro, sitze am Computer, mache meine Arbeit und habe nie Kontakt mit anderen Leuten, nur per E-Mail. Ich hätte gern einen anderen Beruf. Ab und zu kann ich von zu Hause arbeiten. Das gefällt mir besser, weil ich dann wenigstens mit meiner Frau zu Mittag essen kann.

1a 📖 🎧 Read what the people are saying about their jobs. Find the German words for the following:

1	driving licence	5	hairdresser
2	dream job	6	customers
3	working day	7	contact
4	on the move	8	profession

1b 📖 🎧 Read the texts again and complete the table.

	Job	Training	Routine	Opinion
Jasmin	HGV Driver	HGV Licence		
Horst				
Kai				

2 **G** Write five (or more) sentences describing what your ideal workplace would be like, using *würde*, *wäre*, *hätte*, *(es) gäbe*, *könnte* and *müsste*. If you wish, use the phrases below as prompts, but try to include your own ideas.

um … Uhr anfangen	früh nach Hause gehen	Pause machen
wenig Arbeit	bequem	freundliche Kollegen	viel Geld verdienen

3a 🎧 Listen to the recording. These people are answering questions about their jobs, but what were they asked? Match the questions below with the answers you hear.

Beispiel: a *4*

1   Wo arbeitest du?
2   Was für Qualifikationen hast du?
3   Wie viel verdienst du pro Stunde?
4   Wann beginnst du morgens?
5   Warum magst du deine Arbeit?
6   Wie findest du deinen Job?

3b 🎧 Listen again and write down in English as much information as you can for each speaker.

Beispiel: a *Working day starts at 8.45.*

4 🗨 Work with a partner. You should each imagine you have one of the following jobs. Take it in turns to interview one another as if you are a prospective employer for a different job. Use the questions suggested, then make up some of your own. Try to give detailed answers.

Klempner / Klempnerin	Zahnarzt / Zahnärztin
Verkäufer / Verkäuferin	Bauer / Bäuerin
Metzger / Metzgerin	Kellner / Kellnerin

Ich arbeite in … / bei …

Mein Arbeitstag beginnt um … Uhr und endet um … Uhr.

An einem normalen Tag	muss ich	Probleme mit Zentralheizungen lösen. allerlei Fleisch und Wurst verkaufen. meine Patienten untersuchen / behandeln. die Kühe füttern und melken.	
	bediene ich unsere Gäste mit Speisen und Getränken.		
	spreche ich mit vielen Kunden.		
Ich finde meinen Job / meinen Beruf	gut, schlecht, in Ordnung, stressig,	weil die Arbeit	Spaß macht. uninteressant ist.
		da ich	alleine arbeite. immer höflich sein muss.
Ich habe bei … / in …		gearbeitet.	
Es hat mir viel / keinen Spaß		gemacht,	weil / da …
In zehn Jahren möchte ich als … arbeiten.			
Ich würde … verdienen.			

Seite 185

Grammatik

Conditional sentences (revision)

Remember that there are various ways of expressing a conditional in German:

To say 'I would' use *ich würde* plus an infinitive.

To say what something 'would be' or 'would have' use *wäre* and *hätte*.

To say that 'there would be' something use *es gäbe*.

To say 'I could / would be able', use *ich könnte*.

To say 'I would have to', use *ich müsste*.

Look at the texts on page 158: which person uses the conditional form?

Also learn how to use *wen* and *wem*.

See page 161 ➡

- Wo arbeiten Sie?
- Wann beginnt und endet der Arbeitstag?
- Was machen Sie an einem normalen Tag?
- Wie finden Sie Ihren Job? Warum ist das so?
- Wo haben Sie Ihr Arbeitspraktikum gemacht und wie war es?
- Was für einen Job möchten Sie in zehn Jahren machen?
- Wie viel Geld würden Sie dort verdienen?

Strategie 3a

Knowing interrogative pronouns

As most questions start with an interrogative pronoun, it is essential you learn them by heart. Otherwise you will never understand the question!

Strategie 4

Finding out information

Don't limit yourself to answering questions when speaking. Find out information by asking questions. Use as many of the interrogatives you have learnt as possible.

Jobs and employment

1 Copy out the sentences, replacing the underlined time phrase with an alternative expression.

1 <u>Jeden Samstag</u> arbeite ich in einem Friseursalon.

2 Im Geschäft musste ich <u>jeden Morgen</u> und <u>jeden Abend</u> aufräumen.

3 Ich trage <u>jeden Dienstag</u> Zeitungen aus.

4 <u>Jeden Morgen</u> stehe ich früh auf.

5 Zum Glück habe ich <u>jeden Sonntag</u> frei.

Grammatik · Seite 179

Using alternative time phrases

Instead of using *jeden Tag* (every day) you could say *täglich* (daily).

Jeden Morgen / Nachmittag / Abend become *morgens* (in the morning) / *nachmittags* (in the afternoon) / *abends* (in the evening);

With days of the week, *jeden Montag* becomes *montags*, etc. Notice that capital letters are used with these words only when they start the sentence.

The more alternative language you can use, the better your German will sound!

---

2 Identify which form of referring to the future (a)–(h) represent. Choose from: conditional forms, present tense + future indicator, planning, future tense with *werden*.

Beispiel: **a** *conditional*

Mein Traumjob (a) wäre in der Filmindustrie. Ich möchte (b) Schauspielerin werden. Ich bin schon Mitglied in einer Theatergruppe und arbeite am Wochenende im Kino in der Stadtmitte. Ich verdiene zwar nicht viel, aber es macht Spaß, und ich kann die neuesten Filme umsonst sehen. Nächste Woche läuft (c) der neue James Bond Film.

Ich habe vor (d), in fünf Jahren Millionärin zu sein, und wenn ich berühmt bin, werde ich nur einen oder zwei Filme in einem Jahr machen (e). Bis dann muss ich hart arbeiten (f). Nächstes Jahr gehe ich auf die Uni (g), wo ich Medienwissenschaft studieren werde (h). Ich freue mich schon darauf.

Grammatik · Seite 182

Talking about the future (revision)

Remember that there are different ways to talk about the future in German:

Future tense with *werden*. *See page 184* ➡

Present tense (with future time indicators). *See page 184* ➡

Present tense with *ich will*. *See page 182* ➡

People may also use *ich möchte* to say what they would like to do in the future. *See page 182* ➡

Other ways of referring to the future include:

Ich hoffe + zu – I hope to

Ich habe … vor + zu – I am planning to

---

3 Complete these questions with an appropriate interrogative.

Beispiel: 1 *Wie*

1 _____ findest du deinen Arbeitstag?

2 _____ Geld bekommst du pro Tag?

3 _____ kannst du nach Hause gehen?

4 _____ findest du deinen Job so super?

5 _____ ist dein Büro?

6 _____ ist dein Arbeitgeber?

7 Von _____ hast du Informationen über deinen Job bekommen?

8 Mit _____ hast du im Büro gearbeitet und gesprochen?

Grammatik · Seite 188

Interrogatives (revision)

These are some of the words that introduce questions. Can you remember what the following words mean?

wo? ('where?'); *wohin?* ('where to?'); *woher?* ('where from?')

wie? ('how?')

warum? ('why?')

wie viel(e)? ('how much / many?')

welcher(- / s)? ('which?')

The interrogative *wer?* ('who') is often used with prepositions and changes its form. For example:

Für wen? 'For whom?'

Von wem? 'From whom?'

4 Rewrite the following sentences in the perfect tense.

1 Ich finde den Chef sehr angenehm.
2 Wir fangen um acht Uhr an.
3 Meine Kollegin wird ziemlich unfreundlich.
4 Ich komme morgens um 7.45 Uhr an.
5 Schreibst du den Brief schon?
6 Die Chefin fliegt am Montag ins Ausland.
7 Das Arbeitspraktikum gefällt mir nicht.

> **Grammatik** — *Seite 182*
>
> ### Using the perfect tense (revision)
>
> To form the perfect tense, use the correct part of *haben* or *sein* with the past participle at the end of the sentence or clause. Remember that *sein* is used with verbs involving motion (e.g. *gehen, fahren, fliegen, schwimmen*), a change of state (e.g. *sterben* 'to die') and with the verbs *sein* 'to be' and *werden* 'to become'.
>
> *Ich **habe** in einem Büro **gearbeitet**.* – I worked in an office.
>
> *Um halb eins **bin** ich in die Kantine **gegangen**.* – At half past twelve I went in the canteen.
>
> *Der Chef **ist gestorben**.* – The boss has died.
>
> *Ich **bin** in Berlin **gewesen**.* – I have been to Berlin.
>
> *Die Arbeit **ist** leichter **geworden**.* – The work has become easier.

5 Complete the following sentences with the appropriate phrases in German.

1 Mein Bruder arbeitet seit _____ bei der Firma Volkswagen. (*two years*)
2 Ich habe seit _____ einen Samstagsjob. (*one week*)
3 Seit _____ arbeite ich in einer Werkstatt. (*one and a half years*)
4 Meine Mutter arbeitet seit _____ bei Aldi. (*four months*)
5 Seit _____ trage ich morgens Zeitungen aus. (*last week*)

> **Grammatik** — *Seite 186*
>
> ### Using *seit*
>
> To say how long you have been doing something, use *seit* followed by the dative. Notice that you use the present tense rather than the past tense (as you would in English):
>
> *Sie arbeitet seit letzt**em** Monat bei Volkswagen.* – She has been working for Volkswagen since last month.
>
> *Seit ein**er** Woche hat er einen Teilzeitjob in einem Supermarkt.* – He has had a part-time job in a supermarket for a week.
>
> *Ich lerne seit ein**em** Jahr Französisch.* – I have been learning French for a year.

6 Complete these questions with *wen* or *wem* as appropriate. Then translate the sentences into natural English.

Beispiel: 1 *Wen möchten Sie besuchen?*
(Who would you like to visit?)

1 _____ möchten Sie besuchen?
2 Mit _____ haben Sie ein Vorstellungsgespräch?
3 Von _____ hast du die E-Mail bekommen?
4 Für _____ ist diese Tasse Kaffee?
5 _____ haben Sie Unterlagen gegeben?
6 _____ hast du angerufen?
7 _____ würden Sie für diesen Job empfehlen?

> **Grammatik**
>
> ### Using *wen* and *wem*
>
> *Wen* and *wem* (meaning 'whom') are the accusative and dative forms of *wer* ('who'). Although we don't always use 'whom' in English, it is important to use the correct forms in German. Remember that the accusative case is used to show the direct object and the dative is used to show the indirect object:
>
> *Wen kennst du in dieser Firma?* – Who(m) do you know in this firm?
>
> *Mit wem haben Sie gesprochen?* – Who did you speak to? (lit. With whom did you speak?)

Jobs and employment

Topic 8.1 Part-time work and work experience

8.1 F Hast du einen Job? ➡ *pages 148–149*

	abwaschen	to wash up
	anstrengend	exhausting
	aufräumen	to tidy up
der	Bäcker / die Bäckerin	baker
die	Bäckerei	bakery
die	Erfahrung	experience
	mit etw. fertig sein	to be finished with sth.
	im Freien	out in the open
der	Friseursalon	hairdressing salon
	gut bezahlt	well paid
	zum Glück	fortunately
	kochen	to cook, to make (e.g. tea and coffee)
der	Lohn	wages
	eine Menge	a lot of
der	Nachteil	disadvantage
der	Nebenjob	second or extra job, job outside school
	nützlich	useful
den	Rasen mähen	to mow the lawn
	täglich	daily
	verdienen	to earn

8.1 H Wie war dein Arbeitspraktikum?
➡ *pages 150–151*

	angenehm	pleasant
die	Aufgabe	task, job
	behandeln	to treat
	benutzen	to use
	beschäftigt	busy
die	Briefmarke	stamp
der	Briefumschlag	envelope
die	Erfahrung	experience
der / die	Erwachsene	adult
der	Fehler	mistake

die	Firma	firm, company
die	Gelegenheit	opportunity
	herstellen	to make, to manufacture
	höflich	polite
	kleben	to stick, to glue
der	Kollege / die Kollegin	colleague
die	Schichtarbeit	shift work
der	Traum	dream
	überrascht	surprised
die	Verbindung	connection

Topic 8.2 Talking about and getting a job

8.2 F Zukunftspläne ➡ *pages 152–153*

der	Apotheker / die Apothekerin	chemist
der	Bauarbeiter / die Bauarbeiterin	builder
der	Bauer / die Bäuerin	farmer
der	Beamte / die Beamtin	officer
	berühmt	famous
der	Fahrer / die Fahrerin	driver
	faszinierend	fascinating
der	Feuerwehrmann / die Feuerwehrfrau	firefighter
das	Gehalt	salary
der	Hausmann / die Hausfrau	househusband / housewife
der	Ingenieur / die Ingenieurin	engineer
der	Kassierer / die Kassiererin	checkout assistant
der	Kaufmann / die Kauffrau	businessman / businesswoman
der	Maler / die Malerin	painter
der	Pfarrer / die Pfarrerin	vicar
der	Postbote / die Postbotin	postman / postwoman
der	Reiseleiter / die Reiseleiterin	tour guide

der	Schauspieler / die Schauspielerin	actor / actress
das	Studium	study
der	Tischler / die Tischlerin	carpenter

8.2 H Ich möchte mich um diese Stelle bewerben ➡ pages 154–155

	anschreien	to shout at
	begeistert	inspired, enthusiastic
	berühmt	famous
der	Besitzer	owner
	bevorzugen	to prefer, to favour
	einstellen	to take on
	erschöpft	exhausted
	froh	glad
die	Gleitzeit	flexi-time
	kündigen	to hand notice in
	mitteilen	to inform
der	Nachteil	disadvantage
	nötig	necessary
	sammeln	to collect
	schneiden	to cut
der	Topf	pot
	völlig	completely
der	Vorteil	advantage
	wechseln	to change
	zuverlässig	reliable

Topic 8.3 Jobs and communicating in the workplace

8.3 F Am Arbeitsplatz ➡ pages 156–157

die	Anzeige	advertisement
	am Apparat	speaking (when on the phone)
der	Arbeitgeber / die Arbeitgeberin	employer
	besprechen	to discuss
die	Bewerbung	application
der	Durchfall	diarrhoea
die	E-Mail	email
die	Entscheidung treffen	to make the decision
	etwas	something

	genau	exactly
die	Haltestelle	bus / tram stop
	jetzt	now
	kopieren	to copy
	liegen	to be situated
die	Nachricht	message
	sagen	to say
	schicken	to send
	übermorgen	the day after tomorrow
die	Unterlage	document
	unterschreiben	to sign

8.3 H Wie findest du deinen Job? ➡ pages 158–159

	absagen	to cancel, to call off
der	Anstreicher / die Anstreicherin	house painter
der	Bewerber / die Bewerberin	applicant
der	Dolmetscher / die Dolmetscherin	interpreter
	empfehlen	to recommend
	(sich) entschließen	to decide
	frustrierend	frustrating
der	Führerschein	driving licence
das	Gesetz	law
der	Kandidat / die Kandidatin	candidate
der	Kontakt	contact
der	Rechtsanwalt / die Rechtsanwältin	lawyer
	schaffen	to manage
der	Schriftsteller / die Schriftstellerin	writer
	seitdem	since then
	sicherlich	of course, certainly
das	Unternehmen	business
	unterwegs	on the move
das	Vorstellungsgespräch	interview
	wählen	to choose

Higher – Exam practice

info

These pages give you the chance to try GCSE-style practice exam question at grade B-A* based on the AQA Context of Work and education.

Hinweis

Foundation practice exam questions (grades D-C) are available at the end of this Context in the Foundation book.

13 Jahre Schule!

Johann Gerber ist 19 Jahre alt und hat eben die Schule verlassen. Er beschreibt seine Schulkarriere.

Grundschule

Als ich sechs Jahre alt war, bin ich zum ersten Mal in die Grundschule gegangen. Ich habe gehört, dass man in England schon mit 5 Jahren in die Schule geht. Das wäre für mich zu früh gewesen. An meinem ersten Schultag habe ich geweint, als ich ohne Mutti in dem großen Klassenzimmer war. In der Grundschule habe ich mich gut amüsiert, weil ich durch Spielen lernen konnte.

Johanns erster Schultag

Gesamtschule

Als ich die Grundschule verlassen habe, bin ich in eine Gesamtschule gegangen, wo alles ganz anders war. In der Grundschule hatten wir meistens nur einen Lehrer für alle Fächer gehabt. In der Gesamtschule musste ich viele neue Lehrer und Lehrerinnen kennen lernen. Mein Lieblingslehrer war Herr Weber, der Englisch und Französisch unterrichtet hat. Er war sympathisch. Aber einige Lehrer waren ziemlich streng und wir mussten in fast jeder Stunde sehr viel schreiben. Dazu gab es auch Hausaufgaben, was natürlich ganz fürchterlich war.

Viele Schüler und Schülerinnen haben in der Schule geraucht, und in unserer Schule gab es eine Raucherecke hinter der Bibliothek, wo die älteren Schüler rauchen durften. Das habe ich schrecklich gefunden, weil Rauchen stinkt, und man konnte den Gestank in der Bibliothek selbst riechen.

In der Oberstufe habe ich nur 5 Prüfungsfächer gemacht. Da ich mich für Fremdsprachen interessierte, habe ich natürlich Englisch und Französisch gewählt. Ich durfte auch andere Fächer wie Sport machen, aber sie waren nicht so wichtig. Als ich mein letztes Zeugnis gelesen habe, war ich sehr glücklich. In der zwölften Klasse hatte ich eine Drei für Englisch bekommen, aber diesmal hatte ich eine Eins.

Nachdem ich meine Noten bekommen hatte, wurde mir klar, dass ich auf die Uni gehen würde. Die Schulzeit war zu Ende. Ich habe viele gute Freunde in meinem Schulleben gemacht und nächstes Jahr werde ich meine alten Schulfreunde alle vermissen, wenn ich an der Uni bin.

Johannes Kepler Gesamtschule

Zeugnis

Jahrgang 13

Prüfungsfächer	
Englisch	1
Deutsch	2
Mathe	1
Geschichte	3
Französisch	1

1a 📖 Read the text on the opposite page and then work out which four of these eight statements are true.

1 Johann was 5 when he first went to school.
2 He enjoyed primary school.
3 After primary school, he went to a grammar school.
4 His favourite teacher was his maths teacher.
5 He found the homework dreadful.
6 In the sixth form he took 5 subjects.
7 His favourite subjects are languages.
8 Johann has already started university.

Total = 4 marks

1b 📖 Answer the following questions in English.

1 What happened on Johann's first day at school?
2 What did Johann particularly like about primary school?
3 What was the first difference Johann noticed when he went to secondary school?
4 Why did Johann not like the smokers' corner?
5 Why was Johann particularly pleased about his last report?
6 Does Johann look back on his school days in a positive or negative light? Why? (2)

Total = 7 marks

2 🎧 While working in a hotel, you receive a message on the answerphone about a forthcoming conference. Your boss wants to know what it is about. Copy out and fill in the form on the right with the details.

Total = 10 marks

Arrival date (1)................................
No. of double rooms (1)....................
No. of single rooms (1)....................
No. of nights (1)............................
No. of conference rooms (1)..............
Extra equipment required
  (2)..
Times of coffee breaks
  (2)..
And lunch (1)............................

3 📖 Read the text below about Corrina, then answer the questions about her and her work.

Mein Beruf

Ich arbeite jetzt seit fast zehn Jahren als Briefträgerin. Meine Arbeit ist nie langweilig, weil ich jeden Tag mit neuen Leuten spreche. Zu Weihnachten kann es manchmal schwierig sein, da es so viele Pakete zu liefern gibt. Manche Briefträger haben Angst, dass sie von Hunden gebissen werden, aber ich mag alle Tiere und habe noch nie Probleme damit gehabt. Ich mag sogar früh aufstehen: Die Stadt ist oft äußerst ruhig zu dieser Zeit. Ich bin am Mittag fertig und habe den Rest des Tages frei, wenn meine Kinder von der Schule kommen.

Corrina

1 What is Corrina's job? (1)
2 How does she find the work? Why? (2)
3 Give the 2 possible disadvantages she mentions in this job. (2)
4 Give the 2 advantages Corrina gives for getting up early. (2)
5 Do you think she likes her job? Why / Why not? (2)

Total = 9 marks

Total for Reading and Listening = 30 marks

Higher – Speaking

Geld verdienen

You are talking to a German friend about what you do to earn money, any paid work you have done and your career plans for the future.

Your teacher will play the role of the friend. He or she could ask you the following:

1 Do you get money from your parents or family?
2 Do you have a part-time job?
3 Where did you do your work experience?
4 What were your colleagues like?
5 What are your career plans for the future?
6 Would you like to work abroad?
7 !

! Remember you will have to respond to something that you have not yet prepared.

info

Important information:
This sample task is for practice purposes only and should not be used as an actual assessment task. Study it to find out how to plan your Controlled Assessment efficiently to gain maximum marks and / or work through it as a mock exam task before the actual Controlled Assessment.

1 Do you get money from your parents or family?
- say whether you get pocket money and if the answer is yes, say how much you get and from whom
- say what you do to help at home and whether you get paid for it
- give your view on whether you should get paid for helping at home
- mention something you do with the money you get

Strategie

Start your plan. Write a maximum of six words for each bullet point. Here are some suggestions for the first bullet point: *Taschengeld, verdienen, bekommen, Pfund, sparen, kaufen.*

Use *denken, glauben* or *finden* to say why you should (not) be paid. *Ich denke, dass ich dafür Geld bekommen sollte.*

Giving reasons which contain complex language as to why you should (not) get paid for helping out at home will improve your mark.

2 Do you have a part-time job?
- say whether you have a part-time job
- describe what you do
- give your opinion of your job and a reason why
- mention how you get to work and why you prefer this method of getting there

Strategie

Suggested words for your plan: *Teilzeitarbeit, Job, Stunden, abends, Chef, bezahlt.*

If you don't have a part-time job, you could say why not, e.g. no time, pressures of schoolwork. You could also say whether you would like one and why.

Give a reason for your choice of how you get to work. Are you *umweltfreundlich*?

3 Where did you do your work experience?
- say where you did your work experience
- describe a typical day there
- say what the advantages of work experience are
- mention any disadvantages

Strategie

Suggested words for your plan: *Arbeitspraktikum, Aufgaben, Vorteile, Nachteile.* Add two more words to this list.

You will need to use the perfect and imperfect tenses (see page 182) to talk about what you did and describe it.

If you want to say what you had to do, use the imperfect tense of *müssen: Ich musste um halb sieben aufstehen.*

4 What were your colleagues like?
- describe your work colleagues
- say how you got on with them
- mention whether you did things together after work
- say what you think makes a good colleague and / or boss

Strategie

Suggested words for your plan: *geschwätzig, schüchtern, Mittagspause, wieder.* Add two more words to this list.

Again you will need to use the past tense. You can use *ich bin gut / schlecht mit ... ausgekommen* to say 'I got on well / badly with ...', or you could say how you found a particular colleague by using *ich habe ... freundlich / sympathisch gefunden*.

Use the conditional tense of *sein* to describe your ideal boss. *Mein idealer Chef wäre ...*

5 What are your career plans for the future?
- say what sort of job you would like
- mention what sort of qualifications / training you will need
- say what your dream job would be
- explain why you would like it

Suggested words for your plan: *Hochschule, Traumberuf.* Add four more words to this list.

You are now being asked to talk about the future, so you will need to use the future tense with *werden* or the present tense with future indicators.

Other ways of talking about the future might be to use *ich möchte, ich könnte, ich habe ... vor, ich hoffe* or *ich will*. These will all need the infinitive of the other verb at the end of the sentence or clause. Then make it clear that you are talking about the future by adding a time phrase such as *in der Zukunft* or *nach der Schule* to your sentence.

6 Would you like to work abroad?
- say whether you would like to work abroad
- say where you would like to work
- give reasons for your choices
- mention what you think of job opportunities for young people in Europe

Arbeitsmöglichkeiten is the German word for 'job opportunities' and *Freiwilligenjahr* means 'gap year'. Both could make a good addition to your plan. Add four more words of your own.

If you don't yet know where you want to work, you could say *ich habe mich noch nicht entschieden,* or *ich weiß noch nicht, wo ich arbeiten werde*.

7 ! At this point you may be asked to ...
- say whether earning lots of money is important to you, giving justifications
- say whether you think foreign language skills are important for work
- say whether you think it's a good idea to do the same job as your parents
- say if you preferred going to your work experience or to school and why

Think about what the surprise question could be. There are some suggestions in the sub-divisions. Then work out what your answer would be to each of those and any other questions you think might be asked.

You should have four words left to add to your list, so choose carefully, e.g. if your dream job would be a celebrity footballer, then you might want the word *Starfußballer*. Another useful word could be *lieber* for answering the final sub-division.

Pick words that you haven't already used in your preparation, as you're more likely to need help remembering these.

Your answer does not have to be long but it needs to contain a conjugated verb.

Remember to check the total number of words you have used. It should be 40 or fewer.

Hinweis

Foundation sample assessment tasks for this Context can be found in the Foundation book.

Higher – Writing

Das britische Schulwesen

Your local council has asked you to write an article in German for a brochure they are producing to celebrate a twinning relationship with a village in Germany. The article is to be entitled *Das britische Schulwesen*. You could include:

1 a description of your school
2 your school routine
3 your subjects
4 school trips and exchanges
5 your school uniform
6 extra-curricular activities
7 the future.

1 A description of your school

- introduce your school, giving its name and location
- say what type of school it is, e.g. comprehensive, boarding, grammar etc. Also mention the age range
- mention the size of the school and how old it is
- give some information about the history of the school, e.g. when it was opened, what it used to be like, what facilities there used to be
- say what classrooms and facilities there are now

Strategie

Start your plan. Write five or six words for each bullet point. Suggested words for the first bullet point: *Gesamtschule, Schüler, Gebäude, Bibliothek, Gelegenheiten, Umkleideraum.*

Use *es gibt* (there is, there are) and *wir haben* (we have) to describe what there is in the school. Remember that the items that follow will be direct objects and need to take the accusative case.

Use the imperfect tense to say what the school was like in the past. *In der Vergangenheit war meine Schule … Früher gab es …*

2 Your school routine

- give a description of a typical day at school
- say how you get to school and what time you arrive
- say how many lessons you have each day and when they begin
- mention what you do at break and lunchtime

Strategie

Suggested words for your plan: *ankommen, Stunden, anfangen, Stundenplan, Mittagspause, enden.* If you use a verb, check that it is in the infinitive form.

Try to find different things to say for what you do at break and lunchtime to add variety. You could also give your opinion on your school day and how it compares with the typical German school day.

3 Your subjects

- mention compulsory subjects (*Pflichtfächer*) and options (*Wahlfächer*)
- say which subject is your favourite and why
- say which subject is your least favourite and why
- give your view on homework and exam pressures

Strategie

Suggested words for your plan: *Fächer, Lieblingsfach, Hausaufgaben, Druck.* Add two more words to this list.

You can use the perfect tense to say which subjects you have chosen: *Ich habe … als Wahlfach gewählt.*

Link your sentences using words like *weil* and *obwohl.* Check your word order in subordinate clauses. Give more complex reasons for liking / disliking your subjects to improve your mark.

4 School trips and exchanges

- give some information about trips your school organises
- mention any links your school has with schools abroad
- mention a trip or exchange you went on recently
- describe what you did and give your opinion on it and reasons for that opinion

> **Strategie**
>
> Suggested words for your plan: *Schüleraustausch, Ausland, Reise, Verbindungen.* Add no more than two words to this list.
>
> Be creative in your response to this bullet point and show off the grammar you have learnt. Try to use phrases and structures you haven't yet used.
>
> Use different ways to compare your school and schools abroad, e.g. *besser als ..., genauso groß wie ...*

5 Your school uniform

- describe your school uniform
- give and justify your opinion on it
- mention any changes you would make to the uniform
- give your view on German students not having to wear uniform

> **Strategie**
>
> Suggested words for your plan: *Kleidung, abschaffen.* Add three or four words of your own.
>
> Use the conditional to describe what your ideal uniform would be like.
>
> You could give *Vorteile* and *Nachteile* of not having school uniforms in Germany: *Die Vorteile sind, dass ...*

6 Extra-curricular activities

- mention some extra-curricular activities on offer in your school
- mention an activity in which you are involved and say what you think of it
- mention any other activities you would like to do in the future
- say what activities you would like your school to offer in the future

> **Strategie**
>
> Suggested words for your plan: *Sportmöglichkeiten, Theatergruppe.* Add three or four more words of your own.
>
> You can use *man kann* to say what kind of things you can do. Remember to put the infinitive at the end of the sentence or clause when using a modal verb. Try to make these sentences varied rather than one long list.
>
> To say what you would like to do you could use *ich möchte* or *ich würde gern.* To say what the school could offer, use *könnte* from the verb *können*, to be able to.

7 The future

- say what you think your school will be like in the future and mention any new facilities that are planned
- say what sixth form opportunities there are where you live
- mention the courses of study available and give your opinions on them
- say what employment or training prospects there are for 16-year-olds
- finish your article by giving an overall opinion of *das britische Schulwesen*

> **Strategie**
>
> Now count up how many words you have left, ideally about five or six. If you have fewer than this, you may want to go back and take some out of your lists for previous bullet points, as you can only have 40 words in total. Useful words to add to your list for this last bullet point could be *Oberstufe* and *Lehre*.
>
> Future plans may depend on exam results. Use *Es kommt auf meine Ergebnisse an* to start off expressing this.

> **Hinweis**
>
> Foundation sample assessment tasks for this Context can be found in the Foundation book.

Exam technique – Speaking

S10 Showing Initiative

'Showing initiative' does not mean that you suddenly ask your teacher 'What about you, where did you go on holiday?' (although you could do that!). You are generally expected to answer questions. For instance, if you are asked the question *Hast du einen Teilzeitjob?*, you should first answer it directly and then try to develop your answer, e.g. *Ja, ich arbeite samstags bei einer Tankstelle. Die Arbeitszeit ist ziemlich lang, aber die Arbeit ist nicht langweilig.* You were not asked about your hours or opinion of your job, but you decided to add it to your response. It is relevant, linked to what you were asked and follows your developed answer quite naturally. That is 'showing initiative'. Use it to extend your answers and therefore show off extra knowledge of German.

S11 Using different tenses

If you are aiming at grade A, you should also show that you know the pluperfect and the conditional.

S12 Checklist for Speaking success

You will score well in the Speaking task if:

- you say a lot that is relevant to the question
- you have a good range of vocabulary
- you can include complex structures
- you can refer to present, past and future events
- your German accent is good
- you can speak fluently
- you can show initiative
- you can speak with grammatical accuracy.

Grade booster

To reach grade B, you need to …

- Develop most of your answers well, using some complex sentences, e.g. in bullet point 4, go through each option, adding extra details each time, e.g. when describing your colleagues, use at least 2 different adjectives per person and qualifiers where you can. Link up your sentences with appropriate connectives.
- Answer without hesitation, using a good range of vocabulary, e.g. in bullet point 2, use a variety of ways of expressing an opinion and provide different reasons each time.
- Structure your writing well so that the content flows as well as the language.

To reach grade A, you need to …

- Include the three time frames, e.g. use the present tense in bullet point 1 to describe what you do around the house now. Then move to the past (perfect and imperfect) to describe your work experience in bullet point 3 and finally refer to the future in bullet points 5 and 6.
- Express ideas and points of view using complex sentences and a very good range of vocabulary, e.g. in bullet point 3, to give an opinion, go beyond the usual phrases, e.g. *meiner Meinung nach … / ich glaube, dass … / was ich am besten finde, ist dass, … / das Beste / das Schlimmste ist, dass….* Remember that the next verb will go straight after *meiner Meinung nach* but move to the end of sentence or clause after *dass*.

To reach grade A*, you need to …

- Have a wide range of vocabulary and use a number of more complex structures, e.g. in bullet point 2, use the present tense with *seit* to say how long you've worked there, the future tense to say how long you intend to keep your job and the conditional to say whether you would prefer working at different times. Include other complex structures if you can.
- Respond readily and show initiative on several occasions, e.g. in bullet point 5, if you want to go to university, explain how long the course will last and what you will study. Mention some of the advantages of your dream job and why you would like to do it.

Exam technique – Writing

W10 Info about 'Accuracy'

If you are aiming at grade A, your writing is generally correct, although there may still be mistakes, especially in your attempts at more complex sentences. Your use of different verb forms, in particular different tenses, must be mainly accurate.

W11 Ideas for practising

Treat each bullet point as a mini task. Write your answer to one bullet point at a time with the help of your plan. Ask your partner to take a critical look at your work. Take his / her suggestions on board and re-draft your work. Study W12, the Info box that lists what you should do in order to get the best possible mark, and try to improve your work using these hints.

Practise your writing using sample tasks from the AQA website or given to you by your teacher. Write a plan and attempt the task. As you are only allowed 60 minutes to complete the task in your exam, practise using approximately 7 minutes for each bullet point, leaving you 10 minutes or so at the end for a final check. Use that time to check that what you wrote makes sense and that it is as accurate as you can make it.

W12 Checklist for Writing success

You will score well if:

- you communicate a lot of relevant information clearly
- you can explain ideas and points of view
- you have a good range of vocabulary
- you can include complex structures
- you can write long sentences
- you can refer to past, present and future events
- you can write with grammatical accuracy
- you organise your ideas well.

Grade booster

To reach grade B, you need to …

- Be able to explain ideas, using appropriate vocabulary and complex sentences, e.g. in bullet point 3, explain which subjects you had to choose from and what you think of the options system. Give your reasons for your opinions.
- Write with some accuracy. There may be errors in your attempt at more complex sentences but verb and tense formations are usually correct, e.g. in bullet point 2, although the language needed to cover this bullet point is fairly straightforward, it is important that it is as accurate as you can make it. Check verb endings in particular.

To reach grade A, you need to …

- Write 40 to 50 words per bullet point, conveying a lot of relevant information clearly, e.g. in bullet point 7, although you could give a lot of information here, limit yourself to 50 words maximum and focus on the accuracy of the language you have used, e.g. verb endings.
- Try to squeeze as many complex structures as you can into your response to each bullet point. You don't have the capacity to waste your word count, so make sure every sentence is packed with structures that will get you extra marks. Make a list of which ones you want to include before you start to plan and then tick them off as they are incorporated into your writing.

To reach grade A*, you need to …

- Use a wide variety of vocabulary and structures with accuracy, e.g. in bullet point 6, show that you know that modal verbs like *man kann / man sollte / man muss* are all followed by a verb in the infinitive. Try to avoid repetition of vocabulary, e.g. *Schuluniform*. Use *was man tragen muss, unsere Kleider* etc.
- Use more complex structures successfully, e.g. in bullet point 1, use the passive to say when your school was built / renovated. *Meine Schule wurde 1960 gebaut und neulich im Jahr 2010 renoviert.*

(G) Grammatik

(info)

Key to colour coding on the grammar pages

The grammar reference information is divided into four sections, indicated by different colour coding:

grammar to be learnt and used by all GCSE students

grammar to be learnt and used by students working at Higher level, and recognised by students working at Foundation level

grammar to be learnt and used by Higher level students only

grammar to be recognised, but not necessarily used, by Higher students only.

■ Contents

■ Glossary of terms

Adjectives   *die Adjektive*

… are words that describe somebody or something:

groß   big   *blau*   blue

Adverbs   *die Adverbien*

… are words that describe an action:

*Ich laufe **schnell**.* I run fast.

**Articles (definite   *die Artikel*
and indefinite)**

… are the words 'the' and 'a':

der, die, das   the

ein, eine, ein   a

Cases

… tell you what words are doing in the sentence.

The nominative case is used for the subject:

Der Junge spielt Klavier.

The accusative case is used for the object and after some prepositions:

*Amelie kauft **einen Kuli**.*

*Ich fahre durch **die Stadt**.*

The dative case is used for the indirect object and after some prepositions:

*Ich gebe **dem Kind** einen Apfel.*

*Die Katze ist neben **der Lampe**.*

The genitive case is used to indicate possession:

*Hier ist das Auto **meiner Mutter**.*

Infinitive   *der Infinitiv*

… is the name of the verb as listed in the dictionary and always ends in *-en* :

spielen   to play
gehen   to go
haben   to have
sein   to be

Nouns   *die Nomen*

… are words for somebody or something:

*das **Haus***   *die **Tür***
*der **Bruder***   ***Susanne***

Object   *das Objekt*

… is a person or thing affected by the verb:

*Ich esse **einen Apfel**.*

*Ich spiele **Tennis**.*

Prepositions   *die Präpositionen*

… are words used with nouns to give information about where, when, how, with whom:

mit, aus, nach, zu, in, …

Pronouns   *die Pronomen*

… are short words used instead of a noun or name, e.g.:

ich   I
du   you
er   he / it
sie   she / it
es   it

Singular and plural

Singular refers to just one thing or person:

Hund   *Bruder*

Plural refers to more than one thing or person:

Hunde   *Brüder*

Subject   *das Subjekt*

A person or thing 'doing' the verb:

***Martina** lernt Deutsch.*

***Ich** gehe ins Kino.*

***Mein Haus** hat zwei Schlafzimmer.*

Verbs   *die Verben*

… express an action or state:

ich wohne   I live
ich habe   I have
ich bin   I am
ich mag   I like

A Number and gender

Number

Many words in German change according to whether they are **singular** or **plural**. You use the singular when there is only one of something or someone. You use the plural when there is more than one of something or someone:

das Auto	the car	*die Autos*	the cars
ich wohne	I live	*wir wohnen*	we live

Gender

Many words in German also change according to whether they are **masculine**, **feminine** or **neuter**. This is called grammatical gender. It does not exist in English, but it does in most other languages.

The grammatical gender of something has nothing to do with its sex or gender in real life. For instance, in German, 'table' is masculine but 'girl' is neuter!

Articles

Articles are words like 'the' and 'a', and are usually used with nouns. There are three kinds of article in German: **definite** ('the'), **indefinite** ('a') and **negative** ('not a').

The **gender** of an article must match the gender of the word(s) it is with. Its **number** must match the number of the word(s) it is with. In the plural, all genders have the same article.

The definite article: *der, die, das, die*

The definite article means 'the':

masculine	feminine	neuter	plural
der	*die*	*das*	*die*

*Das ist **der** Tisch.*   That is the table.

The indefinite article: *ein, eine, ein*

The indefinite article means 'a' or 'an'. There is no plural because 'a' has no plural!

masculine	feminine	neuter
ein	*eine*	*ein*

*Das ist **ein** Tisch.*   That is a table.

You do not use the indefinite article in German if you are talking about what job someone does or what nationality they are, or for ailments:

Ich bin Lehrerin.	I'm **a** teacher.
Er ist Deutscher.	He's **a** German.
Sie hat Halsschmerzen.	She has **a** sore throat.

The negative article: *kein, keine, kein, keine*

The negative article means 'not a' or 'not any' or 'no'.

masculine	feminine	neuter	plural
kein	*keine*	*kein*	*keine*

*Das ist **kein** Tisch.*   That is not a table / That isn't a table.

Nouns

A noun is a word used to name something. Nouns are objects or things, but not all nouns are things that can be touched (e.g. 'laughter'). A good test of a noun is whether or not you can put 'the' in front of it (e.g. the book ✓; the have ✗).

All German nouns are either **masculine**, **feminine** or **neuter**, and either **singular** or **plural**. When you see a noun, you can often work out its **gender** or **number** from its **article**:

masculine	feminine	neuter	plural
der Tisch	*die Tasche*	*das Heft*	*die Hefte*

Plurals of nouns

There are different ways of making nouns plural in German, just as in English. Unfortunately, there isn't really a quick rule – you just have to get the feel of them!

- Feminine nouns which end in *-e* usually just add *-n*: *eine Katze – zwei Katze**n***
- Some nouns stay the same in the plural: *ein Hamster – drei Hamster*
- Some nouns (mainly those borrowed from English) just add *-s*, as in English: *ein Auto – zwei Autos*
- Some nouns add *-e*: *ein Hund – drei Hunde*
- Some nouns add *-e*, but also take an umlaut (¨) on the first vowel: *eine Maus – hundert Mäuse*
- A few nouns add *-er*: *ein Ei – sechs Eier*
- Some nouns add *-er* and take an umlaut on the first vowel: *ein Mann – zwei Männer*

Weak nouns

There is a small group of nouns that are called weak nouns. They add an **-(e)n** ending in the accusative, dative and genitive singular and all plural forms. (For cases, see Section B.)

	singular	plural
nominative	der Junge	die Jungen
accusative	den Jungen	die Jungen
dative	dem Jungen	den Jungen
genitive	des Jungen	der Jungen

Possessive adjectives

Possessive adjectives are words like 'my', 'your', 'his' and 'her'. Their gender and number must match (or 'agree with') the noun they refer to and their endings change (just like der, ein, etc.).

Their endings follow the same pattern as kein (see page 174):

	masculine	feminine	neuter	plural
my	mein	meine	mein	meine
your	dein	deine	dein	deine
his	sein	seine	sein	seine
her	ihr	ihre	ihr	ihre
our	unser	unsere	unser	unsere
your	euer	eure	euer	eure
their	ihr	ihre	ihr	ihre

mein Bruder	my brother
deine Schwester	your sister
sein Vater	his father
ihre Schwestern	her sisters

Demonstrative adjectives and quantifiers

Demonstrative adjectives are words like 'this' or 'that' and quantifiers are words like 'each' or 'every'. You use them in sentences such as these:

Diese Hose ist schön.   These trousers are beautiful.

Jedes Kind darf mitmachen.   Each child may join in.

masculine	feminine	neuter	plural
dieser Mann	diese Frau	dieses Kleid	diese Röcke
jeder Mann	jede Frau	jedes Kleid	–

Interrogative adjectives

The interrogative adjective 'which' is used in questions (see also Interrogatives, page 188):

Welcher Pullover ist zu klein?   Which pullover is too small?

masculine	feminine	neuter	plural
welcher Mann	welche Frau	welches Kleid	welche Röcke

B Case

Besides number and gender, German nouns and the words that go with them have a **case**. The way cases work is quite complex, but they tell you certain simple things about the noun.

The nominative

A word is in the nominative if it is the **subject** or 'doer' of an action (and actions include words like 'is').

Der Tisch ist braun.   The table is brown.

Mein Bruder wohnt in London.   My brother lives in London.

Diese Katze ist launisch.   This cat is moody.

	masculine	feminine	neuter	plural
the	der	die	das	die
a	ein	eine	ein	–
not a	kein	keine	kein	keine
my	mein	meine	mein	meine
this	dieser	diese	dieses	diese
each	jeder	jede	jedes	–
which	welcher	welche	welches	welche

The accusative

For the **object** of most verbs (like haben or es gibt), and after some **prepositions**, you use the accusative.

Der, ein, mein, etc. are different in the accusative – but only in the masculine form:

Ich habe **einen** Bruder.   I have a brother.

Er hat **keinen** Stuhl.   He hasn't got a chair.

Es gibt **einen** Supermarkt. There's a supermarket.

Er geht in **den** Park.   He goes into the park.

	masculine	feminine	neuter	plural
the	den	die	das	die
a	einen	eine	ein	–
not a	keinen	keine	kein	keine
my	meinen	meine	mein	meine
this	diesen	diese	dieses	diese
each	jeden	jede	jedes	–
which	welchen	welche	welches	welche

The dative

After some **prepositions** (e.g. *zu*, *mit*) you use the dative.

Words like *ein*, *mein*, etc. are different in the dative. You will have to learn them.

mit **dem** Mann   with the man

mit **meinem** Bruder   with my brother

	masculine	feminine	neuter	plural
the	dem	der	dem	den
a	einem	einer	einem	–
not a	keinem	keiner	keinem	keinen
my	meinem	meiner	meinem	meinen
this	diesem	dieser	diesem	diesen
each	jedem	jeder	jedem	–
which	welchem	welcher	welchem	welchen

In the plural, an extra *-(e)n* is added to the end of the noun:

*Ich komme mit meinen Brüder**n**.*   I am coming with my brothers.

Some prepositions combine with *dem*, *der*, *dem* to make shortened forms: see section C.

The genitive

You use the genitive to indicate **possession** (and with certain **prepositions**). Words like *ein* and *mein* are different in the genitive. You will have to learn them.

In English, we say 'my brother's room' but in German you have to say 'the room of my brother'. The 'of my' part is incorporated into one word – *meines*:

*Das Zimmer mein**es** Bruder**s***

*Das Zimmer mein**er** Schwester*

*Das Zimmer mein**es** Kind**es***

Note the extra *-(e)s* on the end of masculine and neuter nouns.

	masculine	feminine	neuter	plural
the	des Bruders	der Schwester	des Kindes	der Kinder
a	eines Bruders	einer Schwester	eines Kindes	–
not a	keines Bruders	keiner Schwester	keines Kindes	keiner Kinder
my	meines Bruders	meiner Schwester	meines Kindes	meiner Kinder
this	dieses Bruders	dieser Schwester	dieses Kindes	dieser Kinder
each	jedes Bruders	jeder Schwester	jedes Kindes	–
which	welches Bruders	welcher Schwester	welches Kindes	welcher Kinder

C Other parts of a German sentence

Prepositions

Prepositions are words that tell you **where** things are (or their 'position'), for example 'on', 'under', 'by', 'at', 'with'.

Prepositions + dative

These prepositions are always followed by the dative:

aus	from, out of	*bei*	at the house of, with
gegenüber	opposite	*mit*	with
nach	after, to	*seit*	since
von	from, of	*zu*	to

Shortened forms:

zu dem ➡ *zum*   *zu der* ➡ *zur*

bei dem ➡ *beim*   *von dem* ➡ *vom*

zur Schule   to school

gegenüber dem Haus   opposite the house

bei ihnen   at their house

Prepositions + accusative

These prepositions are always followed by the accusative:

bis	until	*durch*	through
für	for	*gegen*	against
ohne	without	*um*	around

für meine Freundin	for my friend
um die Ecke	around the corner
ohne Geschenke	without gifts
durch den Tunnel	through the tunnel

Prepositions + dative or accusative

Most of the prepositions you have met are sometimes followed by the dative and sometimes (but not as often) by the accusative. Here is a list of them with their meaning when followed by the dative:

an	at, on (vertical things)	*über*	over, above
auf	on (horizontal things)	*unter*	under, underneath
hinter	behind	*vor*	in front of
in	in	*zwischen*	between
neben	near, next to		

*an **der** Wand*	on the wall
*auf **einem** Tisch*	on a table
*in **seiner** Tasche*	in his pocket
*unter **dem** Bett*	under the bed

Usually when there is movement involved (e.g. 'into' rather than 'in'), these same prepositions are followed by the accusative.

an	up to, over to	*über*	(go) over, across
auf	onto	*unter*	(go) under
hinter	(go) behind	*vor*	(go) in front of
in	into	*zwischen*	(go) between
neben	(go) next to, beside		

*in **die** Schule*	into school
***ins** Schwimmbad*	into the swimming pool
*auf **den** Tisch*	on to the table
*Die Katze geht unter **den** Stuhl.*	The cat goes under the chair.
*Der Hund springt über **die** CDs.*	The dog jumps over the CDs.

Shortened forms:

in das ➡ *ins*		*in dem* ➡ *im*	
an das ➡ *ans*		*an dem* ➡ *am*	

Prepositions + genitive

These prepositions are always followed by the genitive:

(an)statt	instead of	*wegen*	because of
außerhalb	outside of, excluding	*trotz*	in spite of
innerhalb	inside of, within	*während*	during

wegen des Wetters	because of the weather
außerhalb der Stadt	outside of the town
während der Reise	during the journey

Adjectives

Adjectives are words that describe nouns. When adjectives come **after** the noun, they work just like English adjectives:

*Die Blume ist **schön**.*	The flower is pretty.
*Das Haus ist **rot**.*	The house is red.

However, when adjectives come **before** the noun, you have to give them an ending.

Here are the adjective endings for nominative, accusative, dative, genitive and plural nouns after *der / die / das / die*.

	masculine	feminine	neuter	plural
nominative	*der schöne Park*	*die schöne Stadt*	*das schöne Haus*	*die schönen Blumen*
accusative	*den schönen Park*	*die schöne Stadt*	*das schöne Haus*	*die schönen Blumen*
dative	*dem schönen Park*	*der schönen Stadt*	*dem schönen Haus*	*den schönen Blumen*
genitive	*des schönen Parkes*	*der schönen Stadt*	*des schönen Hauses*	*der schönen Blumen*

Here are the adjective endings for nominative, accusative, dative and genitive nouns after *ein / eine / ein*. Note that the genitive and dative adjective endings are all *-en*.

	masculine	feminine	neuter	plural
nominative	ein schöner Park	eine schöne Stadt	ein schönes Haus	schöne Blumen
accusative	einen schönen Park	eine schöne Stadt	ein schönes Haus	schöne Blumen
dative	einem schönen Park	einer schönen Stadt	einem schönen Haus	schönen Blumen
genitive	eines schönen Parkes	einer schönen Stadt	eines schönen Hauses	schönen Blumen

Adjectives as nouns

Adjectives can be used as nouns by giving them a capital letter and adding the correct adjective ending. This is most common when using an adjective of nationality to talk about a person:

deutsch	German
der Deutsche / ein Deutscher	the / a German (male)
die Deutsche / eine Deutsche	the / a German (female)

The noun behaves like an adjective, as if another noun were to follow it.

Adjectives after *etwas* / *nichts*, etc.

After the following words, an adjective changes its form:

etwas (something), *nichts* (nothing), *viel* (much), *wenig* (little), *alles* (all).

If you want to say 'something interesting' or 'nothing new', for example, the adjective gains a capital letter (becomes a noun) and you add **-es** to the end of it:

etwas Interessant**es**

nichts Neu**es**

After *alles* (everything), you just add **-e** to the adjective. You may already be familiar with the form *Alles Gut**e*** (all the best) at the end of informal cards or letters.

Comparative and superlative

Comparative

When comparing two things in English, we usually add **-er**, for example 'quick – quicker'. This applies in German as well:

schnell ➡ *schneller*

There are some exceptions, however, where an umlaut (¨) is added to the vowel. Some common ones are:

alt ➡ *älter*

groß ➡ *größer*

jung ➡ *jünger*

kalt ➡ *kälter*

In English, we stop adding '–er' to longer adjectives and use 'more', e.g. 'more interesting'. In German, though, **–er** is added to all adjectives:

interessant ➡ *interessanter*

To say 'than' when making a comparison, use *als*:

*Mein Haus ist größer **als** deine Wohnung.* My house is bigger than your flat.

Superlative

When talking about 'the quickest', you use the word *am* and add **–sten** to the adjective.

*Ich bin schnell, er ist schneller, aber sie ist **am** schnell**sten**.*

To form the noun for 'the quickest', you add the relevant adjective ending:

der **S**chnellst**e**	die **S**chnellst**e**
das **S**chnellst**e**	die **S**chnellst**en**

Adverbs

Adverbs are used to qualify the action of the verb.

*Der Bus ist **langsam**.* The bus is slow. (adjective)

*Ich gehe **langsam** in die Schule.* I walk to school slowly. (adverb)

In English we add '–ly' to the adverb, but in German the adjective and adverb forms are the same.

Adverbs of frequency and place

immer	always
manchmal	sometimes
selten	rarely
nie	never
normalerweise	normally
oft	often
draußen	outside
dort	there
hier	here

Adverbs of degree (quantifiers / intensifiers)

Adverbs of degree qualify other adverbs and adjectives:

sehr	very
ziemlich	fairly
zu	too
fast	almost
ein bisschen	a little, a bit
viel	a lot
ganz	quite, rather
ein wenig	a little
*Du isst **zu** schnell.*	You eat too quickly.

Interrogative adverbs

Interrogative adverbs are used when asking questions and need to be learnt (see also, Interrogatives page 188):

Wann?	When?
Warum?	Why?
Wo?	Where?
Wie?	How?
Wie viel?	How much?
Wer?	Who?
Was?	What?

Adverbial phrases

Adverbial phrases give additional information about when, where or how an action takes place. Examples are:

nach dem Essen	after the meal
vor der Schule	before school
jeden Tag	every day
ab und zu	now and again
letzte Woche	last week
nächstes Wochenende	next weekend
so bald wie möglich	as soon as possible

Words for 'you'

There are **three** German words for 'you', depending on the number of people and your relationship to them:

du Informal singular – for talking to one young person or friend: *Kommst **du** mit?*

ihr Informal plural – for talking to more than one young person or friend: *Kommt **ihr** mit?*

Sie Formal singular or plural – for talking to one or more than one older person or stranger: *Kommen **Sie** mit?*

N.B. You only need to be able to recognise the *ihr* form at Foundation level. At Higher level, you should be able to use it in your own speaking or writing.

Words for 'it'

The German word for 'it' is not always *es*! It depends on the gender of the noun 'it' refers to. For the nominative case, you use *er* (masc.), *sie* (fem.) and *es* (neut.). So *das Buch* is *es*, but *die Banane* is *sie*. Don't be put off by the fact that *er* and *sie* also mean 'he' and 'she' – it should be clear from the context what the particular meaning is.

*Ich habe einen Apfel. **Er** ist lecker.*
I have an apple. It is delicious.

Subject pronouns

Subject pronouns are words like 'I', 'you', 'he', etc. They are usually used with a verb.

ich	I
du	you (informal singular)
er	he
sie	she
es	it
man	one, people, you (non-specific)
wir	we
ihr	you (informal plural)
Sie	you (formal singular or plural)
sie	they

The subject pronoun *man* is used when you are not talking about anyone in particular. It is used to say 'one', 'people', 'you', 'they' or 'we' (see page 26):

***Man** darf nicht rauchen.*
You're not allowed to smoke.

***Man** muss eine Uniform tragen.*
We have to wear a uniform.

Object pronouns

Object pronouns are used to replace the object in a sentence. **Direct objects** are in the **accusative** and **indirect objects** in the **dative**:

	accusative	dative
me	*mich*	*mir*
you (inf. sing.)	*dich*	*dir*
him/her/it	*ihn/sie/es*	*ihm/ihr/ihm*
us	*uns*	*uns*
you (inf. pl.)	*euch*	*euch*
you (form.)/them	*sie/Sie*	*Ihnen/ihnen*

Nimmst du Toby mit nach Köln? Ja, ich nehme **ihn** *mit nach Köln.* (direct object)

Gibst du mir bitte ein Eis? Ja, ich gebe **dir** *ein Eis.* (indirect object)

Reflexive pronouns

Reflexive pronouns are used with reflexive verbs, which are listed in the infinitive with *sich*, e.g. *sich fühlen, sich waschen, sich treffen*. The reflexive pronoun usually changes as follows:

ich fühle **mich**   *wir fühlen* **uns**

du fühlst **dich**   *ihr fühlt* **euch**

er/sie/es/man fühlt **sich**   *sie/Sie fühlen* **sich**

Some reflexive verbs use *mir* and *dir* (dative reflexive pronouns) instead of *mich* and *dich* (accusative reflexive pronouns):

Ich wasche **mich**.   I wash (lit. I wash myself).

This is the usual accusative reflexive pronoun.

Ich putze **mir** *die Zähne*.   I brush my teeth (lit. I clean the teeth to me).

Du bürstest **dir** *die Haare*.   You brush your hair. (lit. 'You brush the hair to you'.)

These last two examples use dative reflexive pronouns.

Relative pronouns and clauses

Relative pronouns ('who', 'whom', 'which', 'that') are used to introduce a relative clause. In German, they vary according to the **gender** and **number** of the word they refer back to, and their **case** depends on their function in the relative clause. The verb in the relative clause goes to the end.

These examples show the nominative form for each gender:

Das ist mein Bruder, **der** *Jürgen heißt.*
This is my brother, who is called Jürgen.

Ingrid, **die** *sehr schön ist, kommt heute.*
Ingrid, who is very beautiful, is coming today.

Das Meerschweinchen, **das** *sehr klein ist, ist schwarz.*
The guinea pig, which is very small, is black.

Relative clauses can also be introduced by question words like 'where' and 'why':

Meine Schule hat ein Sprachlabor, **wo** *ich Französisch lerne.*
My school has a language lab where I learn French.

Interrogative pronouns

Words for 'whom'

In German, there are two words for 'whom': *wen* and *wem*. Use *wen* after prepositions taking the accusative and *wem* after prepositions taking the dative.

Für wen hatte er das Buch gekauft?

For whom had he bought the book? or more commonly you might say, 'Who did he buy the book for?'

Mit wem hast du gegessen?
With whom did you eat? or Who did you eat with?

When you're using 'who' in a question, use *wer*.

Wer ist dein Chemielehrer?
Who is your chemistry teacher?

If you're asking 'what kind of' in a question, use *was für …?*

Was für einen Hund hast du?
What kind of a dog have you got?

Words for 'when'

Wenn means 'when', 'if' or 'whenever' and is used to refer to the present, future or a habitual action in the past.

Wenn *ich nach Deutschland fuhr, habe ich immer bei meinem Brieffreund gewohnt.*
When I used to go to Germany, I always stayed with my penfriend.

Als means 'when' and refers to a particular event in the past.

Als *ich in Deutschland war, habe ich bei meinem Brieffreund gewohnt.*
When I was in Germany (one occasion) I stayed with my penfriend.

Wann introduces a 'when' question, in any tense.

Wann hast du bei deinem Brieffreund gewohnt?
When did you stay with your penfriend?

D Verbs

The present tense

Verbs are 'doing words' – they describe actions.
You use a **noun** (e.g. *mein Bruder*) or a **pronoun**
(*ich, du*, etc.) as the **subject** or doer of the action.
For each different person or pronoun you need to
use the correct verb ending.

Regular verbs

In the present tense, regular (or weak) verbs (verbs
which follow the usual pattern) have the following
endings:

ich spiele	I play, I'm playing
*du spielst**	you play, you're playing
er spielt	he plays, he's playing
sie spielt	she plays, she's playing
es spielt	it plays, it's playing
man spielt	one plays, one's playing
wir spielen	we play, we're playing
*ihr spielt**	you play, you're playing
sie spielen	they play, they're playing
*Sie spielen**	you play, you're playing

* For *du/ihr/Sie* ('you') see section C, page 179.

Ich *spiele Tennis.* I play tennis.

Mein Onkel *spielt gern Fußball.*
My uncle likes playing football.

Sie *spielen Schach.* They're playing chess.

Other verbs that work like this are:

machen	to do	*wohnen*	to live (location)
kaufen	to buy	*kochen*	to cook

Regular verbs which end in *-ten* (e.g. *antworten* to
answer) add *-est* in the *du* form and *-et* in the *er/sie/
es/man* form.

Warum antwortest du nicht? Why don't you answer?

Irregular verbs

Irregular (or strong) verbs use the same endings
as regular verbs, but there is a difference: the first
vowel usually changes in the *du* and *er/sie/es* forms:

laufen to run, to walk

ich laufe	*wir laufen*
du läufst	*ihr lauft*
er/sie/es/man läuft	*sie/Sie laufen*

essen to eat

ich esse	*wir essen*
du isst	*ihr esst*
er/sie/es isst	*sie/Sie essen*

Other common verbs in this category are: *fallen,
fahren, helfen, schlafen, geben, tragen* and *treffen*.

Some irregular verbs change their vowel sound more
radically, such as *lesen* and *sehen*:

lesen to read

ich lese	*wir lesen*
du liest	*ihr lest*
er/sie/es/man liest	*sie/Sie lesen*

Haben

Another important irregular verb is *haben* (to have)
which drops the **b** in the *du* and *er/sie/es* forms:

haben to have

ich habe	*wir haben*
*du **hast***	*ihr habt*
*er/sie/es/man **hat***	*sie/Sie haben*

Sein

The verb *sein* (to be) is totally different and must be
learnt!

sein to be

*ich **bin***	*wir **sind***
*du **bist***	*ihr **seid***
*er/sie/es/man **ist***	*sie/Sie **sind***

Modal verbs

These are verbs like 'will', 'must', 'can' and 'could',
and they usually have to be used with another verb,
which is in the **infinitive** and goes to the **end** of the
sentence.

Usually, the singular forms of modal verbs are
different from others because the vowel changes. An
exception to this is *sollen* (should, ought to). For all
modal verbs there is no **-e** ending for the first person
singular.

müssen must, to have to	*mögen* to like
*ich **muss***	*ich **mag***
*du **musst***	*du **magst***
*er/sie/es/man **muss***	*er/sie/es/man **mag***
*wir **müssen***	*wir **mögen***
*ihr **müsst***	*ihr **mögt***
*sie/Sie **müssen***	*sie/Sie **mögen***

wollen to want to

ich **will**

du **willst**

er/sie/es/man **will**

wir **wollen**

ihr **wollt**

sie/Sie **wollen**

dürfen may, to be allowed to

ich **darf**

du **darfst**

er/sie/es/man **darf**

wir **dürfen**

ihr **dürft**

sie/Sie **dürfen**

können can, to be able to

ich **kann**

du **kannst**

er/sie/es/man **kann**

wir **können**

ihr **könnt**

sie/Sie **können**

sollen to be supposed to, should

ich **soll**

du **sollst**

er/sie/es/man **soll**

wir **sollen**

ihr **sollt**

sie/Sie **sollen**

Ich **will** mein Geld nicht verschwenden.
I don't want to waste my money.

Sie **soll** das Rauchen aufgeben.
She is supposed to give up smoking.

Separable verbs

Some verbs are in **two parts**. They consist of the **normal verb** and a **separable prefix**.

The normal verb goes in the usual place (second idea), but the prefix goes at the end of the sentence. When listed in a dictionary or Glossary, the separable prefix is always listed first.

Here is a separable verb, *einkaufen* (to shop), in full:

ich **kaufe ein**

du **kaufst ein**

er/sie/es/man **kauft ein**

wir **kaufen ein**

ihr **kauft ein**

sie/Sie **kaufen ein**

Ich **kaufe** am Montag **ein**.   I go shopping on Monday.

Er **kauft** mit seiner Mutter **ein**.
He goes shopping with his mother.

Sie **kaufen** in Berlin **ein**.
They go shopping in Berlin.

These are some other separable verbs you have met:

*abwaschen (ich **wasche ab**)*   to wash up

*aufräumen (ich **räume auf**)*   to tidy up

*aufstehen (ich **stehe auf**)*   to get up

*ausgeben (ich **gebe aus**)*   to spend (money)

*aufmachen (ich **mache auf**)*   to open

*ansehen (ich **sehe an**)*   to look at

*fernsehen (ich **sehe fern**)*   to watch TV

Inseparable verbs

Some verbs look like they might have a separable prefix at the front but are in fact inseparable. These include any verbs starting with:

be-, emp-, ent-, er-, ge-, miss-, ver- or *zer-*

e.g. *benutzen* (to use), *empfehlen* (to recommend), *enthalten* (to contain), *erzählen* (to tell), *gewinnen* (to win), *versuchen* (to try), *zerstören* (to destroy).

So these verbs don't split up like separable verbs and are formed in the normal way in the present tense.

The perfect tense

The perfect tense is used to talk about things that happened in the past.

It is made up of two parts: the **auxiliary** (or 'helping') **verb** and the **past participle**. The auxiliary verb goes in the usual place (second): it is usually *haben*. The past participle goes at the end of the sentence.

The perfect tense with *haben*

To form the past participle, you take the **-en** off the infinitive of the verb. Then you (usually) add **ge-** to the beginning of the word and **-t** to the end.

ich **habe gespielt**   I played, I have played

du **hast gemacht**   you did, you have done

er/sie/es/man **hat gekauft**   he/she/it bought, has bought

wir **haben gespielt**   we played, we have played

ihr **habt gemacht**   you did, you have done

sie/Sie **haben gekauft**   they/you bought, have bought

Verbs which begin with **ver-** and **be-** and verbs which end in **-ieren** do not add the **ge-** to the beginning:

Ich **habe versucht**.   I tried.

Ich **habe** Gabi **besucht**.   I visited Gabi.

Hast du dich **amüsiert**?   Did you enjoy yourself?

With separable verbs, the **ge-** goes after the separable prefix:

Ich **habe** in der Stadt **eingekauft**.
I went shopping in town.

Irregular past participles

Some verbs are irregular in the perfect tense. They still make their perfect tense with *haben*, but the past participle is formed differently. You (usually) change the **vowel** in the participle and keep the **-en** from the infinitive on the end. Here are some you have learnt so far:

essen (to eat)	*gegessen*
lesen (to read)	*gelesen*
sehen (to see)	*gesehen*
finden (to find)	*gefunden*
trinken (to drink)	*getrunken*
nehmen (to take)	*genommen*
schreiben (to write)	*geschrieben*
treffen (to meet)	*getroffen*

Again, verbs which begin with *be-, emp-, ent-, er-, ge-, miss-, ver-* or *zer-* do not add the **ge-** to the beginning of the verb:

Ich habe begonnen.	I began.
Ich habe vergessen.	I forgot.

The perfect tense with *sein*

Another group of verbs form their perfect tense with *sein* (to be). These are usually **verbs of movement**. As with the other verbs, the auxiliary (*sein*) is in second place and the participle at the end of the sentence.

Here are the ones you have learnt so far:

fahren ➡ ich **bin gefahren**	I went / drove, I have gone / driven
gehen ➡ ich **bin gegangen**	I went / walked, I have gone / walked
kommen ➡ ich **bin gekommen**	I came, I have come
fliegen ➡ ich **bin geflogen**	I flew, I have flown
fallen ➡ ich **bin gefallen**	I fell, I have fallen
laufen ➡ ich **bin gelaufen**	I ran, I have run

ich **bin gefahren**
du **bist gegangen**
er/sie/es/man **ist gekommen**
wir **sind geflogen**
ihr **seid gefahren**
sie/Sie **sind gekommen**

With separable verbs, the **ge-** goes after the separable prefix:

Ich **bin** *um 7 Uhr* **aufgestanden**.

The imperfect tense

Regular verbs

The imperfect tense is another way of talking about the past but is not usually used in speech.

To form the imperfect tense, take the infinitive of the verb, remove the **-en** and add the endings as follows:

*ich spiel***te**
*du spiel***test**
*er/sie/es/man spiel***t**
*wir spiel***ten**
*ihr spiel***tet**
*sie/Sie spiel***ten**

Irregular verbs

Irregular (strong) verbs have set stems to which the following endings are added. Note that nothing is added in the *ich* and *er/sie/es/man* forms. This example shows the endings for *fahren* (to travel, to drive):

ich fuhr
*du fuhr***st**
er/sie/es/man fuhr
*wir fuhr***en**
*ihr fuhr***t**
*sie/Sie fuhr***en**

Some common stems are as follows:

beginnen (to begin)	*begann*
essen (to eat)	*aß*
gehen (to go)	*ging*
lesen (to read)	*las*
sehen (to see)	*sah*
trinken (to drink)	*trank*

Some verbs are mixed verbs and have set stems but add regular endings, e.g. *bringen*:

*ich brach***te**
*du brach***test**
*er/sie/es/man brach***te**
*wir brach***ten**
*ihr brach***tet**
*sie/Sie brach***ten**

Other examples are:

denken (to think)	*dachte*
kennen (to know)	*kannte*

The most common irregular forms used, and ones to learn, are:

sein to be	*haben* to have
ich **war**	*ich* **hatte**
du **warst**	*du* **hattest**

er/sie/es/man **war**

wir **waren**

ihr **wart**

sie/Sie **waren**

er/sie/es/man **hatte**

wir **hatten**

ihr **hattet**

sie/Sie **hattet**

It's also useful to remember the imperfect tense for *es gibt* (there is / are) – *es gab* (there was / were).

Modal verbs

These are the imperfect tense forms for the modal verbs you have encountered.

müssen must, to have to

ich **musste**

du **musstest**

er/sie/es/man **musste**

wir **mussten**

ihr **musstet**

sie/Sie **mussten**

mögen to like

ich **mochte**

du **mochtest**

er/sie/es/man **mochte**

wir **mochten**

ihr **mochtet**

sie/Sie **mochten**

wollen to want to

ich **wollte**

du **wolltest**

er/sie/es/man **wollte**

wir **wollten**

ihr **wolltet**

sie/Sie **wollten**

können can, to be able to

ich **konnte**

du **konntest**

er/sie/es/man **konnte**

wir **konnten**

ihr **konntet**

sie/Sie **konnten**

dürfen may, to be allowed to

ich **durfte**

du **durftest**

er/sie/es/man **durfte**

wir **durften**

ihr **durftet**

sie/Sie **durften**

sollen should, ought to

ich **sollte**

du **solltest**

er/sie/es/man **sollte**

wir **sollten**

ihr **solltet**

sie/Sie **sollten**

The pluperfect tense

The pluperfect tense conveys a moment **further back** in time than the perfect tense and is formed with 'had' in English, e.g. 'By the time I was 16, I had moved house three times.' For verbs which form their perfect tense with *haben*, use the correct form of *haben* in the imperfect tense (*hatte*, etc.) plus the past participle.

ich **hatte gekauft** (I had bought)

du **hattest gekauft**

er/sie/es/man **hatte gekauft**

wir **hatten gekauft**

ihr **hattet gekauft**

sie/Sie **hatten gekauft**

For verbs which form their perfect tense with *sein*, use the correct form of *sein* in the imperfect tense (*war*, etc.) plus the past participle.

ich **war gegangen** (I had gone)

du **warst gegangen**

er/sie/es/man **war gegangen**

wir **waren gegangen**

ihr **wart gegangen**

sie/Sie **waren gegangen**

The future tense

Present tense with future meaning

As in English, the present tense can be used to convey a future meaning if a **future time indicator** is used:

Nächstes Jahr gehe ich auf die Uni.
I'm going to university next year.

Future tense with *werden*

To form the future tense, use the correct present tense form of the verb *werden* plus the infinitive:

Ich **werde** *nach Berlin* **fahren**. I will travel to Berlin.*

ich **werde**

du **wirst**

er/sie/es/man **wird**

wir **werden**

ihr **werdet**

sie/Sie **werden**

* Remember that *ich will* doesn't mean 'I will', but 'I want to'.

The conditional tense

The conditional tense (strictly speaking, the conditional 'mood') uses 'would' and is used to talk about actions that are dependent on certain conditions being fulfilled. The easiest way of using a conditional in German is to use the following forms of *mögen*: *möchte / möchtest / möchten* (would like) with the infinitive of the second verb at the end of the sentence or clause.

Ich möchte heiraten und Kinder haben.
I'd like to get married and have children.

To form the standard conditional tense, use …

ich würde, du würdest, er/sie/es/man würde, wir würden etc. plus the infinitive:

Was würdest du mit einem Lottogewinn machen?
What would you do with a lottery win?

Ich würde um die Welt fahren.
I would travel around the world.

The forms of *sollen* are *sollte/solltest/sollten* ('should' in the conditional):

*Ich **sollte** meine Hausaufgaben **machen**.*
I should do my homework.

(This form is the same as the imperfect of *sollen*.)

The forms of *können* are *könnte/könntest/könnten* ('could' in the conditional):

*Ich **könnte** um die Welt **fahren**.*
I could travel around the world.

(Do not confuse this form with *konnte* – 'could' in the past.)

It's also useful to know the forms for 'would have' (*ich hätte, du hättest* etc.) and 'would be' (*wäre, wär(e)st* etc.):

*Wenn ich reich **wäre**, **hätte** ich mein eigenes Flugzeug.*
If I were rich, I would have my own plane.

All of these forms (*würde, möchte, könnte, wäre* etc.) are known as the **imperfect subjunctive** of the verbs. You do not need to learn about subjunctive forms in detail at this stage, but you may want to find out more about them as you progress in your studies.

The passive

The passive is used to describe what is **being done to** someone or something. It is formed by using the verb *werden* ('to become') with a past participle:

*Das Auto **wird gewaschen**.*
The car is being washed.

*Der Film **wird** heute noch einmal **gezeigt**.*
The film is being shown once more today.

You will not have to recognise passive forms in your reading or listening exams at GCSE, but you may wish to use them in your spoken and written work.

Impersonal verbs

Some verbs are 'impersonal', which means they do not have a subject like *ich* or *du*. They are used with the impersonal subject *es* (it).

If you want to say 'there is' or 'there are', you use *es gibt* with the accusative case:

Es gibt einen Supermarkt. There is a supermarket.

If you want to say 'there is no' or 'there are no', use *es gibt + kein(e)(n)* + accusative case:

Es gibt kein Schwimmbad.
There is no swimming pool.

Other examples of impersonal verbs are:

Es tut mir Leid.	I'm sorry.
Es geht.	It's OK.
Wie geht es dir?	How are you?
Mir geht's gut.	I'm well.
Es tut weh.	It hurts.

Infinitive constructions

Um … zu, ohne … zu, anstatt … zu

To say 'in order to', you use the construction *um … zu* plus the infinitive at the end of the clause. Note the comma before the *um*:

*Ich treibe Sport, **um** gesund **zu** bleiben.*
I do sport in order to stay healthy.

Ohne … zu ('without doing something') and *anstatt … zu* ('instead of doing something') work in a similar way. You need to put the object after *um* and the verb in the infinitive after *zu*:

*Ich werde nach Amerika fliegen, **ohne** viel Geld aus**zu**geben.*
I will fly to America without spending a lot of money.*

*Ich werde in den Osterferien Skifahren, **anstatt** auf meine Prüfungen **zu** lernen.*
I will go skiing in the Easter holidays instead of studying for my exams.

* Note that with separable verbs such as *ausgeben*, *zu* goes after the prefix.

Zu + infinitive

After modal verbs, you do not need *zu* (*Ich **will** mit dem Bus **fahren***), but after the following verbs, the use of *zu* is required:

beginnen	to begin
beschließen	to decide
helfen	to help
hoffen	to hope
vergessen	to forget
versuchen	to try
vorhaben	to intend

*Ich **versuche**, Energie **zu sparen**.*
I'm trying to save energy.

Lassen + infinitive

Lassen with an infinitive is used to say 'get/have something done':

*Ich **lasse** meine Waschmaschine **reparieren.***
I'm having my washing machine repaired.

*Ich **lasse** meine Bluse **reinigen.***
I'm having my blouse cleaned.

Imperfect tense: *ich **ließ***

Perfect tense: *ich **habe** … **lassen***

Nicht

Nicht means 'not' and it usually comes after the verb:

*Ich bin **nicht** doof.*   I am not stupid.

However, when there is an object in the sentence, *nicht* comes after the object:

*Lena mag Englisch **nicht**.*   Lena doesn't like English.

(Don't forget that you use *kein* to say 'not a', see page 26.)

Other negatives

nie(mals)	never

Ich gehe nie in die Stadt.   I never go into town.

nicht mehr	no longer

Er lernt nicht mehr Italienisch.
He's no longer learning Italian.

niemand	no-one

Er hat niemanden bei ihr gesehen.
He saw no-one at her house / accompanying her.

And *niemand*'s opposite, *jemand* (meaning someone) is also a good one to know:

Jemand ist in diesem Zimmer gewesen.
Someone has been in this room.

Gern

When you want to say that you 'like doing' something, you use *gern*. It comes after the verb.

*Ich gehe **gern** einkaufen.*   I like going shopping.

When you want to say that you 'don't like' doing something, you use *nicht gern*:

*Ich gehe **nicht gern** einkaufen.*
I don't like going shopping.

Giving instructions (the imperative)

When you give someone instructions (e.g. 'Turn right!') you use a particular form of the verb called the imperative.

- With teachers or adults you don't know very well, use the *Sie* form. The verb goes first, with *Sie* after:

  Sie machen das Licht aus. ➡ ***Machen Sie** das Licht aus!*
  Turn the light out!

- With one friend or family member, use the *du* form without the **-st** ending. Put the verb first and omit *du*:

  *Du **machst** das Licht aus.* ➡ ***Mach** das Licht aus!*
  Turn the light out!

- With more than one friend or family member, use the *ihr* form without the pronoun *ihr*:

  *Ihr **macht** das Licht aus.* ➡ ***Macht** das Licht aus!*
  Turn the light out!

Seit with the present tense

Seit means 'since' and is usually used with the present tense in German:

*Ich **bin** seit 9 Uhr hier.*   I've been here since 9 o'clock.

It is also used to mean 'for', again with the present tense:

*Ich **lerne** seit vier Jahren Deutsch.*
I have been learning German for four years.

(Note that *seit* takes the dative, which is why *Jahren* has an **-n** at the end.)

Seit with the imperfect tense

You can also use *seit* with the imperfect tense in German to imply the pluperfect ('had done') tense.

Ich wohnte seit vier Jahren in München, als meine Tante starb.
I'd been living in Munich for four years when my aunt died.

Seit der Hochzeit war er sehr froh.
He'd been very happy since the wedding.

E Word order

Basic word order

Here is the basic word order in a German sentence:

subject	verb	rest of the sentence
Ich	*spiele*	*Gitarre.*
Lukas	*geht*	*in die Stadt.*

Verb as second idea

In German, the verb is always in second place in a sentence or clause. It's not always the second word, because you can't separate a phrase like *in meinem Zimmer*, but the verb must be the **second idea** or concept in the sentence:

1	2	3	4
[Ich]	[treibe]	[manchmal]	[Sport].

1	2	3	4
[Manchmal]	[treibe]	[ich]	[Sport].

Changing a sentence so that the first idea is no longer the subject is called using **inversion**.

Subordinate clauses

A subordinate clause is dependent on a main clause and does not make sense on its own, e.g. *weil es 11 Uhr ist*.

■ The conjunctions *weil, dass, da, obwohl, als* and *wenn* send the verb to the end of the subordinate clause which they introduce:

*Ich kann nicht gut schlafen, **weil** ich Angst **habe**.*
I can't sleep well because I'm afraid.

*Ich weiß, **dass** er obdachlos **ist**.*
I know that he's homeless.

*Er ist dick, **da** er viel **isst**.* He is fat, as he eats a lot.

*Ich will eine Karriere haben, **obwohl** meine Eltern reich sind.*
I want to have a career even though my parents are rich.

*Er sah fern, **als** seine Mutti wieder nach Hause **kam**.*
He was watching TV when his mum came back home.

*Ich gehe zum Strand, **wenn** die Sonne **scheint**.*
I go to the beach when the sun shines.

■ If two verbs appear in a subordinate clause, the **finite verb** (not the infinitive or past participle) is sent to the end of the clause. The finite verb is often an auxiliary verb (*haben, sein*) or a modal verb (*können, müssen*):

Ich kann im Meer schwimmen. ➡ *Ich gehe gern zum Strand, **weil** ich im Meer schwimmen **kann**.*

Ich bin im Meer geschwommen. ➡ *Der Urlaub war toll, **weil** ich im Meer geschwommen **bin**.*

■ If a sentence begins with the subordinate clause, the verbs meet in the middle, separated by a comma.

***Wenn** die Sonne **scheint**, **gehe** ich zum Strand.*
When the sun shines, I go to the beach.

■ Other subordinate clauses are introduced by *damit, so dass, ob* and *als*.

*Ich schreibe schnell, **damit** ich bald fertig **bin**.*
I'm writing fast, so that (in order that) I finish quickly.

*Ich esse viel Obst, **sodass** ich gesund **bleibe**.*
I eat lots of fruit, so that (as a result) I stay healthy.

*Ich weiß nicht, **ob** er **kommt**.*
I don't know whether he is coming.

***Als** das Wetter gut **war**, **bin** ich zum Strand gegangen.*
When the weather was good, I went to the beach.

Time – manner – place

When you mention when (time), how (manner) and where (place) you do something, you give the time first, then the manner and then the place.

	Time	Manner	Place
Ich fahre	[am Wochenende]	[mit dem Auto]	[nach Paris].

	Time	Place	
Er fährt	[mit dem Zug]	[nach Berlin].	

Conjunctions

Conjunctions are words that join sentences (or clauses, which are parts of sentences) together.

Coordinating conjunctions

Common conjunctions are *und* (and), *oder* (or) and *aber* (but). They do not affect the word order in a sentence:

Er hat kein Geld. Er kann die Sprache nicht verstehen.
➡ *Er hat kein Geld **und** er kann die Sprache nicht verstehen.*

He has no money. He can't understand the language.
➡ He has no money and he can't understand the language.

Ich kenne ein paar Leute. Wir sind keine richtigen Freunde. ➡ *Ich kenne ein paar Leute, **aber** wir sind keine richtigen Freunde.**

I know a few people. We aren't really friends. ➡
I know a few people but we aren't really friends.

* When using *aber* or *denn*, put a comma before it.

> Higher candidates might like to use some of the following, less common, co-ordinating conjunctions in their work:
>
> *denn*   because
>
> *Ich mag ihn, denn er ist klug.*
> I like him because he's clever.
>
> *sondern*   but (only used after a negative)
>
> *Er hat nicht drei, sondern vier Katzen.*
> He doesn't have three but four cats.

* Both *sondern* and *denn* need a comma before them.

Subordinating conjunctions

Some conjunctions including *weil, dass, da, obwohl, als* and *wenn* send the verb in the clause they introduce right to the end (see Subordinate clauses, page 187).

F Asking questions

Verb first

You can ask questions by putting the verb first in the sentence:

Du hörst *Musik.* ➡ **Hörst du** *Musik?*

You are listening to music. ➡ Are you listening to music?

Birgit ist *sportlich.* ➡ **Ist Birgit** *sportlich?*

Birgit is sporty. ➡ Is Birgit sporty?

Interrogatives (question words)

You can ask a question by starting with a question word or interrogative. Most German question words start with **w**:

Wer?	Who?
Wann?	When?
Was?	What?
Welche(r/s)?	Which?
Wie?	How?
Warum?	Why?
Wie viel(e)?	How much/many?
Wie lange?	How long?
Wo?	Where?
Wohin?	Where to?
Woher?	Where from?
Womit?	What with?

Most of these are pronouns or adverbs (see Interrogative adverbs, page 179) and are immediately followed by a verb:

Wer *kommt mit?*	Who's coming with us?
Wann *kommt sie?*	When is she coming?
Wohin fahren *wir?*	Where are we going (to)?

Welche(r/s) and *wie viel(e)* can be used as adjectives and followed by a noun (see Interrogative adjectives, page 175):

Wie viel *Taschengeld bekommst du?*
How much pocket money do you get?

G Numbers and time

Numbers

Cardinal numbers

1 *eins*		23 *dreiundzwanzig*	
2 *zwei*		24 *vierundzwanzig*	
3 *drei*		25 *fünfundzwanzig*	
4 *vier*		30 *dreißig*	
5 *fünf*		40 *vierzig*	
6 *sechs*		50 *fünfzig*	
7 *sieben*		60 *sechzig*	
8 *acht*		70 *siebzig*	
9 *neun*		80 *achtzig*	
10 *zehn*		90 *neunzig*	
11 *elf*		100 *hundert*	
12 *zwölf*		35 *fünfunddreißig*	
13 *dreizehn*		45 *fünfundvierzig*	
14 *vierzehn*		55 *fünfundfünfzig*	
15 *fünfzehn*		65 *fünfundsechzig*	
16 *sechzehn*		75 *fünfundsiebzig*	
17 *siebzehn*		85 *fünfundachtzig*	
18 *achtzehn*		95 *fünfundneunzig*	
19 *neunzehn*		200 *zweihundert*	
20 *zwanzig*		305 *dreihundertfünf*	
21 *einundzwanzig*		411 *vierhundertelf*	
22 *zweiundzwanzig*			

525 *fünfhundertfünfundzwanzig*

1000 *tausend*

2500 *zweitausendfünfhundert*

1984 *neunzehnhundertvierundachtzig* (in dates)

Ordinal numbers

To make the ordinal numbers (first, second, etc.) up to 19th you add **-te** to the cardinal number. There are a few exceptions: first (*erste*), third (*dritte*), seventh (*siebte*) and eighth (*achte*).

1st *erste*	11th *elfte*
2nd *zweite*	12th *zwölfte*
3rd *dritte*	13th *dreizehnte*
4th *vierte*	14th *vierzehnte*
5th *fünfte*	15th *fünfzehnte*
6th *sechste*	16th *sechzehnte*
7th *siebte*	17th *siebzehnte*
8th *achte*	18th *achtzehnte*
9th *neunte*	19th *neunzehnte*
10th *zehnte*	20th *zwanzigste*

To make the ordinal numbers from 20th upwards you add **-ste** to the cardinal number.

*Ich bin auf **den zwanzigsten** Platz gekommen.*
I came in twentieth place.

When giving dates, use *am* before the number and add **-n** (because *am* takes the dative case):

*Ich habe **am zwölften** Dezember Geburtstag.*
My birthday is on the twelfth of December.

The time

To tell the time, you say *es ist* followed by:

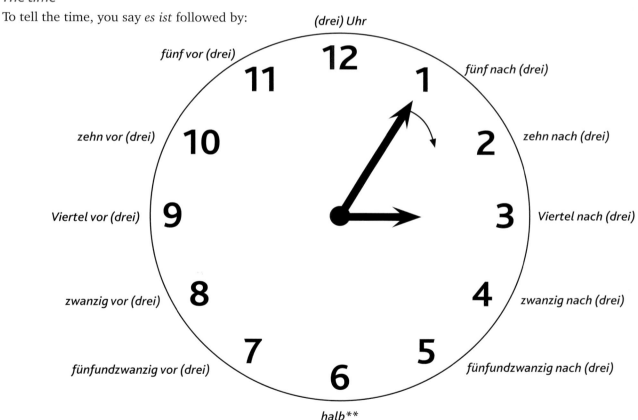

(drei) Uhr
fünf vor (drei) — *fünf nach (drei)*
zehn vor (drei) — *zehn nach (drei)*
Viertel vor (drei) — *Viertel nach (drei)*
zwanzig vor (drei) — *zwanzig nach (drei)*
fünfundzwanzig vor (drei) — *fünfundzwanzig nach (drei)*
halb**

** *Es ist **halb drei*** means 'It's half two', not 'It's half three' – the *halb* indicates **half to the hour**, not half past.

To say at what time something happens, you use *um* followed by the above:

***Um** halb neun gehe ich in die Schule.*
I go to school at half past eight.

Verb tables

H Verb tables

infinitive	present	imperfect	perfect	English
beginnen	beginnt	begann	begonnen	to begin
beißen	beißt	biss	gebissen	to bite
bewegen	bewegt	bewog	bewogen	to move
biegen	biegt	bog	gebogen	to bend
bieten	bietet	bot	geboten	to offer
binden	bindet	band	gebunden	to tie
bitten	bittet	bat	gebeten	to ask
blasen	bläst	blies	geblasen	to blow
bleiben	bleibt	blieb	geblieben*	to stay
brechen	bricht	brach	gebrochen	to break
brennen	brennt	brannte	gebrannt	to burn
bringen	bringt	brachte	gebracht	to bring
denken	denkt	dachte	gedacht	to think
dürfen	darf	durfte	gedurft	to be allowed to
empfehlen	empfiehlt	empfahl	empfohlen	to recommend
essen	isst	aß	gegessen	to eat
fahren	fährt	fuhr	gefahren*	to go, travel
fallen	fällt	fiel	gefallen*	to fall
fangen	fängt	fing	gefangen	to catch
finden	findet	fand	gefunden	to find
fliegen	fliegt	flog	geflogen*	to fly
fliehen	flieht	floh	geflohen*	to flee
fließen	fließt	floss	geflossen*	to flow
frieren	friert	fror	gefroren	to freeze

* Verbs which take *sein* in the perfect and pluperfect tenses.

infinitive	present	imperfect	perfect	English
geben	gibt	gab	gegeben	to give
gehen	geht	ging	gegangen*	to go
gelingen	gelingt	gelang	gelungen*	to succeed
genießen	genießt	genoss	genossen	to enjoy
geschehen	geschieht	geschah	geschehen*	to happen
gewinnen	gewinnt	gewann	gewonnen	to win
graben	gräbt	grub	gegraben	to dig
greifen	greift	griff	gegriffen	to grasp
haben	hat	hatte	gehabt	to have
halten	hält	hielt	gehalten	to stop
hängen	hängt	hing	gehangen	to hang
heben	hebt	hob	gehoben	to lift
heißen	heißt	hieß	geheißen	to be called
helfen	hilft	half	geholfen	to help
kennen	kennt	kannte	gekannt	to know
kommen	kommt	kam	gekommen*	to come
können	kann	konnte	gekonnt	to be able to
laden	lädt	lud	geladen	to load
lassen	lässt	ließ	gelassen	to allow
laufen	läuft	lief	gelaufen*	to run
leiden	leidet	litt	gelitten	to suffer
leihen	leiht	lieh	geliehen	to lend
lesen	liest	las	gelesen	to read
liegen	liegt	lag	gelegen	to lie
lügen	lügt	log	gelogen	to tell a lie
meiden	meidet	mied	gemieden	to avoid
misslingen	misslingt	misslang	misslungen*	to fail

infinitive	present	imperfect	perfect	English
mögen	mag	mochte	gemocht	to like
müssen	muss	musste	gemusst	to have to
nehmen	nimmt	nahm	genommen	to take
nennen	nennt	nannte	genannt	to name
raten	rät	riet	geraten	to guess
reißen	reißt	riss	gerissen	to rip
reiten	reitet	ritt	geritten	to ride
rennen	rennt	rannte	gerannt*	to run
riechen	riecht	roch	gerochen	to smell
rufen	ruft	rief	gerufen	to call
schaffen	schafft	schuf	geschaffen	to manage
scheiden	scheidet	schied	geschieden*	to separate
scheinen	scheint	schien	geschienen	to shine
schlafen	schläft	schlief	geschlafen	to sleep
schlagen	schlägt	schlug	geschlagen	to hit
schließen	schließt	schloss	geschlossen	to shut
schneiden	schneidet	schnitt	geschnitten	to cut
schreiben	schreibt	schrieb	geschrieben	to write
schreien	schreit	schrie	geschrien	to cry
sehen	sieht	sah	gesehen	to see
sein	ist	war	gewesen*	to be
senden	sendet	sandte	gesandt	to send
singen	singt	sang	gesungen	to sing
sitzen	sitzt	saß	gesessen	to sit
sollen	soll	sollte	gesollt	ought to
sprechen	spricht	sprach	gesprochen	to speak
stehen	steht	stand	gestanden*	to stand

infinitive	present	imperfect	perfect	English
stehlen	stiehlt	stahl	gestohlen	to steal
steigen	steigt	stieg	gestiegen*	to climb
sterben	stirbt	starb	gestorben*	to die
stoßen	stößt	stieß	gestoßen	to push
streichen	streicht	strich	gestrichen	to paint
tragen	trägt	trug	getragen	to carry
treffen	trifft	traf	getroffen	to meet
treiben	treibt	trieb	getrieben	to do
treten	tritt	trat	getreten	to step
trinken	trinkt	trank	getrunken	to drink
tun	tut	tat	getan	to do
überwinden	überwindet	überwand	überwunden	to overcome
vergessen	vergisst	vergaß	vergessen	to forget
verlieren	verliert	verlor	verloren	to lose
verschwinden	verschwindet	verschwand	verschwunden*	to disappear
verzeihen	verzeiht	verzieh	verziehen	to pardon
wachsen	wächst	wuchs	gewachsen*	to grow
waschen	wäscht	wusch	gewaschen	to wash
weisen	weist	wies	gewiesen	to show
wenden	wendet	wandte	gewendet	to turn
werben	wirbt	warb	geworben	to advertise
werden	wird	wurde	geworden*	to become
werfen	wirft	warf	geworfen	to throw
wiegen	wiegt	wog	gewogen	to weigh
wissen	weiß	wusste	gewusst	to know
wollen	will	wollte	gewollt	to want to
ziehen	zieht	zog	gezogen	to pull

Glossar

Following each noun, its plural form is indicated in brackets. If the form given is already plural, it is followed by (pl). Following each verb, its past participle is given in brackets.

A

ab off, away, from
ab und zu now and again
der Abend (-e) evening
das Abendessen (-) dinner
abends in the evenings
der Abenteuerfilm adventure film
aber but
die Abfahrt (-en) departure
der Abfall (¨e) waste, litter
der Abfalleimer (-) waste bin
die Abgase (pl) gas emissions
abgesehen davon apart from this
abhängig dependent
das Abitur exams taken at 18 (A-level equivalent)
der Abiturient (-en) Abitur candidate
absagen (abgesagt) to cancel, to call off
der Abschluss final examination
das Abschlusszeugnis (-se) school leaving certificate
der Abstellraum (-räume) storeroom
die Abstinenz abstinence
abtrocknen (abgetrocknet) to dry the dishes
abwaschen (abgewaschen) to wash up
abwechslungsreich varied
abwesend absent
die Achterbahn (-en) rollercoaster
adoptiert adopted
die AG extra-curricular group activity chosen by students
Ägypten Egypt
ähnlich similar
die Ahnung (-en) idea, suspicion
keine Ahnung haben to have no idea
akzeptieren (akzeptiert) to accept
der Alkohol alcohol
der Alkoholiker (-) alcoholic (noun)
alkoholisch alcoholic (adj.)
der Alkoholismus alcoholism

alle/er/es all
alle sein to be all gone, to have run out
allein alone
der/die Alleinerziehende (-n) single parent
alleinstehend single, living alone
die Allergie (-n) allergy
allergisch (gegen) allergic (to)
allerlei all sorts of
alles everything
Alles Gute! All the best!
der Alltag everyday life
die Alpen (pl) the Alps
als ob as though, as if
also so, therefore
das Altenheim (-e) old people's home
das Alter (-) age
älter older
das Altglas waste glass
altmodisch old-fashioned
das Altpapier recycled paper
die Altstadt old part of town
die Ampel traffic lights
amüsant fun
(sich) amüsieren (amüsiert) to enjoy (oneself)
an at, to, close by
die Ananas (-) pineapple
anbieten (angeboten) to offer
anderer/e/es other
die Anderen the others
ändern (geändert) to change
anders different(ly)
anderswo somewhere else
anderthalb one and a half
der Anfang (¨e) beginning
anfangen (angefangen) to begin
die Anfänger (pl) beginners
angeberisch boastful, pretentious
das Angebot (-e) offer
angenehm pleasant
angenommen dass assuming that
der/die Angestellte (-n) employee, office worker
die Angst (Ängste) fear
Angst haben to be afraid
ängstlich fearful
ankommen auf etw. (angekommen) to depend on sth.

es kommt darauf an, ob … it depends on whether …
die Anprobe (-n) changing room
anprobieren (anprobiert) to try on (e.g. clothes)
die Anreise arrival, travel to a place
anrufen (angerufen) to telephone, to ring up
anschreien (angeschrien) to shout at
ansehen (sich etwas) (angesehen) to see, to watch
der Anstieg (-e) rise
der Anstreicher / die Anstreicherin house painter
anstrengend exhausting
die Anzeige (-n) advertisement
(etwas) anziehen (angezogen) to put on (clothes)
(sich) anziehen (angezogen) to get dressed
der Apfel (¨) apple
am Apparat speaking (when on the phone)
April April
die Arbeit (-en) work
arbeiten (gearbeitet) to work
der Arbeitgeber / die Arbeitgeberin employer
arbeitslos unemployed
die Arbeitslosigkeit unemployment
das Arbeitspraktikum (-ka) work experience
die Arbeitsstelle (-n) job, post
der Arbeitstag (-e) working day
die Arbeitszeit (-en) working hours
das Arbeitszimmer (-) study (room)
ärgern (geärgert) to annoy, to irritate
arm poor
der Arm (-e) arm
die Armut poverty
die Art (-en) species
der Arzt / die Ärztin doctor
der Atem breath
atmen (geatmet) to breathe
das Atomkraftwerk (-e) nuclear power station
ätzend lousy
auch also, too
auf on, onto, on top of
auf Achse on the road, out and about

auf dem Lande   in the countryside
auf den Wecker gehen   to get on someone's nerves
auf die Nerven gehen   to get on someone's nerves
auf die Uni gehen   to go to university
Auf Wiederhören!   goodbye (when using the telephone)
Auf Wiedersehen!   goodbye (when in someone's presence)
aufdrehen (aufgedreht)   to turn up
der Aufenthalt (-e)   stay
die Aufgabe (-n)   task, job
aufgeben (aufgegeben)   to give up
aufhören (aufgehört)   to stop
aufmachen (aufgemacht)   to open
aufpassen (auf + accusative) (aufgepasst)   to look after
aufräumen (aufgeräumt)   to tidy up
aufregend   exciting
aufstehen (aufgestanden)   to get up
aufstellen (aufgestellt)   to establish
auftreten (aufgetreten)   to perform
aufwachen (aufgewacht)   to wake up
der Aufzug   lift
die Augen (pl)   eyes
der Augenblick (-e)   moment, instant
August   August
die Aula (-len)   school hall
aus   out, made of
die Ausfahrt   exit (for vehicles)
der Ausflug   trip, excursion
der Ausgang (-̈e)   exit
ausgeben (ausgegeben)   to spend (money)
ausgeglichen   balanced, equal
ausgehen (ausgegangen)   to go out
ausgezeichnet   excellent(ly)
auskommen (ausgekommen) mit   to get on with
die Auskunft (-̈e)   information
auslachen (ausgelacht)   to laugh at
im Ausland   abroad
der Ausländer (-)   foreigner
ausmachen¹ (ausgemacht)   to turn off
ausmachen² (ausgemacht)   to matter

das macht nichts aus   it doesn't matter
ausprobieren (ausprobiert)   to try out
ausschalten (ausgeschaltet)   to turn off
aussehen (ausgesehen)   to look (appearance)
das Aussehen   appearance
außen   outside
der Außenseiter (-)   outsider
außer   besides, apart from
außerdem   besides
außer Betrieb   out of order
außerhalb   outside of
äußerst   extremely
aussetzen (ausgesetzt)   to abandon
die Aussicht (-en)   view
(keine) Aussicht auf Arbeit   (no) prospect of work
aussteigen (ausgestiegen)   to get off (train)
aussterben (ausgestorben)   to die out
der Austausch (-e)   exchange
Australien   Australia
ausverkauft   sold out
die Auswahl   choice, selection
ausziehen (sich) (ausgezogen)   to get undressed
das Auto (-s)   car
der Automat   machine

B

babysitten (babygesittet)   to babysit
backen   to bake
der Bäcker / die Bäckerin   baker
die Bäckerei (-en)   bakery
baden (gebadet)   to bathe
die Badewanne (-n)   bathtub
das Badezimmer (-)   bathroom
die Bahn   railway, train
der Bahnhof (-̈e)   train station
der Bahnsteig (-e)   platform
bald   soon
der Balkon (-e)   balcony
die Banane (-n)   banana
das Bargeld   cash
bauen (gebaut)   to build
der/die Bauer/Bäuerin   farmer
das Bauernhaus   farmhouse
der Baum (-̈e)   tree
die Baumwolle   cotton
beantworten (beantwortet)   to answer
beaufsichtigen   to look after
der Becher (-)   cup
bedeckt   covered
bedienen (bedient)   to serve

bedrohen (bedroht)   to threaten
bedürftig   needy
der/die Bedürftige   person in need
begeistert   inspired, enthusiastic
der Beginn   beginning
beginnen (begonnen)   to begin
begleiten (begleitet)   to accompany
behandeln (behandelt)   to treat
bei   at the house of, with
beide   both
beiliegend   enclosed
bekommen (bekommen)   to receive
Belgien   Belgium
bemerken (bemerkt)   to notice
benachteiligen (benachteiligt)   to disadvantage
benutzen (benutzt)   to use
bequem   comfortable
der Berg (-e)   mountain
der Beruf (-e)   job, profession
beruflich   career-wise, in terms of a job
beruhigen (sich) (beruhigt)   to calm down
berühmt   famous
beschäftigt   busy
beschließen   to decide
beschreiben (beschrieben)   to describe
beschweren (sich) (beschwert)   to complain
besetzt   occupied
besichtigen (besichtigt)   to see (while sightseeing)
der Besitzer (-)   owner
besonders   particularly
besprechen (besprochen)   to discuss
die Besprechung (-en)   discussion, meeting
besser   better
bestehen aus (bestanden)   to be made of, to consist of
bestellen (bestellt)   to order
bestimmt   definitely
besuchen (besucht)   to visit
der Besucher   visitor
beten (gebetet)   to pray
das Bett (-en)   bed
betrunken   drunk
bevor   before (time)
bevorzugen (bevorzugt)   to prefer, to favour
die Bewegung (-en)   movement
sich um etwas bewerben (beworben)   to apply for sth.

der *Bewerber / die Bewerberin* applicant

die *Bewerbung (-en)* application

das *Bewusstsein verlieren* to lose consciousness

bezahlen (bezahlt) to pay

die *Bibliothek (-en)* library

das *Bier (-e)* beer

bieten (geboten) to offer

billig cheap

die *Biokost* organic food

Biologie biology

der *Biomüll* organic waste

die *Birne (-n)* pear

bis until, as far as

Bis bald! See you later!

ein *bisschen* a little

Bitte! please

blau blue

„blau" machen to skip work

bleiben (geblieben) to remain, to stay

der *Bleistift (-e)* pencil

der *Blitz (-e)* lightning

Es *blitzt.* There's lightning.

blöd stupid

der *Blumenkohl* cauliflower

der *Blutdruck* blood pressure

das *Blutgefäß (-e)* blood vessel

die *Bohne (-n)* bean

das *Boot (-e)* boat

böse angry

die *Bratwurst (¨e)* (fried) sausage

brauchen (gebraucht) to need, to use

braun brown

die *Braut (¨e)* bride

der *Bräutigam (-me)* bridegroom

brechen to break

breit wide, broad

brennen (gebrannt) to burn

der *Brennstoff* fuel

der *Brief (-e)* letter

die *Briefmarke (-n)* stamp

der/die *Briefträger/-in* postman/postwoman

der *Briefumschlag (¨e)* envelope

die *Broschüre (-n)* brochure

der *Bruder (¨)* brother

der *Brunnen (-)* fountain, well

das *Buch (¨er)* book

das *Bücherregal (-e)* bookcase

der *Buchstabe (-n)* letter (character)

buchstabieren (buchstabiert) to spell

bügeln (gebügelt) to iron

Bundestagsgebäude German parliamentary buildings

bunt colourful

die *Bürgerinitiative* community action group

das *Büro (-s)* office

der *Bus (-se)* bus

das *Butterbrot (-e)* sandwich

C

der *Cent* cent (100th of a Euro)

der *Chat-Server* chat server

chatten (gechattet) to chat (on the internet)

der *Chef / die Chefin* boss

(die) *Chemie* chemistry

die *Chips (pl)* crisps

der *Chor (¨e)* choir

der *Computer (-)* computer

der *Computerprogrammierer* computer programmer

der *Computerraum (-räume)* computer room

das *Computerspiel (-e)* computer game

der *Cousin / die Cousine* cousin

D

d.h. (das heißt) i.e.

da as, since, there

der *Dachboden (¨)* attic

dafür in favour of something

dagegen opposed to it, against it

damals then, in those days

damit so that, in order that, with that

danach afterwards

Danke (schön)! Thank you!

dann then

dass that

das *Datum* date

dauern (gedauert) to last (time)

dazu with it, in addition

DB Deutsche Bahn (German rail system)

denken (gedacht) to think

das *Denkmal* statue

denn as, since

dennoch nevertheless

deprimiert depressed

der/die *dasselbe* the same

deshalb therefore

deswegen because of this/that

Deutsch German

Dezember December

dick fat

Dienstag (-e) Tuesday

das *Ding (-e)* thing

die *Disko(thek)* disco, club

die *Diskriminierung (-en)* discrimination

doch but, after all, on the contrary

der *Dokumentarfilm* documentary

der *Dolmetscher / die Dolmetscherin* interpreter

der *Dom (-e)* cathedral

der *Donner* thunder

Donnerstag Thursday

Es *donnert.* There's thunder.

doof stupid

das *Doppelhaus (¨er)* semi-detached house

das *Dorf (¨er)* village

dort there (fixed position)

dorthin there (movement towards)

die *Dose (-n)* can

draußen outside

dreckig dirty

das *Dreieck (-e)* triangle

dreieckig triangular

drinnen inside (it)

drittens thirdly

die *Droge (-n)* drug

die *Drogenberatungsstelle (-n)* drugs advice centre

der *Drogenhändler (-)* drug dealer

der/die *Drogensüchtige* drug addict

die *Drogerie* chemist (without dispensing facilities)

drüben over there

der *Drucker (-)* printer

drücken (gedrückt) to push, to press

dumm stupid

das *Düngemittel (-)* fertiliser

dunkel dark

dünn thin

durch through

im *Durchschnitt* on average

dürfen (gedurft) may, to be allowed to

die *Dusche (-n)* shower

duschen to shower

E

eben just (time), even (surface)

echt real

die *Ecke (-n)* corner

Mir ist das egal I don't care about that

egoistisch selfish

ehemalig former

ehrenamtlich voluntary, voluntarily

ehrlich honest

das *Ei (-er)* egg

die *Eierschale* egg shell

eifersüchtig jealous

eigener/e/s own

eigentlich actually, really

die Eigentumswohnung flat (owned rather than rented)

eindrucksvoll impressive

einfach simple, simply

die Einfahrt entrance (for vehicles)

das Einfamilienhaus (¨er) detached house

der Einfluss (¨e) influence

einführen (eingeführt) to introduce

der Eingang entrance (on foot)

eingebildet conceited

die Eingliederung (-en) integration

einige some, a few

einkaufen (eingekauft) to shop, to buy

einkaufen gehen to go shopping

der Einkaufskorb shopping basket

die Einkaufstasche shopping bag

der Einkaufswagen shopping trolley

das Einkaufszentrum (-zentren) shopping centre

die Einladung (-en) invitation

einmal once

einmalig once in a lifetime, unique

einsam lonely

einschalten (eingeschaltet) to turn on

einsteigen (eingestiegen) to get on (train / bus)

einstellen (eingestellt) to take on

der Eintritt admission (ticket)

der Einwanderer (-) immigrant

die Einwegflasche (-n) single-use bottle

der Einwohner (-) inhabitant

einzeln single

das Einzelkind (-er) only child

einziehen (in + acc.) (eingezogen) to move into

das Eis ice cream

die Eisdiele ice-cream parlour

das Eisen iron (substance)

das Eiweiß protein

der Elektriker / die Elektrikerin electrician

das Elektrogeschäft (-e) electrical shop

die Eltern (pl) parents

die E-Mail (-s) e-mail

der Empfänger receiver

der Empfangschef / die Empfangschefin receptionist

empfehlen (empfohlen) to recommend

das Ende end

enden (geendet) to end, to finish

endlich finally

die Energie energy, power

die Energiesparlampe (-n) energy-saving bulb

die Energiewende energy revolution

Englisch English

enorm enormous

entdecken (entdeckt) to discover

entfernt distant

enthalten (enthalten) to contain

die Enthüllung (-en) unveiling

entlang along

entscheiden (sich) (entschieden) to decide

die Entscheidung (-en) decision

eine Entscheidung treffen to make a decision

entschließen (sich) (entschlossen) to decide

Entschuldigung! Excuse me!

entsetzlich terrible

entspannen (sich) (entspannt) to relax

enttäuschend disappointing

entweder ... oder ... either ... or ...

die Entziehungskur (-en) withdrawal treatment

die Erdbeere (-n) strawberry

(die) Erdkunde geography

die Erfahrung (-en) experience

der Erfolg (-e) success

erfolgreich successful(ly)

das Ergebnis (-se) result

die Erholung (-en) relaxation, recovery

erinnern (sich) to remember

erkunden (erkundet) to explore

erlauben (erlaubt) to allow

das Erlebnis (-se) experience

die Ermäßigung reduction

ermüdend tiring

die Ernährung (-en) diet

erschöpft exhausted

erst first

erstens firstly

der/die Erwachsene adult

erwarten (erwartet) to expect

es it

essen (gegessen) to eat

das Essen meal, food

das Esszimmer (-) dining room

das Etagenbett bunk beds

das Etui (-s) pencil case

etwa about, roughly

etwas something

F

die Fabrik (-en) factory

das Fach (¨er) school subject

die Fachhochschule (-n) university of applied sciences

fahren (gefahren) to travel

die Fähre ferry

das Fahrrad (¨er) bicycle

der Fahrradverleih bike hire

die Fahrt (-en) trip, journey

fallen lassen (gelassen) to drop

falsch false, wrong

die Familie (-n) family

fantastisch fantastic

die Farbe (-n) colour

der Fasching see *Karneval*

fast almost

fasten (gefastet) to fast

faszinierend fascinating

faul lazy

faulenzen (gefaulenzt) to laze around

der Faulpelz lazybones

FCKWs CFCs

Februar February

der Fehler (-) mistake

die Feier (-n) celebration

feiern (gefeiert) to celebrate

der Feiertag (-e) holiday (one day)

das Fenster (-) window

die Ferien (pl) holidays (time)

fernsehen (ferngesehen) to watch TV

der Fernseher (-) TV set

mit etw. fertig sein to be finished with sth.

das Fest (-e) festival, celebration

fettarm low fat

fetthaltig fatty

feucht damp

der Feuerwehrmann / die Feuerwehrfrau fireman/ firewoman

das Feuerwerk (-e) fireworks

der Film (-e) film

der Finger (-) finger

der Fingernagel (pl. Fingernägel) finger nail

die Firma (-men) company

der Firmenchef company director

der Fisch (-e) fish

fit bleiben (geblieben) to keep fit

das Fitnesszentrum (-tren) fitness centre

flach flat

die Flasche (-n) bottle

das Fleisch meat
der Fleischer / die Fleischerin butcher
fleißig hard-working
fliegen (geflogen) to fly
das Fließband (¨er) conveyor belt, production line
der Flughafen airport
das Flugzeug (-e) aeroplane
der Flur (-e) hall
der Fluss (¨e) river
die Forelle (-n) trout
fortgeschritten advanced
der Fotoapparat camera
eine Frage stellen to ask a question
Frankreich France
Französisch French
die Frau (-en) woman, wife
frech cheeky, impudent
frei free
das Freibad (¨er) open-air swimming pool
im Freien out in the open
die Freiheit freedom
Freitag Friday
die Freizeit free time
der Freizeitpark theme park
die Fremdsprachen (pl) foreign languages
der Fremdsprachenassistent (-en) foreign languages assistant (m)
(sich auf etw.) freuen (gefreut) to look forward to sth.
der Freund / die Freundin (boy)friend/(girl)friend
freundlich friendly, kind, nice
die Freundschaft (-en) friendship
frieren (gefroren) to freeze
Es friert. It's freezing.
frisch fresh
der Friseur / die Friseurin hairdresser
froh glad
Frohe Weihnachten! Happy Christmas!
der Fruchtsaft (¨e) fruit juice
früh early
der Frühling (-e) spring
das Frühstück (-e) breakfast
frühstücken (gefrühstückt) to have breakfast
frustrierend frustrating
(sich) fühlen (gefühlt) to feel
führen (geführt) to lead, to guide
der Führerschein (-e) driver's licence
funktionieren to work
für for

für jdn sorgen (gesorgt) to look after sb.
furchtbar terrible
der Fuß (¨e) foot
der Fußball football
Fußball spielen (gespielt) to play football
der Fußballplatz (¨e) football pitch
die Fußgängerzone (-n) pedestrian zone

G

die Gallerie (-n) gallery
der Gang (¨e) corridor
die Gans (¨e) goose
ganz completely
die Ganztagsschule (-n) school that lasts all day
gar/überhaupt nicht not at all
der Garten (¨) garden
die Gartenbenutzung (-en) use of a garden
der Gärtner / die Gärtnerin gardener
das Gasthaus (¨er) guesthouse
das Gebäude (-) building
geben (gegeben) to give
das Gebiet district
geboren born
der Geburtstag (-e) birthday
geduldig patient
gefährlich dangerous
gefallen (+ dat) (gefallen) to please
gegen against
die Gegend (-en) area
das Gegenteil (-e) opposite (noun)
gegenüber opposite (prep.)
die Gegenwart present (time)
das Gehalt (Gehälter) salary
gehen (gegangen) to go
das Gehirn (-e) brain
gehören (gehört) (+ dat) to belong to
die Geige (-n) violin
gelb yellow
das Geld money
der (Geld)schein note (money)
das (Geld)stück coin
die Gelegenheit (-en) opportunity
die Gelegenheitsarbeit (-en) casual work
gemein mean
das Gemüse vegetables
gemütlich cosy
genau exactly
genauso just as, equally
genießen (genossen) to enjoy

genug enough
die Gepäckaufbewahrung left luggage
gerade just (now)
geradeaus straight ahead
das Gerät equipment
geräumig roomy
gering low
gern with pleasure
ich spiele gern … I like playing …
Gern geschehen! With pleasure! Done!
gerne willingly
der Geruch smell
die Gesamtschule (-n) comprehensive school
das Geschäft (-e) shop, business
das Geschenk (-e) present
(die) Geschichte history
geschieden divorced
das Geschlecht (-er) sex (male or female)
geschlossen closed
die Geschwister (pl) siblings, brothers and sisters
die Gesellschaft (-en) society
das Gesetz (-e) law
gestern yesterday
gestorben dead
gesund healthy, healthily
die Gesundheit health
das Getränk (-e) drink
getrennt separated
die Gewalt violence
gewaltig powerful, violent
die Gewalttätigkeit (-en) violence, acts of violence
gewinnen (gewonnen) to win
das Gewitter thunderstorm
gewöhnlich usually
die Gewohnheit (-en) habit
es gibt there is / are
das Glas (¨er) glass
glauben (geglaubt) to believe
gleich the same
die Gleichheit equality
gleichzeitig at the same time
das Gleitschirmfliegen hanggliding
die Gleitzeit flexi-time
der Gletscher (-) glacier
Viel Glück! Good luck!
GmbH (-s) Ltd.
der Goldfisch (-e) goldfish
die Gondel gondola
gratis free of charge
grau grey
Griechenland Greece

grillen (gegrillt) to grill, to have a barbeque
groß big, large
die *Größe (-n)* size
die *Großeltern (pl)* grandparents
im *Großen und Ganzen* by and large
der *Großglockner* highest mountain in Austria
die *Großmutter (¨)* grandmother
die *Großstadt (¨e)* big city, metropolis
der *Großvater (¨)* grandfather
großzügig generous
grün green
die *Grünanlage (-n)* green space/ area
gründen (gegründet) to found, to set up
gründlich thoroughly
die *Gruppe (-n)* group
Grüß Gott! Hello! (Austria and S. Germany)
mit freundlichen Grüßen yours sincerely, best wishes
günstig reasonable, at a good price
die *Gurke (-n)* cucumber
gut good
gut bezahlt well paid
gut/schlecht gelaunt good-/ bad-tempered
das *Gymnasium (-ien)* grammar school

H

die *Haare (pl)* hair
haben (gehabt) to have
die *Haferflocken (pl)* rolled oats
der *Hagel* hail
Es *hagelt.* It's hailing.
das *Hähnchen (-)* chicken
halb half (to)
halb neun half past eight
Halb… half-
das *Hallenbad (¨er)* indoor swimming pool
Hallo! Hello!
die *Halsschmerzen* sore throat
halten (gehalten) to keep
die *Haltestelle (-n)* bus stop
die *Hand (¨e)* hand
Handball handball
die *Handschuhe (pl)* gloves
die *Handtasche* handbag
die *Handtücher* towels
das *Handy (-s)* mobile phone
hart hard
hassen (gehasst) to hate

hässlich ugly
Haupt- main, central
der *Hauptbahnhof* main station
das *Haus (¨er)* house
die *Hausaufgaben (pl)* homework
die *Hausfrau / der Hausmann* housewife/-husband
der *Haushalt* household
der *Hausmeister (-)* caretaker
das *Haustier (-e)* pet
die *Hautfarbe (-n)* colour of skin
der *Hautkrebs* skin cancer
das *Heft (-e)* exercise book
heftig violent(ly)
der *Heiligabend (-e)* Christmas Eve
das *Heim (-e)* hostel
das *Heimweh* homesickness
heiraten (geheiratet) to marry, to get married
heiß hot
heiter cheerful
die *Heizung (-en)* heating
helfen (geholfen) to help
hell light, bright
das *Hemd* shirt
herausfinden (herausgefunden) to find out
der *Herbst* autumn
der *Herd (-e)* cooker
herrlich marvellous, magnificent
herrschend ruling, reigning, current
herstellen (hergestellt) to make, to manufacture
herum around
herumlaufen (herumgelaufen) to run or go around
herumreisen (herumgereist) to travel around
herunterdrehen (heruntergedreht) to turn down
herunterladen (heruntergeladen) to download
hervorragend excellent, outstanding
das *Herz (-en)* heart
Herzlichen Glückwunsch zum Geburtstag! Happy birthday!
heute today
heutzutage these days
hier here
die *Hilfe (-n)* help, assistance
hilfsbereit helpful
die *Himbeere (-n)* raspberry

der *Himmel* sky, heaven
das *Hindernis* obstacle
hinfallen to fall
hinter behind
hoch high
hochladen (hochgeladen) to upload
die *Hochzeit (-en)* wedding
hoffen (gehofft) to hope
hoffentlich hopefully
höflich polite
das *Holz (¨er)* wood
der *Honig* honey
der *Horrorfilm* horror film
die *Hose (-n)* trousers
das *Hotel (-s)* hotel
hübsch pretty
der *Hund (-e)* dog
hungern (gehungert) to go hungry
der *Hut (¨e)* hat
die *Hütte* mountain hut

I

ich I
ideal ideal
die *Idee (-n)* idea
illegal illegal
der *Imbiss (-e)* snack
die *Imbissstube (-n)* snack bar
immer always
in in, into
die *Industrie (-n)* industry
das *Industriegebiet* industrial area
die *Informatik* IT
informativ informative
der *Ingenieur / die Ingenieurin* engineer
inkl. (inklusiv) including
das *Insektizid (-e)* insecticide
die *Insel (-n)* island
das *Instrument (-e)* instrument
intelligent intelligent
das *Interesse (-n)* interest
(sich für etwas) interessieren (interessiert) to be interested in
das *Internat (-e)* boarding school
das *Internet* internet
die *Internetseite (-n)* internet site
inzwischen in the meantime
irgendwelche some
irgendwo somewhere
Italienisch Italian

J

Ja! yes!
die *Jacke (-n)* jacket
die *Jahreszeit (-en)* season
das *Jahrhundert (-e)* century

jahrhundertealt centuries-old
Januar January
die Jeans (sing / pl) jeans
jedoch yet
jemand someone
jetzt now
der Job (-s) job
der Jogurt (-e) yoghurt
die Jugendherberge (-n) youth hostel
der Jugendklub youth club
Juli July
jung young
Juni June
Jura law
das Juweliergeschäft (-e) jeweller's

K

der Kaffee coffee
kalt cold
die Kamera (-s) camera
der Kanal (¨e) canal
der Kandidat / die Kandidatin candidate
das Kaninchen (-) rabbit
die Kantine (-n) canteen
die Kappe (-n) baseball cap
kaputt machen (gemacht) to ruin, to wear out
die Karibik the Caribbean
der Karneval carnival (traditional German celebration between Epiphany and Ash Wednesday)
die Karriere (-n) career
die Karte (-n) ticket
die Kartoffel (-n) potato
der Karton (-s) card, cardboard
der Käse cheese
der Kassettenrekorder cassette recorder
der Kassierer / die Kassiererin cashier
die Katastrophe disaster
die Katze (-n) cat
kaufen to buy
das Kaufhaus (-häuser) department store
der Kaufmann / die Kauffrau businessman/woman
der Kaugummi (-s) chewing gum
kaum hardly
kaum vorstellbar barely imaginable
kegeln (gekegelt) to bowl
der Keks (-e) biscuit
der Keller (-) cellar
der Kellner / die Kellnerin waiter/waitress

kennen lernen (gelernt) to get to know
das Kind (-er) child
das Kinn (-e) chin
der Kinnbart goatee beard
das Kino (-s) cinema
die Kirche (-n) church
das Kitzsteinhorn name of a mountain
die Klamotten (pl) clothes
die Klarinette (-n) clarinet
die Klasse (-n) class
Klasse! Great!
die Klassenarbeit (-en) class test
die Klassenfahrt (-en) school trip
der Klassenlehrer / die Klassenlehrerin form teacher, tutor
das Klassenzimmer (-) classroom
das Klavier (-e) piano
kleben (geklebt) to stick, to glue
das Kleid (-er) dress
der Kleiderschrank wardrobe
die Kleidung clothes
das Kleidungsgeschäft clothes shop
klein small
das Kleingeld change
der Klempner / die Klempnerin plumber
klettern (geklettert) to climb
das Klima (-ten) climate
der Klimawandel climate change
der Klingelton (¨e) ringtone
die Klinik (-en) clinic
der Klub (-s) club
klug clever
die Kneipe (-n) pub
der Knoblauch garlic
der Koch / die Köchin cook
kochen (gekocht) to cook, to make (e.g. tea and coffee)
der Koffer suitcase
die Kohle (-n) coal, money (slang)
das Kohlendioxid (-e) carbon dioxide
die Kohlenhydrate (pl) carbohydrates
das Kohlenmonoxid carbon monoxide
der Kollege / die Kollegin colleague
die Kommode chest of drawers
die Komödie comedy
kompliziert complicated
die Konditorei (-en) cake shop
können (gekonnt) can, to be able to

der Kontakt (-e) contact
(sich) konzentrieren to concentrate
das Konzert (-e) concert
der Kopfhörer headphones
das Kopfkissen (-) pillow
die Kopfschmerzen (pl) headache
kopieren (kopiert) to copy, to photocopy
der Körper (-) body
körperlich physical
kosten (gekostet) to cost
kostenlos free
köstlich delicious
das Kostüm (-e) costume
das Krankenhaus (¨er) hospital
der Krankenpfleger / die Krankenschwester nurse
die Krankheit (-en) illness
kraulen (gekrault) to swim the crawl
der Krebs (-e) cancer
die Kreditkarte (-n) credit card
der Kreis (-e) circle
die Kreuzung crossroads
kriegen (gekriegt) to get
der Krimi crime film
die Kriminalität crime
kritisieren (kritisiert) to criticise
die Küche (-n) kitchen
der Kuchen (-) cake
der Kugelschreiber / der Kuli ballpoint pen
kühl cool
der Kühlschrank fridge
kulturell cultural
der Kunde / die Kundin customer
kündigen (gekündigt) to hand notice in
die Kunst (¨e) art
die Kunstgalerie (-n) art gallery
der Kurs course
kurz short, brief
kürzlich shortly
küssen (geküsst) to kiss
die Küste (-n) coast
an der Küste on the coast

L

das Labor (-s) laboratory, lab
lachen (gelacht) to laugh
der Lachs (-e) salmon
der Laden (¨) shop
das Land (¨er) country
die Landschaft (-en) landscape
der Landwirt / die Landwirtin farmer
lang long
langsam slow(ly)

(sich) *langweilen (gelangweilt)* to be bored
langweilig boring
der *Lärm* noise
Latein Latin
leben (gelebt) to live
das *Leben* life
der *Lebenslauf (¨e)* CV
die *Lebensmittel (pl)* food items, groceries
das *Lebensmittelgeschäft* food shop
der *Lebensstil* lifestyle
die *Leber* liver
lecker delicious
das *Leder* leather
ledig single
leer empty
die *Lehre (-n)* apprenticeship
der *Lehrer / die Lehrerin* teacher
das *Lehrerzimmer (-)* staff room
lehrreich educational
leicht easy, light
die *Leichtathletik* athletics
Es tut mir Leid! I'm sorry!
leiden (gelitten) to stand, to suffer, to bear
leider unfortunately
der *Leihwagen (-)* hire car
leisten (geleistet) to afford
der *Leistungsdruck* pressure to achieve
lesen (gelesen) to read
letzter/e/es last
die *Leute (pl)* people
das *Licht* light
lieb kind, nice, lovely
lieben (geliebt) to love
lieber rather
Lieblings- favourite
am *liebsten* best of all
das *Lied (-er)* song
liegen (gelegen) to be situated in
lila purple
das *Lineal (-e)* ruler
die *Linie (-n)* route, line
links to the left
die *Lippen (pl)* lips
der *Lippenstift* lipstick
der *LKW (Lastkraftwagen)* lorry
der *LKW Fahrer / die LKW Fahrerin* lorry driver
der *Lohn (¨e)* wage(s)
losgehen (losgegangen) to get going, to get started
die *Luft* air
die *Luftverschmutzung* air pollution

die *Lunge (-n)* lung
der *Lungenkrebs* lung cancer
die *Lust (¨e)* desire, pleasure
lustig fun
die *Magenschmerzen (pl)* stomach ache

M

magersüchtig anorexic
die *Mahlzeit (-en)* meal
Mai May
mailen (gemailt) to send (by e-mail)
malen (gemalt) to paint
malerisch picturesque
manchmal sometimes
der *Mann (¨er)* man, husband
die *Mannschaft (-en)* team
der *Mantel (¨)* coat
die *Marke (-n)* brand
der *Markt (¨e)* market
der *Marktplatz (¨e)* market place, market square
März March
(die) *Mathe(matik)* maths
die *Maus (¨e)* mouse
der *Mechaniker / die Mechanikerin* mechanic
(die) *Medienwissenschaft* media studies
das *Medikament (-e)* medicine, medication
die *Medizin* medicine
das *Meer (-)* sea
das *Meerschweinchen (-)* guinea-pig
der *Meeresspiegel* sea level
mehr more
das *Mehrbettzimmer* room for multiple occupants
mehrere several
das *Mehrfamilienhaus (¨er)* house for several families
die *Mehrwegflasche* recyclable bottle
mein my
meinen (gemeint) to think
die *Meinung (-en)* opinion
am *meisten* most (of all)
eine *Menge* a lot of
der *Mensch* person
messen (gemessen) to measure
das *Metal (-le)* metal
der *Metzger / die Metzgerin* butcher
die *Metzgerei (-en)* butcher's shop
mies rotten, lousy
mieten (gemietet) to rent
die *Mietwohnung* rented flat
die *Mikrowelle (-n)* microwave oven

die *Milch* milk
die *Milchprodukte (pl)* dairy produce
mindestens at least
das *Mindesthaltbarkeitsdatum (-ten)* best-before date
das *Mineralwasser* mineral water
mit with, by (transport)
miteinander with one another
mitgehen (mitgegangen) to go with sb.
das *Mitglied (-er)* member
mitkommen (mitgekommen) to come with sb.
mitmachen (mitgemacht) to join in
Mittag (-e) midday
das *Mittagessen (-)* lunch
die *Mitte* middle
mittelalterlich medieval
mittelgroß medium-sized, of average height
mitten in in the middle of
Mitternacht midnight
die *mittlere Reife* intermediate school certificate
Mittwoch Wednesday
mobben (gemobbt) to bully
möbliert furnished
die *Mode (-n)* fashion
modisch fashionable
mögen (gemocht) to like
möglich possible
die *Möglichkeit (-en)* possibility
der *Moment (-e)* moment
der *Monat (-e)* month
der *Mond (-e)* moon
Montag Monday
montags on Mondays
morgen tomorrow
der *Morgen* morning
morgen früh tomorrow morning
morgens every morning
der *Motor (-en)* engine
der *MP3-Spieler (-)* MP3 player
mühsam laboriously
der *Müll* waste, rubbish
die *Mülltonne (-n)* dustbin
multikulturell multicultural
München Munich
der *Mund (¨er)* mouth
das *Museum (-een)* museum
die *Musik* music
Musik hören (gehört) to listen to music
musikalisch musical
das *Müsli (-s)* muesli

müssen (gemusst) must, to have to
die *Mutter (¨)* mother
der *Muttertag* Mother's Day
die *Mütze (-n)* hat
MwSt (Mehrwertsteuer) VAT

N

nach after
nachdem after, afterwards
nachdenken to think about
nachforschen (nachgeforscht) to research
nachher afterwards
der *Nachmittag (-e)* afternoon
die *Nachricht (-en)* message, piece of news
nachsitzen (nachgesessen) to have detention
nächster/e/es nearest, next
die *Nacht (¨e)* night
der *Nachteil (-e)* disadvantage
nachts at night
der *Nachttisch (-e)* bedside table
nagelneu brand new
nah near
die *Nähe* vicinity, neighbourhood
in der *Nähe* nearby
die *Nahrung* food
die *Nase (-n)* nose
die *Nase voll haben* to have had enough, to be fed up
nass wet
natürlich naturally, of course
das *Naturschutzgebiet (-e)* conservation area
die *Naturwissenschaften (pl)* science
der *Nebel* fog
nebelig foggy
neben next to
der *Nebenjob (-s)* second or extra job, job outside school
Es ist *neblig.* It's foggy.
nehmen (genommen) to take
Nein! No!
nerven (genervt) to annoy, irritate
nervös nervous
nett nice
neu new
neulich recently
nicht not
nicht fit unfit
nicht mehr no longer
nicht nur ... sondern auch ... not only ... but also ...
nichts nothing
nie never
die *Niederlande (pl)* the Netherlands

niemals never
niemand no one
nirgendwo nowhere
noch still
noch einmal once more
noch nicht not yet
der *Norden* north
im *Norden* in the north
nördlich to the north
die *Nordsee* the North Sea
normalerweise usually
die *Not (¨e)* need
der *Notausgang* emergency exit
die *Note (-n)* mark
der *Notendruck* exam pressure
nötig necessary
notwendig necessary
November November
nun now
nur only
die *Nudeln (pl)* pasta, noodles
nützlich useful
nutzlos useless

O

ob whether
obdachlos homeless
die *Obdachlosen* the homeless
die *Oberstufe* sixth form
oben above
das *Obst* fruit
der *Obst- und Gemüseladen (¨en)* greengrocer's
obwohl although
oder or
offen open
die *Öffentlichkeit* public
in der *Öffentlichkeit* in public
die *öffentlichen Verkehrsmittel (pl)* public transport
öffnen (geöffnet) to open
oft often
ohne without
die *Ohrenschmerzen (pl)* earache
Oktober October
das *Oktoberfest (-e)* Munich beer festival in October
das *Öl (-e)* oil
die *Oma (-s)* granny, grandma
der *Onkel (-)* uncle
der *Opa (-s)* granddad, grandpa
die *Oper (-n)* opera (house)
das *Orchester (-)* orchestra
in *Ordnung* fine, okay
organisch organic
organisieren (organisiert) to organise
der *Ort (-e)* place
der *Osten* east
im *Osten* in the east

das *Osterei* Easter egg
Ostern Easter
Österreich Austria
Osteuropa Eastern Europe
östlich to the East
die *Ostsee* the Baltic Sea
das *Ozonloch (¨er)* hole in the ozone layer
die *Ozonschicht (-en)* ozone layer

P

ein *paar* a couple
das *Papier (-e)* paper
die *Pappe (-n)* cardboard
das *Paradies* paradise
der *Parkplatz (¨e)* car park
passen (gepasst) to fit
Es *passt dir.* It fits you.
passieren (passiert) to happen
die *Pause (-n)* break, breaktime
das *Pech* bad luck
peinlich painful, embarrassing
die *Pension (-en)* guesthouse
die *Person (-en)* person
das *Personal* personnel / staff
pessimistisch pessimistic
das *Pestizid (-e)* pesticide
das *Pfand* deposit
das *Pferd (-e)* horse
Pfingsten Whitsun
der *Pfirsich (-e)* peach
pflanzen (gepflanzt) to plant
die *Pflaume (-n)* plum
das *Pflichtfach (¨er)* compulsory subject
das *Pfund (-e)* pound
(die) *Physik* physics
die *Pizzeria (-s)* pizzeria
das *Plakat (-e)* poster
der *Plan (¨e)* plan
das *Plastik* plastic
die *Plastikflasche* plastic bottle
der *Platz (¨e)* space, room
plaudern (geplaudert) to chat
pleite skint
plötzlich suddenly
PLZ (Postleitzahl) postcode
Polen Poland
die *Polizei* police
der *Polizist / die Polizistin* policeman/woman
die *Pommes (frites) (pl)* chips
das *Portemonnaie* wallet, purse
die *Portion (-en)* portion
das *Postamt (¨er)* post office
praktisch practical, practically
die *Praxis (plural = Praxen)* practice (e.g. a medical or law practice)

der Preis (-e) price
preiswert cheap, good value
prima great
pro per
probieren (probiert) to try
der Profi (-s) professional
die Prüfung (-en) exam
der Pulli (-s) pullover
die Pute (-n) turkey
putzen (geputzt) to clean
der Putzmann / die Putzfrau
     cleaner

Q

die Qualifikation (-en)
     qualification
qualifiziert qualified
die Qualität (-en) quality
die Quantität (-en) quantity
quatschen (gequatscht)
     to chat
die Quelle (-n) source
die Quittung (-en) bill, receipt

R

der Rabatt (-e) reduction
das Rad (¨er) wheel, bicycle
Rad fahren (gefahren)
     to go cycling
der Radweg (-e) cycle path
Rasen mähen (gemäht)
     to mow the lawn
der Rassismus racism
der Rassist (-en) racist person
rassistisch racist
das Rathaus (¨er) town hall
rauchen (geraucht) to smoke
der Raucher / die Raucherin
     smoker
die Raucherecke (-n) smokers'
     corner
der Raucherhusten smoker's
     cough
das Rauschgift (-e) drug, narcotic
die Realschule (-n) secondary
     modern school
recherchieren (recherchiert)
     to research
Recht haben (gehabt) to be
     right
das Rechteck (-e) rectangle
rechts on/to the right
der Rechtsanwalt / die
     Rechtsanwältin lawyer
die Rechtsanwaltspraxis (-xen)
     lawyer's practice
recyceln (recycelt) recycle
reden (geredet) to speak
reduziert reduced
das Regal shelf

regelmäßig regularly
der Regen rain
der Regenwald rain forest
regnen (geregnet) to rain
Es regnet. It's raining.
reich rich
reichen (gereicht) to be
     enough
das Reihenhaus (¨er) terraced
     house
reinigen (gereinigt) to clean
der Reis rice
die Reise (-n) journey
der Reisebus (-se) coach
reisen (gereist) to travel
der Reiseleiter / die Reiseleiterin
     tour guide
das Reiseziel holiday destination
reiten gehen (gegangen)
     to go riding
der Rektor / die Rektorin
     headmaster/-mistress
die Religion (-en) religion, RS
der Rentner pensioner
reparieren (repariert)
     to repair
reservieren (reserviert)
     to reserve
die Reservierung (-en)
     reservation
das Restaurant (-s) restaurant
retten (gerettet) to save
die Rezeption (-en) reception
der Rhein Rhine
richtig right
die Richtung (-en) direction
riechen (gerochen) to smell
das Riesenrad (¨er) big wheel
riesig gigantic
das Risiko (-ken) risk
das Risiko eingehen, etw. zu tun
     to run the risk of doing sth.
rosa pink
der Rock (¨e) skirt
der Rollstuhl wheel chair
der Rosenmontag (-e) Monday
     before Ash Wednesday
rot red
der Rotwein red wine
die Rückenschmerzen backache
die Ruhe peace, quiet
ruhig calm, peaceful
das Rührei (-er) scrambled egg
rund round
die Rundfahrt sightseeing tour
der Rundflug (¨e) a sightseeing
     tour by plane
Russland Russia

S

die S-Bahn local train
die Sache (-n) thing
sagen (gesagt) to say
die Sahne cream
der Salat (-e) salad
das Salz salt
sammeln (gesammelt)
     to collect
Samstag Saturday
das Satellitenfernsehen satellite
     TV
satt full
es satt haben to have had
     enough of sth.
sauber clean
sauer cross
saurer Regen acid rain
das Schach chess
die Schachtel (-n) box
schade it's a shame
schaden (geschadet) to
     damage
schädlich damaging
schaffen (geschafft) to
     manage, to pass
der Schal (-s) scarf
die Schallplatte record
der Schatten (-) shadow
schauen (geschaut) to look
schauspielen to act
der Schauer (-) shower (of rain)
die Scheibe (-n) slice
(sich) scheiden (lassen) (scheiden
     gelassen) to get divorced
scheinen (geschienen) to
     seem, to shine
die Schichtarbeit shift work
schick stylish, chic
schicken (geschickt) to send
das Schiff (-e) ship
der Schinken (-) ham
der Schirm (-e) umbrella, screen
schlafen (geschlafen) to sleep
das Schlafzimmer (-) bedroom
schlank slim
schlecht bad, badly
schlecht gelaunt bad-tempered
schließen (geschlossen)
     to shut, to close
schließlich in the end, finally,
     eventually
schlimm terrible, awful
Schlittschuh laufen
     (gelaufen) to go ice skating
das Schloss (¨er) castle
schmecken (geschmeckt)
     to taste
Es schmeckt. It tastes good.

... schmeckt mir (nicht) I (don't) like the taste of ...

der Schmuck jewellery

schmutzig dirty

ein Schnäppchen machen to pick up a bargain

der Schnee snow

schneiden (geschnitten) to cut

schneien (geschneit) to snow

Es schneit. It's snowing.

schnell quick, quickly

die Schokolade (-n) chocolate

der Schokoriegel (-) chocolate bar

schon already

schön beautiful

Schöne Ferien! Have a great holiday!

Schottland Scotland

der Schrank (¨e) cupboard

schrecklich terrible

schreiben (geschrieben) to write

die Schreibmaschine typewriter

das Schreibwarengeschäft (-e) stationer's

der Schriftsteller / die Schriftstellerin writer

der Schuh (-e) shoe

Schuld an etw. sein to be to blame for sth.

die Schule (-n) school

der Schüler / die Schülerin pupil, student

der Schulhof (¨e) playground

die Schulordnung (-en) school rules

die Schulter (-n) shoulder

das Schulwesen school system

die Schuluniform (-en) school uniform

schützen (geschützt) to protect

der Schützenzug (¨e) parade of riflemen

schwarz black

schwatzen (geschwatzt) to gossip, to chatter

das Schwefeldioxid (-e) sulphur dioxide

die Schweiz Switzerland

schwer difficult, hard

die Schwester (-n) sister

Schwieger- -in-law

schwierig difficult

die Schwierigkeit difficulty

schwimmen (geschwommen) to swim

der Schwimmverein swimming club

das Schwimmbad (¨er) swimming pool

der See (-n) lake

die See (-n) sea

segeln (gesegelt) to go sailing

sehenswert worth seeing

die Sehenswürdigkeit (-en) sight (thing worth seeing)

Sehr geehrte Dame Dear Madam

Sehr geehrter Herr Dear Sir

sehr very

die Seifenoper soap opera

sein (gewesen) to be

seit since, for (a length of time)

seitdem since

die Seite (-n) page, side

der Sekretär / die Sekretärin secretary

der Sekt sparkling wine, champagne

selbstständig independent

selten rarely

die Sendung (-en) TV programme

sensibel sensitive

September September

die Serie TV series

der Sessel (-) armchair

sicher sure, safe

sicherlich of course, certainly

das Silber silver

Silvester New Year's Eve

simsen (gesimst) to send text messages

sitzen bleiben (geblieben) to repeat a school year

die Sitzung (-en) meeting, session

Skateboard fahren (gefahren) to go skateboarding

der Skatepark skateboarding park

Ski fahren (gefahren) to go skiing

Ski laufen to ski

das SMS (-) text message

so ... wie as ... as

so viel ... wie as many ... as

das Sofa (-s) sofa

sofort straight away

sogar even

der Sohn (¨e) son

die Solarenergie solar power

sollen (gesollt) should, ought to

der Sommer summer

der Sommerschlussverkauf end of summer sales

das Sonderangebot (-e) special offer

der Sonnabend Saturday

die Sonne sun

sonnen (sich) (gesonnt) to sunbathe

der Sonnenbrand (¨e) sunburn

die Sonnenterrasse (-n) sun terrace/deck

sonnig sunny

Es ist sonnig. It's sunny.

Sonntag (-e) Sunday

sonst else, otherwise

die Sorge (-n) worry

sorgen für (gesorgt) to ensure

das Souvenir (-s) souvenir

sowohl ... als auch both ... and

das soziale Netzwerk social networking site

der soziale Wohnungsbau social housing

Spanien Spain

Spanisch Spanish

sparen (gespart) to save

der Spaß fun

Spaß haben (gehabt) to have fun

spät late

später later

spazieren gehen (gegangen) to go for walks

speichern (gespeichert) to save (files on a computer)

die Speise (-n) dish, food

die Spende (-n) donation

spenden (gespendet) to donate

der Spiegel mirror

das Spiegelei (-er) fried egg

das Spiel (-e) game

spielen (gespielt) to play

der Spielplatz (¨e) playground

der Spinat spinach

Spitze! Great!

Sport PE

Sport treiben (getrieben) to take part in sports

die Sportart (-en) type of sports

die Sporthalle (-n) sports hall

der Sportplatz (¨e) playing fields

die Sportsachen (pl) things for sport (PE kit)

die Sportschuhe (pl) trainers

der Sportverein sports club

das Sportzentrum (-zentren) sports centre

die Sprachkenntnisse (pl) knowledge of the language

das Sprachlabor (-s) language laboratory

die Spraydose (-n) aerosol

die Spritze (-n) syringe

spritzen (gespritzt) to inject

der *Sprudel* sparkling water
die *Spülmaschine (-n)* dishwasher
die *Staatsangehörigkeit (-en)* nationality
das *Stadion (-ien)* stadium
die *Stadt (¨e)* town
der *Stadtbummel* stroll around town
die *Stadtführung* guided tour of town
die *Stadtmitte / das Stadtzentrum* town centre
der *Stadtrand (¨er)* outskirts of town
am *Stadtrand* on the outskirts of town
der *Stadtteil / das Stadtviertel* area of a town, quarter
stattfinden (stattgefunden) to take place
der *Stau (-s)* congestion, traffic jam
staubsaugen (staubgesaugt) to vacuum
stecken (gesteckt) to put
stehlen (gestohlen) to steal
Es *steht dir.* It suits you.
die *Stelle (-n)* job, position
sterben (gestorben) to die
Stief- step-
die *Stiefel (pl)* boots
Stimmt! That's right!
stinken (gestunken) to stink
die *Stofftasche* textile bag
stolz proud
stören (gestört) to bother, to disturb
der *Strahl (-en)* ray
der *Strand (¨e)* beach
die *Straße (-n)* street
die *Straßenbahn (-en)* tram
(sich) *streiten (gestritten)* to argue
streng strict
der *Stress* stress
stressig stressful
das *Stück (-e)* piece
studieren (studiert) to study (at university level)
der *Stuhl (¨e)* chair
die *Stunde (-n)* hour, lesson
der *Stundenplan (¨e)* timetable
der *Sturm (¨e)* storm
stürmisch stormy
suchen (gesucht) to look for
die *Sucht* addiction
süchtig addicted
der *Süden* south
im *Süden* in the south
südlich to the south
surfen (gesurft) to surf
süß sweet

die *Süßigkeit (-en)* sweet
sympathisch nice, kind

T

der *Tabak (-e)* tobacco
diese *Tabletten* these tablets
der *Tag (-e)* day
tagsüber during the day
täglich daily
das *Tal (¨er)* the valley
die *Tante (-n)* aunt
der *Tante-Emma-Laden* corner shop
tanzen (getanzt) to dance
die *Tasche (-n) (Schultasche)* bag (schoolbag)
das *Taschengeld* pocket money
tauchen (getaucht) to dive
die *Technologie (-n)* technology
der *Tee* tea
teilen (geteilt) to share
teilnehmen (teilgenommen) to participate
Teilzeit- part-time
das *Telefon (-e)* telephone
telefonieren (telefoniert) to telephone
die *Telefonnummer (-n)* telephone number
der *Tellerwäscher / die Tellerwäscherin* dish washer (person)
die *Temperatur (-en)* temperature
Tennis spielen (gespielt) to play tennis
der *Tennisplatz (¨e)* tennis court
der *Teppich (-e)* carpet
teuer expensive
das *Theater (-)* theatre
das *Thema (-men)* topic
der *Tiefkühlschrank (¨e)* freezer
das *Tier (-e)* animal
der *Tierarzt / die Tierärztin* vet
tippen (getippt) to type
der *Tisch* table
die *Tochter (¨)* daughter
die *Toilette (-n)* toilet
toll great
die *Tomate (-n)* tomato
die *Tonne* bin
der *Topf (Töpfe)* pot
tot dead
total totally
töten (getötet) to kill
der *Tourismus* tourism
der *Tourist (-en)* tourist
der *Tourismussektor (-en)* tourist sector
die *Touristeninformation* tourist information

die *Tradition (-en)* tradition
tragen (getragen) to wear
trainieren (trainiert) to train
der *Traum (¨e)* dream
traurig sad
der *Trauring* wedding ring
die *Trauung* wedding
(sich mit) *treffen (getroffen)* to meet (with)
treiben (getrieben) to drive, to do
der *Treibhauseffekt (-e)* greenhouse effect
(sich) *trennen (getrennt)* to separate
treu faithful
trinken (getrunken) to drink
trocken dry
der *Trommler (-)* drummer
die *Trompete* trumpet
diese *Tropfen (pl)* these drops
trotzdem nevertheless
der *Truthahn* turkey
Tschüss! Bye!
das *T-Shirt (-s)* T-shirt
tun (getan) to do
die *Türkei* Turkey
türkis turquoise
der *Turm (¨e)* tower
turnen (geturnt) to do gymnastics
die *Turnhalle (-n)* gymnasium
der *Turnschuh* trainer (shoe)
die *Tüte (-n)* bag
typisch typical

U

die *U-Bahn (-en)* the underground
über over, above
überall everywhere
die *Überdosis* overdose
übergewichtig overweight
überhaupt nicht not at all
übermorgen the day after tomorrow
übernachten (übernachtet) to stay the night
die *Übernachtung* overnight stay
überrascht surprised
die *Überstunden (pl)* overtime
übrig bleiben (geblieben) to be left
sieben *Uhr* hour, 7 o'clock
um at, around
die *Umfrage (-n)* survey
die *Umgebung (-en)* surrounding area
der *Umkleideraum (¨e)* changing room
umschauen (umgeschaut) to look around

umsteigen (umgestiegen) to change (trains, buses etc.)

umtauschen (umgetauscht) to exchange

die *Umwelt* environment

umweltbewusst environmentally aware

umweltfeindlich environmentally unfriendly

das *Umweltproblem* environmental problem

umweltfreundlich environmentally friendly

umziehen (umgezogen) to move house

der *Umzug ("e)* parade, (house) move

unabhängig independent

unbedingt without fail, definitely

und and

unfair unfair

ungefähr about

ungerecht unjust

ungesund unhealthy, unhealthily

unglaublich unbelievable

das *Unglück* disaster

die *Uni(versität) (-en)* university

unmöglich impossible

unnötig unnecessary

unordentlich untidy

Unrecht haben (gehabt) to be wrong

unsicher unsure

unten underneath, below

unter below, under

unterbringen (untergebracht) to accommodate

(sich) *unterhalten (unterhalten)* to talk

die *Unterkunft ("e)* accommodation

das *Unternehmen (-)* business

unternehmen (unternommen) to undertake, to do

unternehmungslustig likes doing lots of things (adj.)

der *Unterricht* lessons, classes

der *Unterschied (-e)* difference

unterschiedlich different

unterschreiben (unterschrieben) to sign

unterwegs on the move

der *Urlaub (-e)* holiday (trip)

die *Urlaubspläne (pl)* holiday plans

usw. (und so weiter) etc.

V

der *Vandalismus* vandalism

der *Vater (")* father

der *Vegetarier / die Vegetarierin* vegetarian

vegetarisch vegetarian

Venedig Venice

(sich) *verabschieden (verabschiedet)* to say goodbye

die *Veranstaltung (-en)* event

die *Verantwortung (-en)* responsibility

verbessern (verbessert) to improve

die *Verbesserung (-en)* improvement

verbieten (verboten) to forbid, to ban

die *Verbindung (-en)* connection

das *Verbrechen (-)* crime

verbringen (verbracht) to spend (time)

verdienen (verdient) to earn

der *Verein (-e)* club, society

die *Vergangenheit* past

vergessen (vergessen) to forget

der *Vergleich (-e)* comparison

vergleichen (verglichen) to compare

Mit *Vergnügen!* with pleasure!

das *Verhältnis (-se)* relationship

verheiratet married

verkaufen (verkauft) to sell

der *Verkäufer / die Verkäuferin* shop assistant, salesperson

der *Verkehr* traffic

das *Verkehrsamt ("er)* tourist information

verkleidet dressed-up, disguised

verlassen (verlassen) to leave

(sich auf etw.) *verlassen (verlassen)* to rely on sth.

sich *verletzen* to get hurt / injured

verlobt engaged

der/die *Verlobte (-n)* fiancé(e)

vermeiden (vermieden) to avoid

die *Verpackung (-en)* packaging

verpesten (verpestet) to pollute

verrückt crazy

die *Versammlung (-en)* assembly

verschieden different

die *Verschmutzung* pollution

verschwenden (verschwendet) to waste

verschwinden (verschwunden) to disappear

verstecken (sich) (versteckt) to hide

verstehen (verstanden) to understand

(sich mit) *verstehen (verstanden)* to get on with

versuchen (versucht) to try

verursachen (verursacht) to cause

der/die *Verwandte (-n)* relation

verwenden (verwendet) to use

Verzeihung! Sorry!

viel a lot, much, many

viele lots of

vielleicht perhaps

viereckig quadrangular

Viertel nach quarter past

Viertel vor quarter to

der *Virus* virus

die *Vitamine (pl)* vitamins

der *Vogel (")* bird

voll full

völlig completely

die *Vollpension (-en)* full board

Vollzeit- full-time

von from, by, of

vor in front of, before, ago

vor kurzem until recently

im *Voraus* in advance

vorausgesetzt dass provided that

vorbei past, by

vorgestern the day before yesterday

der *Vorhang ("e)* curtain

vorher before

der *Vormittag (-e)* morning

der *Vorort* suburb

vorschlagen (vorgeschlagen) to suggest

vorsichtig careful

vorstellen (vorgestellt) to introduce

das *Vorstellungsgespräch (-e)* job interview

der *Vorteil (-e)* advantage

das *Vorurteil (-e)* prejudice

vorwärts forwards

vorziehen (vorgezogen) to prefer

W

wählen (gewählt) to choose

das *Wahlfach ("er)* optional subject

während while

wahrscheinlich probable, probably

der Wald (¨er)   forest, wood
das Waldsterben   dying of the
   forests
die Wand (¨e)   wall
der Wandel   change
   wandern (gewandert)   to hike,
   to go on walks
die Wanderung   walk, hike
   wann?   when?
   warm   warm
   warten   to wait
der Wartesaal   waiting room
   warum?   why?
   was?   what?
(sich) waschen (gewaschen)   to wash
die Waschküche (-n)   laundry
   room
das Wasser   water
die Webseite (-n)   webpage
   wechseln (gewechselt)   to
   change
   weder ... noch ...   neither ...
   nor ...
   wegen   due to, because of
   weglaufen   to run away
   wegwerfen (weggeworfen)
   to throw away
... tut weh   ... is hurting
   Weihnachten   Christmas
der Weihnachtsmarkt (¨e)
   Christmas market
   weil   because
   weinen (geweint)   to cry
die Weintraube (-n)   grape
   weiß   white
   weit   far
   weiterstudieren
   (weiterstudiert)   to do
   further study
   welcher/e/es?   which?
der Wellensittich (-e)   budgie
die Welt   world
   weltberühmt   world famous
die Weltreise (-n)   tour of the
   world
   weniger   less
   wenigstens   at least
   wenn   if, when
   wer?   who?
   werden (geworden)   to become
das Werken (pl)   D&T
der Westen   West
im Westen   in the West
   westlich   to the West
der Wettbewerb   competition
das Wetter   weather
der Wetterbericht (-e)   weather
   report
die Wettervorhersage (-n)
   weather forecast
der Wettkampf   competition

   wichtig   important
Das Wichtigste ist, ...   The most
   important thing is, ...
   wie?   how?
   wie lange?   how long?
   wie viel(e)?   how many?
   wieder   again
   wiegen (gewogen)   to weigh
Herzlich willkommen!   Welcome!
der Wind (-e)   wind
   windig   windy
Es ist windig.   It's windy.
der Winter   winter
der Wintergarten   conservatory
   wirklich   really
   wissen (gewusst)   to know
   wo?   where?
   woanders   somewhere else
die Woche (-n)   week
das Wochenende (-n)   weekend
   woher?   where from?
   wohin?   where to?
sich wohlfühlen   to feel well
die Wohltätigkeit   charity
die Wohltätigkeitsveranstaltung
   charity event
der Wohnblock (-s)   block of flats
   wohnen (gewohnt)   to live (in
   a particular place)
die Wohnung (-en)   flat
der Wohnwagen (-)   caravan
das Wohnzimmer (-)   living room
die Wolke (-n)   cloud
   wolkig   cloudy
Es ist wolkig.   It's cloudy.
die Wolle   wool
   wollen (gewollt)   to want to
   womit?   what with?
   wunderbar   wonderful
   wunderschön   gorgeous, very
   beautiful
   wünschen (sich)
   (gewünscht)   to wish, to
   want
die Wurst (¨e)   sausage
die Wüste   desert

Z

   z.B. (zum Beispiel)   for
   example
der Zahn (¨e)   tooth
der Zahnarzt / die Zahnärztin
   dentist
die Zahnschmerzen   toothache
der Zeichentrickfilm   cartoon
   zeichnen (gezeichnet)
   to draw
der Zeitpunkt (¨e)   point in time
die Zeitschrift (-en)   magazine
die Zeitung (-en)   newspaper

   Zeitungen austragen
   (ausgetragen)   to deliver
   newspapers
die Zeitverschwendung   waste of
   time
das Zelt (-e)   tent
   zelten (gezeltet)   to camp
das Zentrum (-tren)   centre
das Zeug   thing
das Zeugnis (-se)   school report
   ziemlich   quite
die Zigarette (-n)   cigarette
das Zimmer (-)   room
der Zoll (¨e)   customs
der Zoo (-s)   zoo
   zu   to, too, by
das Zuckerfest   Islamic festival of
   breaking the fast
   zuerst   first
   zufällig   by chance
   zufrieden   content, happy
das Zuhause   home
die Zukunft   future
   zumachen (zugemacht)
   to close
   zunehmend   growing,
   increasing
   zurück   back
   zusammen   together
   zusammenleben
   (zusammengelebt)   to
   cohabit
der Zuschlag (¨e)   supplement (to
   pay)
   zustimmen   to agree
   zu viel   too much, too many
der Zweck (-e)   purpose, goal
ohne Zweifel   without a doubt,
   doubtless
der Zweig   branch
   zweitens   second(ly)
die Zwiebel (-n)   onion
die Zwillinge (pl)   twins (noun)
   Zwillings-   twin (adj.)
   zwischen   between
   zwitschern (gezwitschert)
   to twitter
der Zug (¨e)   train
   zuverlässig   reliable

Acknowledgements

Kathy Baxendale pp 12, 13, 21, 59, 73; Mark Draisey: page 16, 62, 143; Tony Forbes: page 22, 39, 57; Abel Ippolito: page 33, 35, 80, 81; Dave Russell: page 104

The authors and the publisher would also like to thank the following for permission to reproduce material:
p7, Design Pics Inc./Alamy; p9, Shutterstock; p11, iStockphoto; p16 topic banner: iStockphoto; p18, Shutterstock; p 20, Fotolia; p23, both: Fotolia; p24, four teenagers: iStockphoto; p26, Paul Thompson Images/Alamy; p32, topic banner: iStockphoto; p34, Jasmin: iStockphoto, Lutz: Bubbles Photolibrary/Alamy, Natascha: Art Directors & TRIP/Helene Rogers/Alamy; p36, iStockphoto; p38, top to bottom: Shutterstock, Andreas Keuchel/Alamy, Fotolia; p40, dbimages/Alamy; p42, Claudia: 123rf.com, Bodo: BigStockPhoto. com; p48, Fotolia; p56, topic banner: Fotolia, Karim and Hannah: Nelson Thornes; p58, Kornelia and Natascha: BigStockPhoto.com, Erika: 123rf.com, Andreas: BigStockPhoto.com, Kal: 123rf.com; p60, 1,2 and 3: iStockphoto, 4 and 5: Fotolia, 6: iStockphoto, Nina: Fotolia, Saed and Christian: iStockphoto; p64, top: Fotolia, bottom: Shutterstock; p65, iStockphoto; p72, topic banner and beach image: iStockphoto; p74, top: Fotolia, bottom: iStockphoto; p77, a: Fotolia, b: BigStockPhoto.com, c, d and e: iStockphoto, f and g: Fotolia; p78, Olaf: Fotolia, all others: iStockphoto; p82, all: Fotolia; p84, all: Fotolia; p88, iStockphoto; p96, topic banner: Fotolia, a: iStockphoto, b: Shutterstock, c: iStockphoto, d: Shutterstock, e, f and g: iStockphoto; p97, Fotolia; p98, Fotolia; p102, iStockphoto; p105, a and b: 123rf. com, c: Fotolia, d, e and f: BigStockPhoto.com; p106, Karneval: BigStockPhoto.com, fireworks: Fotolia, market stall: Shutterstock; p112, topic banner: iStockphoto, 1: Fotolia, 2 and 3: iStockphoto, 4 and 5: Fotolia; p114, all: Shutterstock; p115, both: Shutterstock; p116, INSADCO Photography/Alamy; p117, a: 123rf.com, b: BigStockPhoto. com, c: Fotolia, d: BigStockPhoto.com, e and f: Fotolia; p118, litter: Fotolia, park: BigStockPhoto.com; p124, all: Fotolia; p132, topic banner: iStockphoto, top: Fotolia, bottom: 123rf.com; p134, Paula: iStockphoto, Tom: 123rf.com, notebooks background: BigStockPhoto. com; p136, 1: BigStockPhoto.com, 2: iStockphoto, 3: Fotolia; p138, iStockphoto; p140, Fotolia; p142, all: iStockphoto; p148, topic banner: Shutterstock, Karin and Georg: BigStockPhoto.com, Monika: iStockphoto; p152, Shutterstock; p156, Shutterstock; p158, iStockphoto; p164, top: Fotolia, bottom: iStockphoto.

Every effort has been made to trace the copyright holders but if any have been inadvertently overlooked the publisher will be pleased to make the necessary arrangements at the first opportunity.